THE ANNALS OF UNSOLVED CRIME

ALSO BY EDWARD JAY EPSTEIN

---

*Inquest: The Warren Commission
and the Establishment of Truth*

Counterplot: Garrison vs. the United States

News from Nowhere: Television and the News

Between Fact and Fiction: The Problem of Journalism

Agency of Fear: Opiates and Political Power in America

Cartel

Legend: The Secret World of Lee Harvey Oswald

*The Rise and Fall of Diamonds:
The Shattering of a Brilliant Illusion*

*Who Owns the Corporation?:
Management vs. Shareholders*

*Deception: The Invisible War Between
the KGB and the CIA*

*The Assassination Chronicles:
Inquest, Counterplot, and Legend*

Dossier: The Secret History of Armand Hammer

The Big Picture: Money and Power in Hollywood

*The Hollywood Economist:
The Hidden Financial Reality Behind the Movies*

Three Days in May: Sex, Surveillance, and DSK

THE ANNALS OF UNSOLVED CRIME

BY EDWARD JAY EPSTEIN

MELVILLE HOUSE
BROOKLYN · LONDON

THE ANNALS OF UNSOLVED CRIME

Melville House Publishing
145 Plymouth Street
Brooklyn, NY 11201

www.mhpbooks.com

ISBN: 978-1-61219-048-8

First Melville House Printing: February 2013

Book design: Christopher King

Manufactured in the United States of America

1 2 3 4 5 6 7 8 9 10

Library of Congress Cataloging-in-Publication Data

Epstein, Edward Jay, 1935-
   The annals of unsolved crime / Edward Jay Epstein. -- 1st ed.
     pages cm
   ISBN 978-1-61219-048-8
   1. Assassination--History. 2. Assassination--Investigation.
   3. Criminal investigation. I. Title.
   HV6281.E67 2013
   364.152'3--dc23
                              2012049984

This book is dedicated to the memory of a wise teacher,
James Q. Wilson (1931–2012)

CONTENTS

EDWARD JAY EPSTEIN

PREFACE

The idea for *The Annals of Unsolved Crime* grew out a trip to Moscow in 2007 to investigate the case of a radioactive corpse. The victim was Alexander Litvinenko, an ex-KGB officer, who had become deeply involved in the political intrigues of the billionaire Boris Berezovsky, an oligarch in exile in London, and those of Yukos, the immensely powerful oil company that Vladimir Putin was then in the process of expropriating from its owners. What made the case interesting to the intelligence services of at least four countries was the way the corpse in London had become radioactive: Litvinenko had been poisoned by an extremely rare radioactive isotope, polonium-210, which had immense value to parties seeking to go nuclear because it could be used to trigger an early-stage nuclear weapon. For this reason, it was one of the most tightly controlled and most carefully monitored substances on earth. So how, and why, were Litvinenko and some of his associates exposed to it? When I read through the relevant files in Moscow, I realized that this question might never be answered. The files had come to me by a circuitous route. The Crown Prosecutor in London had supplied their counterparts in Moscow with some evidence that they had in the case to support an extradition request for a suspect, Anatoli Lugovoi, who had also been exposed to polonium-210. What the files made clear was that, even though this was supposed to be a joint British-Russian investigation, the autopsy report, the hospital records, the toxic analysis, the radiation readings in London, and other evidence concerning the polonium-210 were being retained by the British government as state secrets. For their part, the Russians would not allow Lugovoi (whom I interviewed for many hours in Moscow) or any other Russian citizen to be extradited, and they would not furnish any information about the leakage or smuggling of polonium-210. Nor, as of December 2012, would the British allow the coroner to complete his report on Litvinenko's death or release the autopsy files.

Even if officially the case of the radioactive corpse remains an unsolvable crime, we can still learn a great deal from the barriers that block us from solving it. I have found in my journalistic career that even with the unstinting financial and editorial support of magazines such as *The New Yorker*, *Vanity Fair*, *The Atlantic*, *New York*, and *Reader's Digest*, the cases from which I learned the most—and that most intrigued me— were cases that I could not solve. Some of the most high-profile crimes in history also lack a satisfactory solution because the basic facts of the case remain suspect. Napoleon defined history "as the version of past events that people have decided to agree upon," which raises the question of whether such agreements proceed from facts or from political expediency. The problem of establishing truth has concerned me since I began my thesis at Cornell on the assassination of President John F. Kennedy in 1965 by posing it to seven of the most powerful men in America, the members of the Warren Commission. Some of these men, including a former director of the CIA, a former U.S. high commissioner for Germany, and the minority leader of the House of Representatives, pointed to inherent difficulties faced by a Presidential Commission, such as pressure of time, the lack of truly independent investigators, and the need to reach a consensus even if they disagreed. Other commissions from the military tribune that investigated the assassination of President Abraham Lincoln have confronted similar problems. So do prosecutors whose careers turn on their ability to appear to resolve cases of great interest to the public. For the past four decades, in seeking to cast light on this limitation, I have tended to focus on crimes that may contain elements beneath the surface that have never been fully reported. In this regard, *New York Times* columnist Joe Nocera was correct when he suggested that I believe "that conspiracies are more common than most journalists credit." But conspiracies do exist—indeed, over 90 percent of federal indictments for terrorism since the 9/11 attacks in 2001 have contained a conspiracy charge, according to the Center on Law and Security at New York University, which tracks all federal terrorism cases. It is also true that many cases that initially appear to be conspiracies, such as the putative plot against the Black Panthers in the late 1960s, turned out, as I discovered when I reported about it for *The New Yorker*, to be the unconnected acts of lone individuals.

Some obvious problems with the puzzles presented by unsolved crimes are that they may be missing critical pieces, contain pieces that have been falsified, or contain pieces of evidence that belong in other puzzles. Even so, unsolved crimes have commonalities that can help us understand why they defy resolution. Although the taxonomy of such an elusive subject may be imperfect, I have classified these cases in four categories: loners, disguised crimes, cold cases, and crimes of the state.

The category of "loners" has long intrigued me. A lone gunman shoots someone and then is himself killed. There is no doubt that he fired the shots and was the only perpetrator at the crime scene, but was he alone? Conspiracies can hire a lone assassin, such as the killer in the book and movie *The Day of the Jackal*, to minimize the chances of being detected. Consider, for example, the assassination that had probably the most momentous consequences in history, the shooting of Archduke

Franz Ferdinand, the Hapsburg heir to the Austro-Hungarian throne, in Sarajevo on June 28, 1914. The bullet that killed him, and that ignited World War I, was fired by Gavrilo Princip. The immediate circumstances suggested a happenstance shooting. The archduke was on his way to an unscheduled visit to Sarajevo Hospital in his open Gräf and Stift Double Phaeton limousine. The driver made a wrong turn, got lost, and then while he backed up toward a bridge, the giant car stalled. The archduke, in his easily recognizable gold-braided uniform and plumed hat, was in the back seat, waiting for the driver to crank the car. At that very moment, Princip, a nineteen-year-old Serbian nationalist, was finishing his coffee at a café on the corner. He spied the archduke, rushed over to the stalled car, and fatally shot him in the neck. Since no one could have known in advance that the archduke would be at that place at that time, it initially appeared to be a random shooting by a lone Serb. Austrian authorities, however, intercepted Serbian communications that revealed that this was a conspiracy planned and orchestrated by Serbian intelligence and that Princip was one of a dozen assassins positioned along the archduke's route. At least three, including Princip, had received their weapons, training, and a suicide cyanide capsule from their Serbian case officers. It was the discovery of this plot that led to a war in which nine million soldiers were killed, and to the demise of the Hapsburg empire.

Investigations that stop at the singleton killer may, for better or worse, leave open the door to an unsolved crime. When the stakes are high, as when a head of state is assassinated, the decision of whether to stop at the singleton killer or pursue a possible conspiracy may not be entirely free of political considerations. I first came across this political dimension when I interviewed the members and most of the staff of the Warren Commission in 1965. I was given this unique access to the Commission because my investigation—later published as a book,

Inquest: The Warren Commission and the Establishment of Truth—was of interest to Chief Justice Earl Warren. One of the first commissioners I interviewed was John J. McCloy, who had served as the U.S. High Commissioner of Germany. As we sat in his forty-sixth floor office in the Chase Manhattan building, he described how the Commission had wrestled over how to deal with the loner issue. He said that all the commissioners agreed that the evidence was overwhelming that Lee Harvey Oswald had fired the shots that killed President John F. Kennedy. Their difficulty lay in resolving whether or not they could say that he was the sole author of the assassination. The chief justice, supported by most of the other commissioners, wanted to close the case by stating categorically that Oswald was a "loner." McCloy said that he objected because the Commission did not have access to information about Oswald's liaisons with the security services of Cuba and Russia, and therefore it could not rule out the possibility that Oswald's connections with them made him more than a lone actor. He told the chief justice the Commission could say only that it had found no credible evidence of any other conspirators. As Warren wanted an unanimous report, he went along with McCloy and inserted a paragraph saying that, as it was not possible to prove a negative, the Commission could not rule out the possibility that Oswald had help. That qualification, though buried in the verbiage of the Commission's report, as McCloy put it, "left the door ajar." The "loner" issue has never really been resolved.

Political climates can also change, and when they do, what begins as a conspiracy could end up pinned on a loner. Consider, for example, the initial conclusions about the assassination of President Abraham Lincoln in 1865. Immediately after the assassination, with the South still seen as the enemy, the Military Commission appointed by the new president, Andrew Johnson, concluded that John Wilkes Booth, the assassin who was killed during his escape, was part of a conspiracy sponsored by leaders of the defeated Confederate States. Four of his associates were hanged as co-conspirators, and an arrest warrant was issued for former Confederate States President Jefferson Davis. But when the political climate in America changed, and the reunification of the North and South proceeded, the government vacated the warrants against Southern leaders and abandoned the Military Commission's conspiracy case. Instead, John Wilkes Booth was viewed as a deranged loner.

What makes this issue vexing is that there is no single answer. Some crimes are committed by loners operating on their own, others by a singleton working on the behalf of a group. In the realm of fiction, the public readily accepts that a lone murderer can be carrying out a contract for a conspiracy that does not expose itself. In the movie based on Mario Puzo's book *The Godfather*, no fewer than six mob leaders are slain by a lone killer retained by Michael Corleone. In Frederick Forsyth's book *The Day of the Jackal*, a group of French conspirators hire a lone assassin to kill President Charles de Gaulle, sure that the man cannot be traced back to them. Such arrangements also occur in the realm of reality. The 1967 *CIA* Inspector General's *Report on the Plots to Assassinate Fidel Castro* describes how the CIA hired singleton assassins, such as Rolando Cubela (code-named AMLASH), to kill Castro between 1961 and 1963. If Cubela (or any of the other assassins) had succeeded, the CIA would claim he was a disgruntled Cuban acting on his own. How common are such conspiracies in political crimes? From the perspective of U.S. prosecutors at least, conspiracies are not rare when it comes to political murder. The interesting issue is sorting out loners who act alone from loners who act for others.

Another category of interest is disguised murder. To protect itself against pursuit, a party can disguise a murder as a suicide or accident in such a way that the issue becomes: Was there a crime? My interest here was piqued by James Jesus Angleton, the legendary counterintelligence chief of the CIA. In 1977, he described to me six connected suicides that had occurred in Germany in late 1968. First, on October 8, Major-General Horst Wendland, the deputy head of the BND, the German equivalent of the CIA, was found shot dead with his own service revolver in his own office. That same day, Admiral Hermann Ludke, the deputy head of the logistics department of NATO, was found fatally shot by a dum-dum bullet from his own Mauser rifle in a private hunting preserve in Germany's Eifel Mountains. Then, within days, four more bodies turned up: Lt. Colonel Johannes Grimm, who worked in the German Defense Ministry, shot; Gerald Bohm, his colleague in the Ministry, drowned in the Rhine river; Edeltraud Grapentin, a liaison with the Information Ministry, poisoned with sleeping pills; and Hans-Heinrich Schenk, a researcher at the Economics Ministry, hanged. All were declared apparent suicides. After he reeled them off, Angleton made his point. These were not unrelated deaths. All six apparent suicides had access to highly classified secrets and were all under investigation as suspected spies or for leaks of NATO documents. The secret investigation of these men had proceeded from the discovery of a strip of film taken on a Minox camera of top-secret NATO documents. The camera had then been traced to Admiral Ludke. This discovery was of immense interest to Angleton, who in 1968 was a liaison with the BND, because Admiral Ludke had "need-to-know" access to the top secrets in NATO, including the location of the depots in which nuclear weapons were stored. Next, a Czech defector supplied a lead that pointed directly to Major-General Wendland and the German Defense Ministry. But before the investigation could go further, both Ludke and Wendland were shot to death on the same day, followed by four other suspects in the case suddenly meeting violent ends. How was such a coincidence possible? Angleton supplied one theory: the KGB had eliminated them to protect its espionage. I said, "But they were ruled suicides."

He corrected me: "Apparent suicides," and he added, "Any thug can commit a murder, but it takes the talents of an intelligence service to make a murder appear to be a suicide." He pointed out that coroners look for a murder signature, such as rope burns or bruises, and, if those are not present, they declare the death apparent suicide or natural death. Those signatures can be erased, as Angleton explained, in what is termed in intelligence-speak "surreptitiously-assisted deaths."

The death of Hamas commander Mahmoud al-Mabhouh in Dubai in 2010 is also instructive in this regard. Since his body had no telltale signs of violence, the Dubai coroner initially concluded that he died from natural causes. But then security cameras revealed that al-Mabhouh had been under surveillance by a group of suspicious individuals shortly before his death and, at the insistence of Hamas, his body fluids were re-analyzed by a lab in Switzerland with highly sophisticated equipment. The lab discovered in the fluids minute traces of succinylcholine, a quick-acting, depolarizing, and muscle-paralyzing drug that would have rendered a person incapable of resisting. Then Dubai authorities came up with a new verdict: Mabhouh had been murdered by first giving him this drug, then smothering him to death with his own pillow. The coroner explained that it was a disguised homicide "meant to look like death from natural causes during sleep."

A variation of disguised murder is the arranged accident. A plane, for example, disappears in the ocean and is consumed in a fire. There is no evidence found: Was it an accident or a crime? Even if possibly incriminating evidence is recovered from the wreckage, it requires interpretation. Consider, for example, the crash over the Atlantic ocean of TWA flight 800 on July 17, 1996, that resulted in the death of 230 people. Much of the wreckage was recovered from the ocean and, from it, the FBI lab in Washington, D.C., identified traces of three different explosives, RDX, PETN, and nitroglycerin, on pieces of the plane. All three chemicals are used in bomb-making, and they could be interpreted as signatures of sabotage. They also could have been the result of prior security tests—airlines use live explosives on planes to test their sniffer dogs and other detection equipment—or of the transportation of troops during the 1991 Gulf War. When this discovery was considered in the context of other evidence, the National Transport Safety Board concluded that the latter had occurred and ruled that the crash was the result of an accidental gas leak, not sabotage.

It became evident to me how contentious and complex air-craft investigations could be when I went to Pakistan to investigate the plane crash that killed General Zia-ul-Haq, the military dictator of that country, in 1988. Even with sophisticated forensic analysis by the plane's manufacturer, it could not be determined why the plane had crashed, because crucial evidence was missing: the government had disposed of the bodies of the pilots before they could be medically examined.

Corpses do not necessarily stay in the ground in this ghoulish age of exhumation, especially if a historic case takes on a political dimension. Consider, for example, Simón Bolívar, the revered liberator of South America from Spain and then, in his own right, dictator of Venezuela. He died on December 17, 1830, after a prolonged battle with tuberculosis, according to the historical record. But in 2010, Hugo Chávez, the president of modern Venezuela, raised the issue of whether Bolívar died a natural death or whether he was murdered. After appointing a commission to reexamine his medical symptoms for any signs of arsenic poisoning, Chávez ordered Bolívar's 180-year-old remains exhumed from his monument in Caracas so further forensic tests could be conducted. Exhumations often raise more questions than they answer. Eight years after Yasser Arafat, the president of the Palestinian National Authority, died on November 11, 2004, at the Percy Military Hospital in Clamart, France, his remains were exhumed, because his shoes and other personal effects showed traces of polonium-210 (the same radioactive isotope that killed Litvinenko in 2006). Even though the 558 pages of Arafat's medical records clearly establish that Arafat died from a cerebrovascular failure caused by cirrhosis, and not from any kind of radiation poisoning, the polonium-210 signature on his personal effects raised an even more intriguing mystery: How had Arafat come in such close proximity to an extremely rare isotope that could be used as an early-stage nuclear weapon trigger and in miniaturized surveillance devices used by intelligence services?

Then there are cases in which investigators simply cannot find clues to pursue. Such crimes enter the limbo of a police cold-case file, but they also generate a profusion of speculation. Consider the so-called Jack the Ripper case in late-nineteenth-century London. As the city was shrouded in fog and there was little illumination from street lamps, there were no witnesses (other than one fatally wounded victim who said he was attacked by two boys). Fingerprint matching did not yet exist, nor did analysis of blood, hair, or clothing fiber. The police had no evidence and never caught the killer or killers. The same absence of evidence allowed future writers to cast Jack the Ripper in the guise of any personage of the period, including a member of the royal family.

Even with modern forensics, police cannot pursue a case, or even prove there was a crime, if the putative victim is missing: For examples, New York Supreme Court Justice Joseph Force Crater, who vanished in 1930 (he remained in a missing persons file for fifty years) and labor leader James Hoffa, who vanished in 1975. Vanishings of course may be voluntary. Michael Hand, for example, who had worked closely with intelligence services, and whose Nugan Hand Bank conducted large scale money laundering for the CIA, disappeared without a trace in June of 1981. After his partner Frank Nugan was found shot to death in his Mercedes Benz and $40 million in bank funds were found missing, Hand disguised himself as a local butcher in Sydney named Alan Glenn Winter, and under this false identify went to New York City. He was never found.

Next, there are crimes of state in which governments make a solution virtually impossible. What might be considered an "obstruction of justice" if performed by an individual may be done by a government on the grounds of national security. Documents can be sealed or expunged, witnesses can be sequestered or intimidated, physical evidence can be suppressed, and other measures can be taken to protect a state secret. State cover-ups can take many forms. In Thailand, King Ananda Mahidol was found shot to death in his bed in the Bangkok royal palace in 1946. When the official story of an accident failed to gain traction, the government charged, tried, convicted, and executed three young servants who were almost certainly innocent. That, together with strict censorship in which disparagement of the king is a crime, ended any further public discussion of King Ananda's death in Thailand. Crimes of state can also become inseparable from the political context of crimes. For example, in December 2011, I went to Kiev to interview Leonid Kuchma, the ex-president of Ukraine, about the unsolved decapitation of a journalist in 2000. Kuchma had been implicated in the crime and was then facing a criminal trial. Also implicated was his former Minister of Internal Affairs, Yuri Kravchenko, who had been found dead in 2005 with two gunshot wounds to his head and a suicide note. Kuchma suggested to me in our interview that all the evidence against him had been forged by a foreign intelligence service to destabilize Ukraine and that Kravchenko's apparent suicide was a disguised murder. Government concealment of such enterprises, and crimes, is a true art of the state.

It should also be recognized that conspiracies need not resemble the intricately crafted intrigues found in movies and novels. They come in a multitude of different forms; some are plotted in advance and other are enacted opportunely after the fact to take advantage of circumstances. The 1972–1973 Watergate scandal, for example, involved a number of different conspiracies. The first, which grew out of a covert operation called Gemstone, involved seven conspirators, all of whom had formerly worked for the CIA or the FBI. All went to prison. The second conspiracy was the after-the-fact cover-up organized by the White House, and its exposure led to conviction of Attorney General John Mitchell and ten other high-ranking officials. A third possible conspiracy involved government officials clandestinely distributing protected data, including FBI 201 files, to select journalists in order to weaken, if not destroy, the Nixon Administration. That the release was "deliberately coordinated," rather than a spontaneous act of whistle-blowing, is suggested by CIA memoranda, written by CIA officers Martin Lukoskie and Eric Eisenstadt (published as an appendix in Jim Hougan's book *Secret Agenda*), one "for the record" and the other for the CIA's deputy director of plans. The memos discuss how Lukoskie's operation "has now established a 'back door entry' to the Edward Bennett Williams law firm, which is representing the Democratic Party in its suit for damages resulting from the Watergate incident," and had also managed to feed stories to the *Washington Post* via Bob Woodward on the understanding that there be no attribution to the CIA operation. If the purpose of this effort by an intelligence service was to unseat elected officials, it would constitute a conspiracy within a conspiracy.

This brings us to the final section, induced miscarriages of justice. When someone corrupts the legal system by fabricating evidence or otherwise usurps it to damage an opponent, this produces a crime within a crime that may go undetected. And once such a perversion of justice is established as the "truth" in the public mind, the situation is not easily remedied. One of the most notorious examples of this crime-within-a-crime is the imprisonment of Captain Alfred Dreyfus on Devil's Island. The affair began in Paris in 1894 as an espionage case after French military intelligence discovered that a traitor with access to documents from the General Staff was in contact with the German embassy. The mole hunt immediately focused on Captain Dreyfus, the only officer of Jewish descent on the French Army's General Staff. In 1895, he was court-martialed, sentenced to life imprisonment, and put in solitary confinement on the penal colony of Devil's Island. The following year, French intelligence discovered that the mole was actually Major Ferdinand Esterhazy. But instead of suffering the embarrassment of exonerating Dreyfus, the intelligence agency concealed the discovery, Esterhazy was allowed to escape to Britain, and an intelligence officer forged documents further implicating Dreyfus. In 1899, in response to public outcry, Dreyfus was given a second trial and, on the basis of the fabricated evidence, re-convicted. It was not until 1906 that Dreyfus was fully exonerated. But there was another crime here that was not pursued: the corruption of justice by French intelligence officers that destroyed Dreyfus' career. Such perversions of justice take many forms, including frame-ups, setups (illegal entrapments), and deliberate prosecutorial abuses of power.

The mysteries in *The Annals of Unsolved Crimes* include political assassinations, kidnappings, airplane crashes, arson, vanishings, mass murders, serial killings, poisonings, nuclear-weapon smuggling, and bioterrorism. Whereas some of the cases, such as that of the Reichstag fire, changed the course of world history, all captured the public imagination through intense media coverage, speculation, and the proliferation of conspiracy theories. For this book, I have included both cases that I have investigated personally and for which I have done extensive interviews, and historic cases in which I have relied on books, court documents, and archival material. I have divided each unsolved crime into three parts: a narration of the basic evidence in the case, a presentation of the basic theories, and my own assessment, based on my view of the best sense of the current state of the evidence. The length of the chapters varies since more convoluted cases, such as that of the headless Ukrainian journalist, require a longer presentation. The common thread running through them all is the difficulty of establishing truth in high-profile crimes.

PART ONE

"LONERS": BUT WERE THEY ALONE?

CHAPTER 1

THE ASSASSINATION OF PRESIDENT LINCOLN

Shortly after the American Civil War came to an end, President Abraham Lincoln was murdered. The assassination had immense consequences; it disastrously delayed the reconstruction of the South for nearly a century. The man who shot Lincoln was John Wilkes Booth. Was he a lone assassin or part of a conspiracy aimed at changing history?

At about 10:15 p.m. on Friday, April 14, 1865, in Washington, D.C., assassins launched nearly simultaneous attacks against President Lincoln and Secretary of State William Seward. At Ford's Theater, John Wilkes Booth, who was then one of the world's celebrated actors, slipped into the unguarded president's box and fatally shot President Lincoln in the head. At the Washington home of Secretary of State Seward, Lewis Powell, who had served in the Confederate secret service, stabbed Seward—but, unlike Lincoln, Seward survived the attack. A third alleged member of the conspiracy, George Atzerodt, who owned a carriage repair business in Maryland, stalked Vice President Andrew Johnson with a loaded pistol that night and was arrested. Powell was arrested at the home of Mary Surratt in Surrattsville, Maryland. Surratt was also arrested for harboring the accused would-be assassins. Meanwhile, David Herold, who had gone with Powell to Seward's home that night, escaped with Booth from Surrattsville to Virginia.

On April 26, Federal troops trapped Booth and Herold in a barn in Virginia. In the ensuing gun battle, Booth was killed and Herold captured.

Meanwhile, Johnson, who succeeded Lincoln as president, declared that there was "evidence in the Bureau of Military Justice that the atrocious murder of the late president, and the attempted assassination of the Hon. William H. Seward, Secretary of State, were incited, concerted and procured," by leaders of the defeated Confederate States. They placed a $100,000 reward on the head of its president, Jefferson Davis, and established a Military Commission to mete out justice.

On May 1, 1865, eight alleged conspirators, including Powell, Herold, Atzerodt, and Mary Surratt, were tried before that Commission. Over the course of seven weeks, the Commission heard 371 witnesses. According to the prosecution's witnesses, the Confederate Congress had appropriated five million dollars in 1864 for covert operations run out of Canada by Jacob Thompson, the former secretary of the interior, and Clement Clay, a former senator. One prosecution witness described a failed covert operation sponsored by the Confederate States to deliver clothing that had been "carefully infected in Bermuda with yellow fever" to the White House. Another prosecution witness testified that the goal of the April plot was not only to kill Lincoln but also to "leave the government entirely without a head" by killing those in the line of succession. To this end, Thompson allegedly met in Montreal with John Wilkes Booth and John Surratt, Jr., the son of Mary Surratt (he escaped to Canada after the assassination), and approved plans to attack Lincoln on April 6, 1865. According to a Canadian banker's testimony, Thompson withdrew $184,000 from the more than $600,000 in his private Montreal account just after the meeting with Booth. The prosecution also introduced a coded letter found in Booth's possession, which, according to its forensic experts, was traced to a cipher machine recovered from the code room in the Confederate headquarters in Richmond. That cipher putatively authorized an earlier plot to abduct Lincoln on March 17, 1865. George Atzerodt admitted at the trial that he had planned, along with Herold, Booth, and other conspirators, to abduct Lincoln as he was returning from a matinee performance at the Campbell Hospital on the outskirts of Washington. (The scheme failed when the president canceled his trip.)

The prosecutor said in his summation that the evidence showed "that John Wilkes Booth was in this conspiracy; that John Surratt was in this conspiracy; and that Jefferson Davis and his several agents named, in Canada, were in this conspiracy."

The Military Commission then found Powell, Herold, Mary Surratt, and Atzerodt (who had admitted his involvement in the earlier plot) guilty of participating in the April conspiracy and sentenced them to death by hanging. On July 7, 1865, the four condemned prisoners were hanged (making Mary Surratt the first woman ever executed by the federal government). The other four defendants were found guilty of helping the assassins escape and sentenced to prison.

John Surratt, the remaining conspirator, was captured in Egypt in November 1866. By that time, military commission trials had been ruled unconstitutional, so he was tried in 1867 by a state court in Maryland. Since the statute of limitations had expired on all the lesser charges, he was tried only for murdering Lincoln. As part of his defense, he freely admitted that he had been a Confederate spy and had conspired with Booth to kidnap Lincoln, but he denied any involvement in the subsequent assassination. When the jury failed to agree on a verdict, the judge declared a mistrial, and Surratt was set free.

In light of the momentous consequences of the assassination and the flawed judicial process of the Military Commission, there was no shortage of theories. To begin with, there was the theory of the Commission itself that John Wilkes Booth and his five fellow plotters were part of a covert action designed to decapitate the federal government by killing the president, vice president, and secretary of state. According to this theory, as articulated by Secretary of War Stanton, this assassination plot was authorized by the high command of the Confederate States and paid for through its intelligence arm in Canada. An alternative theory subscribed to by many, if not all, Civil War historians is that there was an earlier failed plot to kidnap Lincoln that was hijacked by Booth. According to this theory, the Confederacy had backed an earlier covert action in March 1865 to ransom Lincoln for the exchange of Confederate prisoners of war. The Confederacy authorized the transfer of money to Surratt for this purpose via a ciphered message and even positioned troops to transport the abducted president to the South. Booth, John Surratt, Powell, Herold, and Atzerodt were all participants in this plot (as Atzerodt and Surratt admitted at their trials). When the kidnapping plot failed, Booth deceived or coerced the others into participating in his unauthorized assassination. There is also a theory implicating Jesuit priests in the assassination. General Thomas Harris, who had served as a prosecutor on the Military Commission, advanced this theory in his 1897 book *Rome's Responsibility for the Assassination of Abraham Lincoln.* According to this theory, John Surratt, who had been convicted in absentia and was one of the most pursued fugitives in American history, was smuggled out of America by Jesuit priests to the Vatican in Rome, where he was enrolled under false documentation in the Swiss Guard and, when discovered there, allowed to escape to Egypt. This anti-papist theory has received no support from modern historians.

My assessment is that the attacks on President Lincoln and Secretary of State Seward on the night of April 14, 1865, as well as the planned attack that night on Vice President Johnson, were part of a coordinated plot aimed at eliminating those in the immediate line of succession to the presidency. It was, in modern terms, a decapitation strike. There can be little doubt that the perpetrators were acting in concert: two of them, John Wilkes Booth and David Herold, the latter of whom was an accomplice in the attempted assassination of Seward, escaped together to Virginia and engaged in a gun battle with their pursuers. George Atzerodt, who had the job of shooting the vice president, had Booth's bank book in his possession and, just before he was hanged, confessed to the minister attending him that Booth had told him in advance of the plan to shoot Lincoln and had designated Herold as his backup to assassinate the vice president. Lewis Powell, who stabbed Secretary of State Seward, was placed by witnesses at a meeting with Booth and Herold at the Surratt boarding house, and at his trial, the defense offered by his lawyer was that he was a soldier following orders. We also know that Booth, Herold, Powell, and Atzerodt had been involved in a plot to kidnap Lincoln (which Atzerodt described in detail in his confession) less than a month earlier.

The remaining question of whether this conspiracy was state-sponsored by the Confederacy is more difficult to answer. We know that as Lincoln was about to begin his second term in 1864, the Confederate Congress allocated five million dollars to a Confederate Secret Service operation in Canada run by Jacob Thompson and Clement Clay. It sponsored a number of lethal covert acts in the United States from 1864 to 1865, including a plan to spread the smallpox virus and blow up the White House. We further know that Thompson met with Booth in Montreal in the fall of 1864. I believe that a strong indication of the close relationship between the Confederate Secret Service and Booth is a ciphered letter sent to Booth on October 13, 1864, asking whether Booth's "friends would be set to work as directed." After the assassination, the cipher was matched to one used by the Confederate Secret Service in Richmond and Canada. Since intelligence services do not share their ciphers with people not involved in their activities, it seems likely that

Booth was acting for the Confederate Secret Service, at least in October 1864. This relationship may have extended to the plot by Booth and his associates to kidnap Lincoln on March 17, 1865, since Confederate military records show that on that day its elite cavalry unit's troops were positioned along the route on which Booth planned to transport the kidnapped president to the South. Certainly, his co-conspirators in the kidnap plot believed that it was backed by the Confederacy.

It is less clear, however, that this Confederacy backing extended to the assassination. Booth wrote in his diary, which was captured after he was killed, "For six months we had worked to capture, but our cause being almost lost, something decisive and great must be done." This suggests that Booth may have decided to act without authorization after the Confederacy surrendered on April 12. If so, Booth likely hijacked the earlier conspiracy to accomplish his purpose. The problem here is that Booth tore eighteen pages out of the diary that bore on this crucial issue. Without them, it cannot be definitely ruled out that Booth, realizing that the diary might be captured, engaged in a final cover-up of the plot's command structure.

The lesson to be drawn from the Lincoln assassination is how political context may shape our understanding of a crime. The interpretation of evidence of a conspiracy in this case proceeded from the prevailing political exigencies. The military tribunal had evaluated the case under wartime conditions. Although the Confederacy had surrendered, its top leaders had escaped to Canada and were still considered a threat to the nation. No doubt the tribunal viewed the testimony through a prism colored by concerns over further acts of terrorism aimed at destabilizing the fragile union and, in piecing together this evidence, saw a plot directed by the Confederacy leadership and coordinated by John Surratt, the Confederate liaison with Booth. These wartime jitters, however, had faded away by the following year, and by the time Surratt was captured and brought to trial, in 1867, the nation's focus had changed from war to peace, and the charges against Surratt were dropped. In the decades that followed this turmoil, the reunited government no longer found it expedient to give credence to the evidence that the military tribunal had used to hang four people for participating in a wider conspiracy. The version that then established itself in the public's mind coalesced into one featuring a deranged assassin acting as a loner. The changing verdicts in this case suggest the degree to which reasons of state weigh on the scales of justice in cases that impinge on urgent issues of war and peace.

CHAPTER 2

THE REICHSTAG FIRE

In 1933 in Berlin, in the midst of bitter political struggle between the Nazis and the Communists for control of a fragile
German democracy, the Reichstag, the home of the German
Parliament, was set ablaze. The conflagration would have consequences far beyond Germany, and even Europe. It brought
Adolf Hitler to power. Was this a political act—or was it the
mad act of a loner?

The fire began on the evening of February 27, 1933. At 9:25
p.m., the Berlin fire department received a call that the Reichstag, the symbol of the German state, was burning. By the time
firemen and police arrived at the scene, the building was a
sheet of flames. After the fire was brought under control, police found Marinus Van der Lubbe hiding in the still-smoldering
building. They also found twenty bundles of inflammable materials in the same area, and arrested Van der Lubbe on a charge
of arson. Van der Lubbe told police that he was a Dutch Communist who had come to Germany to find work as a bricklayer.

When Adolf Hitler, the leader of the Nazi party, arrived at
the fire that night, he was met by Hermann Göring, his second
in command, who told him, "This is a Communist outrage! One
of the Communist culprits has been arrested." Hitler instantly
termed the fire a "sign from heaven." The next day, proclaiming
the fire part of a wider Communist plot in Moscow to overthrow the German government, he persuaded President Paul

von Hindenburg to sign the "Reichstag Fire decree," which temporarily suspended civil liberties in Germany and allowed the mass arrest of Communists. As a result, Hitler's Nazi Party gained control of Parliament. And, after a snap election, Hitler's Nazi Party won enough votes to make Hitler dictator.

As Hitler demanded the Communist conspirators be brought to justice, police arrested three top Communists: Georgi Dimitrov, a Bulgarian Communist, and Stalin's chief of covert operations in central Europe, and his associates, Vasil Tanev and Blagoi Popov. Together with Van der Lubbe, they were charged with conspiracy to overthrow the government.

The trial began in Leipzig on September 21, 1933, presided over by judges from Germany's highest court. As one of the first trials to be globally broadcast live via radio, it was also an international media event. The first prosecution witness was Van der Lubbe. He admitted setting the fire and claimed he had acted entirely on his own. The prosecution then proceeded to make the case that he could not have been the sole arsonist by calling as witnesses firemen and police who testified about the locations of bundles of inflammable material, and arson experts who testified that Van der Lubbe, who was half-blind and infirm, could not have both placed and rigged all these incendiary devices. For nearly a month, through these witnesses, the prosecution made the case that the fire was the work of a conspiracy, not a loner.

The real defendant was Dimitrov, accused of organizing the conspiracy on behalf of the international Communist Party. Though not a lawyer by training, he acted as his own defense lawyer. When he took the stand, he surprised the court, saying that he fully agreed with the prosecutors that the fire had been set by a conspiracy. In his role as defense lawyer, he even went so far as to cross-examine Göring about the role he played in the investigation. He also challenged Göring's recollection of the sequence in which evidence was uncovered, inconsistencies in his testimony, and Nazi views about Communism. These latter questions provoked heated exchanges between himself and Göring on the nature of Communism.

Four months later, the judges rendered their verdict. They said they were convinced by the testimony that the fire was the work of a conspiracy, but that the prosecution had failed to prove that Dimitrov or his associates were part of it. Dimitrov and his two Communist associates were thus acquitted. (Dimitrov later became President of Bulgaria.) The only person convicted was Van der Lubbe, who was beheaded in 1934.

During the trial in Leipzig, a so-called "counter-trial" was held in London. It had been organized by Willi Münzenberg, the propaganda chief for the Communist International, and it also became an international media event. Indeed, newsreels cut between the two trials in the summer of 1933. The counter-trial produced evidence in the form of revelations from masked men who claimed to be Nazi defectors. One, for example, who identified himself as a former Nazi storm trooper, testified that his unit in Berlin had set the fire on direct orders from Göring. Another witness identified Van der Lubbe as the homosexual lover of a top Nazi commander and said that the Nazis used him as a convenient fall guy. At the end of the London trial, Göring was convicted of burning down the Reichstag to bring Hitler to power. It subsequently turned out that almost all the testimony had been faked by Münzenberg's propaganda staff. The masked witnesses were not Nazi defectors but actors reading scripted parts. (The "Nazi storm trooper" was played by Albert Norden, the editor of a Communist newspaper in Germany.)

The evidence was not reexamined until the end of World War II. When the Soviet Army captured Berlin in 1945, it took control of the Gestapo archive, including some 50,000 pages of legal proceedings and Gestapo investigation records bearing on the Reichstag fire. Stalin had this trove of documents transported under seal to Moscow, where, for over three decades, they remained a state secret until the collapse of the Soviet Union. Finally, in 1990, over a half-century after the Reichstag fire, this archive was partly opened to researchers. The released material showed no evidence that any organized conspiracy was behind the Reichstag fire. It did, however, contain evidence showing that the Nazis had been preparing to arrest Communists *before* the fire. It also contained a Gestapo report that a Berlin prison guard had told police investigators that a prisoner named Adolf Rall had told other prisoners that he had been part of a Nazi squad that entered the Reichstag through a tunnel and sprinkled inflammable liquid inside the building. But there is no record of Rall's interrogation by the Gestapo before Rall was himself murdered on the outskirts of Berlin in November 1933. In any case, since the Gestapo and KGB each had custody of an archive and neither agency was above tampering with documents, the third-hand report about a dead witness has no real evidentiary value.

There are three main theories about the Reichstag fire. First, there is the Hitler-Göring theory that the fire was set on the orders of Stalin's Comintern in Moscow to create chaos in Germany. It was also the theory of the prosecution in the Leipzig trial. According to the prosecution, Van der Lubbe was one of a group of Communist arsonists. Second, there is the theory advanced at the Comintern-sponsored "counter-trial" in London: that the fire was set by a group of Nazi SS agents acting under the orders of Göring himself. According to this theory, the fire was an act of provocation to allow the Nazis to seize power and Van der Lubbe was merely a pawn recruited under a false flag to convince the German public that Communists had set the fire. Finally, there is the loner theory that holds that Van der Lubbe was a deranged drunk who set the fire on his own. He had no help, support, or encouragement from any other person or group. This is the view of the German judiciary that, in January 2008, overturned the 1933 conviction of Van der Lubbe on the grounds that he was incompetent to stand trial.

Assessing the evidence in such a propaganda-charged case presents a problem. The value of evidence depends on the integrity of the process by which it is gathered, selected, and maintained; and this process is not immune to political pressures surrounding it. In the case of the burning of the Reichstag, the political stakes were enormous, both for Hitler in Berlin, who wanted to use the incendiary event as a stepping-stone to seizing power, and to the Communist International in Moscow, which wanted to use it to discredit Hitler. Not only did both sides go to great lengths to fake, hide, and distort the facts surrounding this case, but six years later, the archives were captured by the Soviet Army and consigned to the machinations of the Russian intelligence services. What we do know for certain is that there was no credible evidence produced at either the Leipzig or the London trial that linked the arsonist Van der Lubbe to any accomplice. Nor has any such evidence emerged afterward. Since Van der Lubbe had a prior record as a pyromaniac in the Netherlands and went to Germany, as he himself admitted, to protest against the Nazis, the most plausible explanation is also the simplest one: Van der Lubbe acted alone.

A lesson to be drawn here is that in even the most politically charged crimes, history tends to gravitate toward a simple story that provides closure. As the possibility of finding further witnesses recedes over generations, the explanation of an individual mad act becomes more attractive than an open-ended conspiracy, if only because it requires no further conjectures about possible political machinations.

CHAPTER 3

THE LINDBERGH KIDNAPPING

By 1932, aviator Charles A. Lindbergh had become depression-era America's most celebrated hero. Seven years earlier, at the age of twenty-five, he had been the first person to fly solo from New York to Paris, a feat that so captured the imagination of the world that when he landed, a French crowd of some 150,000 spectators at Le Bourget Airport hoisted him above their heads for nearly half an hour; millions turned out for ticker-tape parades in America; and he received commendations from presidents, kings, and dictators. His apotheosis into a celebrity hero was complete when he was married in a fairytale wedding to Ann Morrow, a beautiful fellow aviator and the daughter of a powerful banker at J.P. Morgan. When his only child, eighteen-month-old Charles Augustus Lindbergh, Jr., was kidnapped from his New Jersey home, it became, as H.L. Mencken famously put it, "the biggest story since the Resurrection."

The crime took place on the evening of March 1, 1932. The police were notified at around 11:30 p.m. and arrived at the Lindbergh home in rural East Amwell, New Jersey, shortly before midnight. It had been raining heavily that night, so the police could find no identifiable footprints or other clues outside the house, other than scratches indicating that a ladder had been used to gain entry to the window of the second-floor nursery. The child was last seen in his crib in the nursery by his nurse, Betty Gow, at 8:00 p.m. The nursery itself contained no fingerprints whatsoever, not even those of Gow, other servants, or the family members who had searched the room after the child was found missing. This absence suggested to police that the room had been wiped clean before the police had arrived. The only evidence of a kidnapping in the room was a poorly scribbled ransom note demanding "25000$ in 20$ bills 15000$ in 10$ bills and 10000$ in 5 bills. After 2–4 days we will inform you were [sic] to deliver the mony [sic]. We warn you for making anyding [sic] public or for notify the Police The child is in gut [sic] care. Indication for all letters are singnature [sic] and three holes."

There were interconnected red and blue circles below the signature and three punched holes. In searching the grounds, police found three sections of a home-built ladder in a thicket. Fingerprint experts found 400 partial prints on it, but because they were fragmentary, they had no value in identifying anyone who might have used it. Since it would reach the second-floor window when two sections were assembled, police theorized that it could have been used to gain access to the nursery. But there were wide and irregular spaces between the rungs which would have made it extremely difficult for a person carrying a baby to descend on it on a dark and rainy night. Therefore the police theorized that the intruder or intruders had escaped through the house itself.

Lindbergh said that he heard a noise about 9:30 p.m., and, about a half-hour later, learned from the nurse, Betty Gow, that she had found the child missing. He then armed himself with a Springfield rifle and searched the room and premises, discovered the ransom note on the windowsill, and called the police.

At this point, police had little to go on. No witnesses could be found who saw a car arrive or leave between 8:00 and 10:00 p.m. Nor was there any evidence of the intrusion, other than the note. Even the specks of mud found in the nursery could have come from Lindbergh himself. So could many of the fragmented footprints found on the grounds.

EDWARD JAY EPSTEIN

The lack of evidence fed speculation that some powerful criminal organization or a foreign government had stolen "the Eaglet," as the baby was called in the press. President Herbert Hoover, who had personally decorated Lindbergh after his solo flight, vowed to "move Heaven and Earth" to recover the child. And J. Edgar Hoover—no relation to the President—took the kidnapping as a mandate to expand the FBI, which he had headed since its creation, into a national police agency.

For his part, Lindbergh chose not to cooperate with the FBI agents that Hoover sent to New Jersey. Instead, he first went to William "Wild Bill" Donovan (who would go on to head America's wartime intelligence service, the Office of Strategic Services), then sought out shady intermediaries who claimed to have underworld connections. At this point, he seriously contaminated the police investigation by supplying these intermediaries with the only real secret information in the case, the precise contents of the ransom note. They then provided it to the *New York Daily News*, which, engaged in a circulation war, published most of it. As a result, extortionists, who had nothing to do with the kidnapping, could make bogus requests for the money that Lindbergh, in newspaper ads, was offering to pay. On April 1, 1932, for example, a purported kidnapper answered the ad, claiming that he would return the Eaglet for $100,000. Lindbergh packaged $50,000 in gold certificates and, following instructions, went to St. Raymond's Cemetery in the Bronx, where he gave the money to a man called "John." "John" then handed Lindbergh a note saying that his son was in good health, cared for by two women, on a boat called "The Nelly" docked at Martha's Vineyard. Lindbergh again did not wait for the police. He overflew the docks in his private plane but found no sign of his son—nor the boat (which, it turned out, did not exist). In all, Lindbergh received twelve ransom notes.

Then on May 12, 1932, the corpse of a decomposed child was found in the woods about four and a half miles from the

Lindbergh home. Even though both hands and the left leg were missing, Lindbergh identified the remains from the toes on the right foot. In response to the public outrage, Congress rushed through what became known as the Lindbergh Law, making kidnapping a federal offense.

Meanwhile, unable to find any credible evidence of a kidnapping gang, police began focusing on the possibility of an inside job. The absence of fingerprints after the room had been searched by the Lindbergh family suggested that the room had been wiped clean by someone with something to hide. An inside job would also explain how the kidnapper could have escaped carrying a thirty-pound child. Inside information could also account for how the kidnapper knew not only the child's whereabouts but which was the unlocked window in the nursery. Violet Sharp, a pretty twenty-eight-year-old serving maid, who had told contradictory stories about where she was on the night of the kidnapping, became a prime suspect. The police and FBI were particularly interested in associates of hers with suspected criminal associations. In June 1932, police announced their intentions to take Sharp to police headquarters for questioning, but when they arrived at the Lindbergh house, they found her dead. An autopsy determined that she had died of cyanide poisoning, and the coroner ruled it an apparent suicide.

No further evidence developed, and in 1933, the new President, Franklin Delano Roosevelt, met with J. Edgar Hoover and ordered that the entire kidnapping investigation be centralized under the FBI. Finally, on September 18, 1934, a gold certificate from the ransom that Lindbergh had paid in the Bronx graveyard turned up at a gas station. That clue led police to the home of Bruno Richard Hauptmann, a thirty-four-year-old carpenter, who had a criminal record in his native Germany. A search of his garage turned up about one-third of the ransom money. Hauptmann claimed that the gold certificates had been left with him by his former business partner, Isidor Fisch (who had died after returning to Germany in 1933). Although he denied any knowledge of the kidnapping, Hauptmann was arrested and charged with kidnapping and murder.

At the trial, the prosecutor, New Jersey Attorney General David Wilentz, presented a chain of evidence tying Hauptmann to the $50,000 ransom that Lindbergh had paid for bogus information: handwriting experts found his style consistent with the note; he had part of the ransom money in his garage; and Lindbergh identified his voice as matching that of the man he spoke to in the cemetery. But there was much less evidence placing him anywhere near the scene of the actual kidnapping. One witness who testified that he saw someone looking like Hauptmann driving in the area turned out to be legally blind. The only physical evidence was the ladder used in the kidnapping itself. The state's expert witness rendered an opinion, based on his examination of a floorboard taken from Hauptmann's attic, that it was consistent with one strut of wood in the ladder. But "consistent" merely means that it could have been cut from wood in his attic, not that it had been. The provenance of the wood was also questionable, since it was not found in the original search. It also turned out that none of the partial prints on the ladder or ransom notes matched those of Hauptmann. Despite the lack of direct evidence, Hauptmann was convicted on February 13, 1935, and sentenced to death. Even though New Jersey Governor Harold Hoffman offered to commute his death sentence if Hauptmann would confess, he maintained his innocence, and he was executed by electric chair on April 3, 1936.

The prosecution theory was that Hauptmann acted alone. He built a ladder himself, drove alone to the Lindbergh home in New Jersey, used the ladder to enter the unlit nursery through an unlocked window, left a ransom note that he had prepared, and stole the child. In making his escape, he accidentally killed the child. He then contacted Lindbergh about the ransom, went alone to the cemetery, and collected the $50,000 from Lindbergh.

The problem with the loner theory is that it does not account for how Hauptmann would have known about the movements of the Lindbergh family, who had just returned from New York City, or that the child would be alone in his crib, or which was the unlocked nursery window. An alternative theory is that the kidnapper had an inside source of information. This was the theory of the New Jersey police investigators when they came to arrest Violet Sharp. According to it, the kidnapper was tipped off that the Lindbergh family had returned from New York City, that the child would be alone in the nursery, that the nursery window would be left unlocked, and that there were no alarms or guard dogs that would prevent him from escaping through the house. If he had such inside help, he may even have entered through the house and left the ladder as a diversion for the police. Since Lindbergh restricted police access to his wife and servants—and Violet Sharp died of cyanide before she could be questioned—the police were unsuccessful in pursuing this theory.

A third theory is that the kidnapping story was part of the cover-up of an accidental killing or murder. According to this theory, the child died as the result of domestic violence, his body was buried, and then the responsible party in the household left the ransom note to explain the missing child. Two investigators of the case, Gregory Ahlgren and Stephen Monier, go so far as to suggest in their book *Crime of the Century: The Lindbergh Kidnapping Hoax* that Lindbergh himself accidentally killed his son and then wrote the ransom note to cover up the accident. However, in my view, Lindbergh's actions, including paying the ransom and his relentless searches for his son, are not consistent with the theory that he had killed and buried his son.

Finally, there is the theory that Hauptmann was part of a

gang of swindlers, not kidnappers. According to this theory, Hauptmann or his accomplices, after reading the newspaper stories about the kidnapping, decided to collect the ransom by pretending that they were holding the baby. Since the ransom note had been published, forging similar handwriting would not be difficult. The swindler theory would account for why most of the $50,000 was not found in Hauptmann's home— or anywhere. Another $3,000 of it was later traced to Jacob Novitsky, a convicted forger. Novitsky, who was arrested for another crime, reportedly told a cellmate that he had been involved in the extortion plot but not the kidnapping.

Any assessment of this case needs to take into account how deeply it was corrupted by the media circus. Within an hour of the reported kidnapping, a swarm of reporters trampled through the crime scene, literally muddying up potential footprint and fingerprint evidence. Lindbergh himself gave a copy of the ransom note, the secrecy of which was critical to the investigation, to intermediaries who provided it to the *New York Daily News*. Copies were later sold for five dollars apiece. Other reporters attempted to bribe Lindbergh's servants. The *New York Journal* provided Hauptmann with a flamboyant lawyer, Edward Reilly, who made sensational but false statements to the press, and the Hearst newspapers offered Hauptmann $90,000 to confess. What was lost in this circus is that there were no fingerprints, footprints, fibers, or witnesses that showed Hauptmann was ever in the Lindbergh house or even in the vicinity.

My view is that a perpetrator cannot, even prior to the era of DNA, stage a crime of this magnitude and complexity without leaving a trace of his presence at the crime scene. The possible match of the wood in the ladder to a wood sample taken from Hauptmann's former home is, at best, only probative evidence. So I do not believe that the evidence proves that Hauptmann either kidnapped or killed the baby.

The evidence that Hauptmann came to the cemetery and collected Lindbergh's $50,000 ransom is convincing. I believe that he was part of a gang of swindlers who decided to cash in on the crime. They answered the ad that Lindbergh had placed in the newspapers requesting a meeting, misrepresenting themselves as the kidnappers, and they stole the real kidnappers' ransom. We know that Hauptmann was not alone in this enterprise because he turned over most of the money to others, including $3,000 to Novitsky, an expert forger, who probably wrote the note. As for the kidnapping itself, none of the evidence identifies the perpetrator or perpetrators. The circumstances surrounding the crime suggest that the kidnapper either knew someone inside the household or had other means of learning the Lindberghs' schedule and the layout of the home. Whatever evidence might have pointed to an insider was lost when the nursery was wiped clean of fingerprints. As a result, it is not possible to know how many people were involved in the "crime of the century."

One lesson to be taken away from the Lindbergh case is that the evidence of a crime can be lost forever if the crime scene is not immediately sealed off from journalists, curiosity-seekers, unauthorized law enforcement officers, and family members. The trampling, muddying, and erasure of evidence in and around the Lindbergh home left investigators with no convincing way to determine the identity of the intruder or intruders. With tighter crime-scene procedures, the evidence necessary to resolve this case may have been discovered. Instead, the holes in the case, spotlighted by journalists, have kept this crime unsolved.

CHAPTER 4

THE ASSASSINATION OF OLOF PALME

Olof Palme was the young, dynamic, and charismatic prime minister of Sweden with a radical foreign policy that had attracted worldwide attention—and concern. His assassination in 1986 bedeviled, divided, and haunted the country for over a decade.

On February 28, 1986, at 11:21 p.m., while walking home with his wife from the Grand Cinema on Sveavägen Street in Stockholm, Prime Minister Palme was fatally shot from behind at close range as he neared a subway station. His wife, Lisbet Palme, was then shot by the assassin and critically wounded, but she survived. Palme had no bodyguards or escorts, and no one witnessed the shooting. By the time Lisbet turned in his direction, the shooter, wearing a heavy overcoat, was calmly jogging away. He then disappeared from Lisbet's view through a tunnel at the end of the street.

No one else saw him, and no murder weapon, or any other physical evidence, was found at the crime scene. The Swedish police were able to methodically reconstruct the timeline of the Palmes' movements from cell phone records, but the inferences they drew only added to the mystery. Calls made between Palme and his wife and their son Marten established that the decision to go to the 9:00 p.m. movie was made at 8:00 p.m. The police checked and found no bugs on any of their phones. So, if this was a pre-planned murder, someone would have had to follow Palme to the movie theater and then wait for him to emerge at 11:00 p.m. The assassin would then presumably have followed the Palmes to the deserted street leading to his Hötorgart subway station, shot them both with .357 magnum bullets, and escaped the crime scene. Since the murder weapon was a revolver, no cartridge case was left behind for the police to match to the weapon. Nor was ballistic matching possible on the fragmented bullets. So the killer left no trace. There were two possible explanations: either this was a professional killer who knew how to cover his tracks, or a deranged person who left no evidence by pure chance.

The Swedish investigation focused for the next twenty-one months on the latter possibility, searching Stockholm for a deranged loner who might have been on the street that night and who had a prison record for drug abuse. Then, in December 1988, Lisbet Palme picked out of a police lineup Christer Pettersson, a brain-damaged drug user, who had previously been convicted of manslaughter. Even though she had only seen a man running away from the murder scene, Pettersson was arrested, tried, and convicted of Palme's murder. The only evidence against him, other than that he fit the police's profile of a loner, was Mrs. Palme's testimony.

On appeal, however, that verdict was thrown out because no motive had been established and no murder weapon had been found. The court found inconsistencies in Mrs. Palme's testimony. Pettersson was subsequently acquitted on all charges, released, and died in 2004 from a head injury. No gun was ever found, although, in 2006, a Smith & Wesson .357 revolver, consistent with the type of gun used to kill Palme, was recovered from a lake. But the Swedish National Laboratory of Forensic Science was unable to match it through ballistics to the bullets fired in the assassination. No one else has ever been arrested. Even a $7 million reward failed to produce any further evidence or credible witnesses. So, although the Palme investigation generated some 700,000 pages of documents and cost over $45 million, the case remains unresolved.

There have been many theories offered to explain this unsolved crime. Even after the acquittal of Christer Pettersson, police tended to stick to the loner theory. A gunman saw an unprotected Palme as a target of opportunity, and he simply walked up to him, shot him, shot his wife, and disposed of the weapon. Another theory claimed that the Kurdish militant organization "PKK" had organized the assassination because Palme was cutting off their sources of finance. After receiving a number of tips, Swedish police arrested a number of Kurdish refugees in Stockholm. As there was no evidence placing them at the scene of the crime, and because most of them had alibis, they were released. Fifteen years later, Kurdish PKK leader Abdullah Ocalan was questioned by Swedish investigators in prison in Turkey, but he denied any Kurdish involvement.

Finally, there is the theory that the South African intelligence service killed Palme because he was about to make a deal with its archenemy, the outlawed African National Congress. This theory grew out of the testimony of Eugene de Kock in 1996 to the South African Supreme Court in Pretoria. De Kock, a former high-ranking South African police officer during the apartheid era, said that Craig Williamson, a former police colleague, had organized the plot and hired Anthony White, a former Rhodesian Selous Scout, as the triggerman. The code name for the covert action, according to de Kock, was Operation Longreach.

My assessment is that the assassin was not a spur-of-the-moment amateur. All the evidence points to a professional killer who had carefully stalked his prey and then chose a time and place in which there were no witnesses. He had also planned to kill Lisbet Palme. If she had not survived, no one would have known what had happened. The fact that the weapon was not found, and that the bullets were never traced, are also the marks of a professional hitman. It is also likely he had the false documentation and other support necessary to escape Sweden. We have such a candidate in "Operation Longreach." So I find plausible Eugene de Kock's testimony to the South African Supreme Court that a South African covert-action unit sent a professional assassin to kill Palme. It had a motive in Palme's dealings with the African National Congress. It had the means to get an assassin in and out of Sweden under a false identity. And it had an opportunity in Palme's lack of security. Since de Kock had been granted immunity and had no obvious reason to lie, I believe that Palme was killed by an assassin dispatched from South Africa.

The lesson of this case is that absence of evidence is evidence of absence, which Sherlock Holmes famously referred to as "the dog that did not bark in the night-time" in Sir Arthur Conan Doyle's story "Silver Blaze." After the Palme murder, Swedish police searched high and low for the murder weapon for more than a quarter century without success, including tracking down all the reported stolen Magnum revolvers and test-firing more than 400 other weapons. The absence of a weapon, as well as the absence of any clues at the crime scene, is part of the modus operandi of a professional hitman, who, if successful in his work, commits unsolved crimes.

CHAPTER 5

THE ANTHRAX ATTACK ON AMERICA

The anthrax attack in September 2001 was an act of biological warfare involving the first use of a weapon of mass destruction. It came less than three weeks after the 9/11 attack on the World Trade Center in New York and the Pentagon in Washington, D.C. Accompanying the lethal biological agent were photocopies of two handwritten notes dated 09/11/2001. T he first note was sent along with anthrax to NBC and to the *New York Post*. The note read: "THIS IS NEXT. TAKE PENACILIN [sic] NOW. DEATH TO AMERICA DEATH TO ISRAEL ALLAH IS GREAT." The second note was sent to U.S. Senator Patrick Leahy, chairman of the Senate Judiciary committee, and to Senate majority leader Tom Daschle. This note read: "YOU CANNOT STOP US. WE HAVE THIS ANTHRAX. YOU DIE NOW. ARE YOU AFRAID. DEATH TO AMERICA DEATH TO ISRAEL ALLAH IS GREAT." The anthrax in the envelopes was the most virulent of all anthrax, the deadly Ames strain. Even though the secret technology for turning anthrax spores, which tend to clump together, into an aerosol remains a closely guarded state secret, the letters contained a powdered anthrax that, once they were opened, transformed into a cloud of billions of spores of anthrax. This anthrax in aerosol so thoroughly contaminated the Senate Office Building that it had to be closed down for nearly three months. The anthrax also was not pure. It contained a signature of silicon—the anthrax in the *New York Post* letter was 10 percent silicon when the bulk material was measured by mass—and also contained traces of tin. The anthrax powder had been packed in standard, pre-stamped, 3 ½-inch-by-6 ¼ inch white envelopes. They were postmarked "Trenton, New Jersey," and a test of mailboxes in that postal zone indicated that at least one had been sent from Princeton.

The victims provided no further clues. There were five deaths from the inhalation of the anthrax, and seventeen other people were hospitalized. But most appeared to be random exposures caused by anthrax leakage in the postal system.

In the midst of the panic that ensued in the fall of 2001, the government, which had information that it declined to make public, also became uneasy. The CIA had learned that in 1999, al-Qaeda had employed a Malaysian scientist, Yazid Sufaat, to build an anthrax lab near the Kandahar airport in Afghanistan. Had al-Qaeda used anthrax, as the letters themselves suggested? This possibility could not be neglected by the Defense Department, since most of its military personnel had not yet been vaccinated against anthrax. Secretary of Defense Donald Rumsfeld therefore dispatched a top deputy to FBI headquarters to ascertain if the anthrax put U.S. troops at risk. The FBI considered the subject so sensitive at the time that the deputy was not allowed to bring any of his aides to the meeting. He later described the secret briefing as an eye-opener into the FBI's approach to this biological attack. The FBI assistant director reassured the deputy that it was only a matter of time before they identified the perpetrator. Based on the psychological profile it had already assembled, the view of the FBI task force was that a "lone wolf" American scientist, acting alone, had perpetrated all the attacks. The FBI had narrowed the list down to between 150 and 200 scientists who both had access to lab samples of the Ames strain of anthrax and were located within range of the postal district from which the letters were mailed. The deputy assured the Defense Department executive that all were under surveillance, so there was little danger of another attack. He expressed confidence that they would quickly determine the guilty party by giving each one of the suspects a polygraph examination. When the Defense Department executive then asked him if the FBI was also investigating and polygraphing foreigners who had access to anthrax (since the Ames strain had been sent to several labs abroad), the FBI assistant director told him that they were focusing on the American scientists, and that he expected that the guilty party would soon reveal himself. That was in 2001.

But the FBI polygraph effort, which went on for another seven years, never produced a culprit. No suspect ever broke. Although the FBI investigation code-named "Amerithrax" consumed "hundreds of thousands of investigator work hours," making it the most massive inquest in the history of American law enforcement, it produced no further actual evidence identifying the party behind the attack.

The FBI did not find a single witness to the theft, preparation, or mailing of the anthrax. It did not find any of the equipment used to make the powdered anthrax or any growth media that added silicon, tin, or any other of the trace elements found in the envelopes containing the killer anthrax. It did not find anthrax in the homes, automobiles, personal effects, or even garbage of any of the scientists it was investigating. It did not find the original letter from which the photocopies were made, or the photocopy machine on which it was made (although it examined tens of thousands of such devices). On the four letters and envelopes, or tape sealing them closed, it found no fingerprints, hairs, fibers, or DNA, nor could it identify the handwriting, other than to ascertain that four letters—A,T,T, and A—had been emphasized. Nor did surveillance cameras in the vicinity of the mailbox in Princeton show any of the suspected scientists. The perpetrator had effectively erased any evidence of his or her involvement in the crime.

The first fatality of the attack was Robert Stevens, a photo editor at American Media in Boca Raton, Florida. There was a prior possible anthrax exposure in Florida. Dr. Christos Tsonas, a doctor at the Holy Cross Hospital in Fort Lauderdale, Florida, informed the FBI after Stevens' death that two months earlier he had prescribed an antibiotic for an emergency-room patient named Ahmed Alhaznawi, who had a suspicious black lesion on his leg. At the time, Dr. Tsonas was unfamiliar with anthrax. When he was shown pictures of anthrax lesions in October 2001, he then described Alhaznawi's lesion as "consistent with cutaneous (skin) anthrax." Alhaznawi was a pilot, one of the four hijackers of United Airlines Flight 93 on September 11. Since he was incinerated in the crash, the FBI could not pursue this lead.

Without any direct evidence, other than the attack anthrax itself, the FBI tightened the surveillance on American scientists. One such scientist was microbiologist Perry Mikesell, who had access to anthrax in 1999 when he worked at the Battelle Memorial Institute in Columbus, Ohio. The FBI scrutiny of Mikesell became so intense that, according to family members, he began to drink heavily. Although he died from a heart attack in October 2002, family members said that he drank himself to death. The FBI then turned its attention to Dr. Steven J. Hatfill, a virologist who in 1999 worked at the U.S. Army Medical Research Institute of Infectious Diseases (USAMRIID) in Fort Detrick, Maryland, which was experimenting with the Ames strain of anthrax. Hatfill showed stress on a polygraph exam, and he had taken the antibiotic Cipro, which protects against anthrax infection, prior to the attack, and he attracted the attention of a bloodhound trained to react to the anthrax letters. The FBI surveillance agents followed him so closely that one FBI tail car actually ran over his foot. The FBI searched his home, property, girlfriend's apartment, and workplaces, after the media was alerted. As a result, Hatfill lost his job, consulting contracts, and contact with many associates. Even isolated,

Hatfill did not break under the pressure. Instead, he sued the government. A federal judge expressed outrage that the FBI had pursued him for five years without a "scintilla of evidence," leading the Department of Justice to exonerate him and pay him $5.82 million in August 2008.

Meanwhile, the FBI had contracted with The Institute for Genomic Research (TIGR) for an analysis of the DNA of the anthrax that could more closely pinpoint its origins. It used the DNA of minute changes, or "morphs," in the spores as "genetic fingerprints." Of all the samples the FBI had collected from different labs using the Ames strain, only one matched the "fingerprints" of the killer anthrax in the letters. It was from flask RMR-1029 in Dr. Bruce Ivins' lab. This anthrax had been created in 1997 at the Dugway Proving Ground and sent to Ivins at USAMRIID for vaccine tests. If the match was correct, the FBI finally had the "murder weapon." The custodian for this flask had been Ivins, a microbiologist researcher working on anthrax vaccines. It was part of his job to dispense anthrax to other scientists in the world doing approved research.

Even though Ivins had passed his polygraph exam, he now replaced Hatfill as the prime suspect. The FBI then worked to eliminate all the other scientists to whom Ivins had given access to RMR-1029, for one of three reasons: a scientist had not worked solo in a lab and therefore lacked the privacy needed to process the wet spores into dry powder; a scientist lacked the skill set to do the job; a scientist was located too far away from Princeton to mail the letters. Through this Sherlock Holmes process of elimination, the FBI narrowed the list to one man: Ivins. He worked alone in his lab, he had the skill set, and he could have made the nine-hour round-trip drive to Princeton.

The FBI now needed to break Ivins or find evidence that would hold up in court. It spared no effort. It even attempted to trace back to him the 6¾-inch "Federal Eagle" pre-franked 34-cent envelopes in which the anthrax was mailed, even though nearly 70 million of these virtually identical envelopes had been manufactured for the U.S. Postal Service. To narrow this Augean task, an FBI task force attempted an exotic technique called "microscopic print defect analysis." The idea is that each time a manufacturer prints a new order of envelopes for an area of the country, at some point in the printing process, errors occur. The strategy used was to compare the microscopic errors in the anthrax envelopes to a sample of envelopes collected from different areas of the county. From this analysis, the task force determined that those envelopes were likely received by the Dulles Stamp Distribution Office, which distributed to post offices inside the Capital Beltway and southern Maryland. This was undoubtedly great forensic work. The problem was that this area included the employees of a large number of bio-technology facilities that dealt with anthrax. It also covered areas where many employees of intelligence services, foreign embassies, and defense contractors reside. To tie the envelopes, the FBI sought to find them in the search of Ivins' home, office, and past mailings, but came up with no matches. The envelopes could not even be definitely traced to his local post office in Frederick, Maryland, because the office had returned all its stamped envelopes when postal rates changed.

In late 2007, Ivins was harshly interrogated. By this time almost everything he had, including his home, computer, car, and personal effects were searched. Yet no trace of anthrax was found on any of his personal effects. His twin children were then offered a $2.5 million reward to provide evidence against their father, but they did not provide any. Meanwhile, his security clearance was withdrawn, barring him from his work. Even though he had passed his polygraph exam, the intensive searches produced no evidence that he had ever handled anthrax outside his lab or had driven to the Princeton-Trenton area in September 2001, and the FBI came up with no evidence

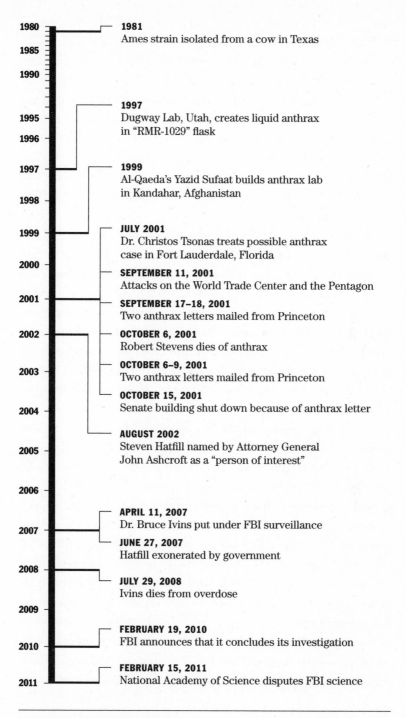

1980
1985
1990

1995
1996

1997

1998

1999

2000

2001

2002

2003

2004

2005

2006

2007

2008

2009

2010

2011

1981
Ames strain isolated from a cow in Texas

1997
Dugway Lab, Utah, creates liquid anthrax
in "RMR-1029" flask

1999
Al-Qaeda's Yazid Sufaat builds anthrax lab
in Kandahar, Afghanistan

JULY 2001
Dr. Christos Tsonas treats possible anthrax
case in Fort Lauderdale, Florida

SEPTEMBER 11, 2001
Attacks on the World Trade Center and the Pentagon

SEPTEMBER 17–18, 2001
Two anthrax letters mailed from Princeton

OCTOBER 6, 2001
Robert Stevens dies of anthrax

OCTOBER 6–9, 2001
Two anthrax letters mailed from Princeton

OCTOBER 15, 2001
Senate building shut down because of anthrax letter

AUGUST 2002
Steven Hatfill named by Attorney General
John Ashcroft as a "person of interest"

APRIL 11, 2007
Dr. Bruce Ivins put under FBI surveillance

JUNE 27, 2007
Hatfill exonerated by government

JULY 29, 2008
Ivins dies from overdose

FEBRUARY 19, 2010
FBI announces that it concludes its investigation

FEBRUARY 15, 2011
National Academy of Science disputes FBI science

linking him to the killer anthrax. However, the FBI found creepy behavior in Ivins' personal life. He collected pornography, had web aliases, and admitted that he had become obsessed with a sorority girl. As the pressure continued, and his legal fees threatened to bankrupt him, he drank heavily, took prescription mind-altering drugs, acted erratically, and had a psychiatric breakdown. Finally, his life a shambles, on July 29, 2008, he killed himself with a Tylenol overdose. Though he was never charged or brought before a grand jury, the FBI identified him as the anthrax killer.

Less than a week after Ivins' apparent suicide, the FBI declared him to have been the sole perpetrator of the 2001 anthrax attacks and released bizarre emails that he had written which, though unrelated to anthrax, suggested that he was a disturbed individual. Even though Ivins had not been indicted, and none of the case against him had ever been tested in a legal process, the FBI justified its extraordinary finding of guilt on the basis of the scientific evidence, which, it suggested before Congress, proved that Ivins, and Ivins alone, was behind the anthrax attack.

I had been investigating this case for seven years at this point, and I had interviewed scientists with whom Ivins had worked or who were otherwise familiar with his lab work. All of them told me that they did not believe that Ivins had the means to grow and then convert the liquid lab anthrax into the powdered attack anthrax without others in the lab observing this process. Jeffrey Adamovicz, one of the lab scientists I interviewed, wrote me: "Even if Bruce (or anyone else) wanted to use the fermentor in our labs, [and it] was non-operational, this person would have been observed even if it were operational." I also found out that the FBI had never reverse-engineered or otherwise replicated the process by which the anthrax was produced. Indeed, almost all the attempts failed to reproduce the silicon content found in the anthrax in the letter sent to the

New York Post. After I reported this FBI failure in a commentary in the *Wall Street Journal* on January 25, 2010, D. Christian Hassell, assistant director of the FBI Laboratory, replied to the *Wall Street Journal*, "The FBI is confident in the scientific findings that were reached in this investigation. We utilized established biological and chemical analysis techniques and applied them in an innovative manner to reach these findings." But had the science actually validated the FBI's conclusions?

To validate the science that the FBI had used to narrow the search to Ivins, the FBI contracted with the prestigious National Academy of Sciences (NAS) to conduct an independent assessment of its methods. The NAS took until February to complete its assignment. The result was not what the FBI expected. The NAS report concluded that the FBI's key assertion that its genetic fingerprinting showed that the killer anthrax could only have come from the flask in Ivins' custody was flawed. "The scientific data alone do not support the strength of the government's repeated assertions that RMR-1029 was conclusively identified as the parent material to the anthrax powder used in the mailings," it stated. "It is not possible to reach a definitive conclusion about the origins of the B. anthracis in the mailings based on the available scientific evidence alone." Without a valid scientific basis for tracing the killer anthrax to Ivins' lab, the FBI case against him is based on inference from his suspicious behavior.

The NAS report also raised questions as to where the anthrax was stolen from and where it was processed into powder. It revealed that the killer anthrax in the *New York Post* letter had a silicon content of "10 percent by mass." Ivins' lab anthrax had no silicon. The FBI had suggested that the silicon could have come naturally from the mixture of water and nutrients in which the anthrax was grown. But when the FBI attempted to test this theory by having the Lawrence Livermore National Lab grow anthrax in broth laced with silicon, it failed to match the silicon signature. Out of fifty-six tries, most results were a whole order of magnitude lower, with some as low as .001 percent. The FBI had other labs attempts to reverse-engineer the killer anthrax, but the closest it came to the silicon signature was in some results from Dugway Proving Ground.

Ivins could still have committed the crimes, but he would have needed a collaborator at Dugway or elsewhere who had access to the powdered anthrax or the process to make it. This complication led Senator Leahy to tell FBI Director Robert Mueller, "I do not believe in any way, shape, or manner that [Ivins] is the only person involved in this attack on Congress." Although the FBI did not agree, the case remains unsolved a decade later.

There remain a number of viable theories of the case. The FBI's theory is that Ivins, and Dr. Ivins alone, was behind the attack. Senator Leahy's theory is that Dr. Ivins may have been guilty, but that he could not have acted alone. Finally, there is the theory that a terrorist or foreign intelligence service was behind the attack. The NAS report found that, though the results were inconsistent, some samples collected abroad from an unnamed location possibly matched the attack anthrax.

My assessment is that the FBI failed to find the perpetrator of the anthrax attack. Indeed, it failed twice. Its first wrong man was Dr. Steven J. Hatfill, whose career was ruined by its 24/7 investigation of him; the second wrong man was Dr. Bruce Ivins, who committed suicide under its relentless pressure. In a case such as the anthrax attack, in which the weapon leaves microscopic traces everywhere, the equivalent of Sherlock Holmes' dog-that-did-not-bark is the conspicuous absence of evidence. The FBI investigation was possibly the most massive in history in terms of expended man-hours. Consider then what evidence the FBI did not find that would have implicated their final suspect, Dr. Ivins.

First, no traces of anthrax were found in Ivins' home, car,

clothing, garbage, or personal effects, so there is no evidence that Ivins ever removed anthrax from his lab.

Second, none of the dozens of scientists, technicians, and security guards that worked or visited Ivins' lab, and were relentlessly interviewed by the FBI, ever witnessed him with the apparatus or growing vats necessary to process liquid anthrax (which was stored in a lab flask) into the powdered anthrax used in the attack. Yet to grow and dry this attack anthrax required gallons of media, as well as drying equipment such as a fermentor, which, according to other scientists who worked with him (and whom I interviewed), were not available to Ivins.

Third, the FBI was not able to find tollbooth records, gas purchases, or surveillance-camera evidence that Ivins drove his car to Princeton, or was in Princeton, during the period when the anthrax letters were mailed. If he was there, no one saw him, and he did not leave a trace of his presence.

Finally, the FBI could not trace the copies of the anthrax letters to any photocopying machine available to Ivins (or any other scientist at Fort Detrick). Nor could it find any pre-paid envelopes in Ivins' home that matched those in which the anthrax letters were mailed. In short, there is no physical evidence actually linking Ivins to the anthrax attack.

Since the science by which the FBI attempted to eliminate all other suspects also turned out to be flawed, according to the exhaustive review by the National Academy of Science panel, it is not certain that the attack anthrax originated at the Fort Detrick lab. It could just as likely have come from the Battelle Memorial Lab in Ohio or the Army's Dugway Proving Ground in Utah. In fact, the silicon signature in the anthrax points directly to Dugway. The Dugway lab had been making dry anthrax there, using the same strain of anthrax, since the late 1990s to test anthrax-detection devices. The concern here was that Iraq would use anthrax against U.S. forces, so Dugway scientists employed a multi-stage process to mill test anthrax using a silica-based flow enhancer that was not available at Ivins' facility at Fort Detrick. As there had been a number of security breaches at Dugway during this period, it is plausible that someone at Dugway stole a minute ampule of anthrax anytime after 1997 and, like any classic espionage operation, delivered it to another party, either foreign or domestic, who used it in the September 2001 attacks.

The lesson to be taken away from this unresolved crime is the vulnerability of even the most massive investigations to a preconception embedded in a behavioral profile. Just weeks after the attack, the FBI had arrived at a "behavioral assessment" pointing to a lone American scientist. It described, as David Willman reports in his 2011 book *Mirage Man*, a well-educated "single person" with "legitimate access to select biological agents," who is "stand-offish," and who prefers not to work in a "group team setting." It was this assessment that steered the FBI first to Hatfield and then to Ivins. When the FBI's behavioral science unit was created in 1972, its primary mission was profiling unknown serial killers by using historical data. But in the case of the anthrax attack, there was only one prior case of bioterrorism in the United States, the deliberate contamination with salmonella of salad bars in ten restaurants in Oregon. But this biological attack, which resulted in the poisoning of 751 individuals, was not perpetrated by a lone American. It was the act of a conspiracy in which the main perpetrators were foreign-born followers of the Indian spiritualist Bhagwan Shree Rajneesh. Nor did the text of the anthrax letters themselves point to a single American scientist, since it used the plural "we," contained the misspelling of the word "penicillin," and also had jihadist formulations, such as "Death to America." If, as the FBI assumed, the text was a deliberate deception, it left little material to support its profile of a lone American scientist. Yet, by clinging to this profile, it neglected investigative paths that may have resolved this crime.

CHAPTER 6

THE POPE'S ASSASSIN

On May 13,1981, Mehmet Ali Agca, a twenty-three-year-old Turkish citizen, who was amidst a throng of people in the piazza in front of St. Peter's Basilica in Vatican City, suddenly raised a Browning semi-automatic pistol, and shot Pope John Paul II no fewer than four times. The fusillade of bullets gravely wounded the pope, who survived the attack. Agca was captured gun in hand at the scene by Vatican security and Italian police. He had arrived in Rome by train only three days earlier. Under interrogation, Agca freely admitted firing the shots and said that he acted alone. Two years earlier, Agca had been sent to prison in Turkey for assassinating Abdi Ipekci, the editor of the newspaper *Milliyet*, a crime he confessed to on Turkish television. He had also threatened in a letter to kill Pope John Paul II, whom he called "the Commander of the Crusades" against Islam. He escaped from prison in November 1979. Based on his confession, the Italian investigation concluded that he acted as a lone fanatic when he shot the pope. In July 1981, he was tried in Rome, convicted, and sentenced to life imprisonment. Even with the conviction, it was not a closed case.

Within months, the case was transformed from a lone-assassin scenario to a possible conspiracy. The driving force for this new narrative was investigative journalism. In Turkey, journalist Ugur Mumcu was able to piece together an intriguing trail for Agca. It began with his well-planned escaped from a high-security Turkish prison in 1979, an escape in which he walked out disguised as a soldier, and it continued as he assumed various other aliases, assisted by false travel documents through a half-dozen countries, including Bulgaria, Germany, Syria, and Iran, to Italy. According to Mumcu's research, the jailbreak was organized by a Turkish terrorist organization called "The Grey Wolves," which also supplied him with money, weapons, and documents. Meanwhile, in America, two separate journalistic investigations—one for the *Reader's Digest* by Paul Henze, the CIA station chief in Turkey from 1974 to 1977; the other by Claire Sterling, who had written *The Terror Network*—uncovered evidence suggesting that Agca had been working for the Bulgarian intelligence service at the time of the assassination attempt. They also named a number of Bulgarian officials in Rome who they said may have been involved in the plot. As the firestorm grew in the Italian media, Agca was re-interrogated in prison. After being shown pictures of the Bulgarian officials in Italy, Agca changed his story. He now said he had two Bulgarian accomplices in Rome. He said one of them was Sergei Antonov, the representative in Rome of Balkan Air, the Bulgarian national airline, who drove him to St. Peter's Square to shoot the pope. Antonov denied knowing Agca and having any involvement in the plot. Nevertheless, he was arrested by Italian authorities and put on trial for complicity in the attempt to kill the pope. During the trial, which extended over two years, Agca again changed his story, exonerating Antonov in rambling and incoherent testimony. Antonov was acquitted in 1986, returned to Bulgaria, became the subject of a novel called *The Executioner* by Stefan Kisyov, and died in 2007. His lengthy trial produced no evidence to substantiate the media stories that Agca was paid by the Bulgarian intelligence. For his part, Agca had made so many contradictory claims in the trial that his testimony was of little value in resolving the question of conspiracy. After the pope recovered and asked that Agca be shown mercy, Agca was extradited to

Turkey, and then, after twenty-eight years in prison, was released on January 18, 2010.

As for why he attempted to assassinate the pope, there are three main theories. First, that he acted on his own, believing, as he wrote prior to the attempt, that the pope was an enemy of Islam. According to this view, Agca, no matter who helped him escape from prison, earned money through smuggling and other criminal activities in Bulgaria and Germany. He used this money to buy a false passport, train tickets, and the weapon he used to shoot the pope. His conspiratorial confessions were either delusional or attempts to win favor from the Italian authorities. A second theory is that he was working for a Muslim extremist group, such as the Grey Wolves, who recruited him in prison, because of the threats he had made against the pope, and arranged his escape. In this view, Agca's trips to Syria, where Agca himself said he had received terrorist training, were sponsored by the Islamic group that recruited him. That his target was not beyond the scope of such Islamic extremist groups was demonstrated, according to this theory, by the failed attempt by Ramzi Yousef, who was the organizer of the first attack on the World Trade Center in 1993, to assassinate Pope John Paul II in the Philippines on January 15, 1995. Finally, there is the theory, advanced in the books of Sterling and Henze, that the papal assassination had been organized by the Bulgarian intelligence service on behalf of the Soviet Union's KGB. The motive, according to this theory, was that Pope John Paul II, the first Polish pope, had been secretly funding the anti-Soviet Solidarity involvement in Poland. This alleged KGB plot was the prosecution's theory in the 1984–86 trial of Antonov.

My own assessment is that Agca acted alone. His own contradictory statements demonstrate, if anything, that he was opportunistic in inventing stories. There is no doubt that he had assistance from the Grey Wolves in escaping prison, as Mumcu convincingly shows, but there is no evidence that this organization supported or even stayed in contact with him when he went to Europe. And there is no persuasive evidence that he had ever been connected to either Bulgarian or Russian intelligence. At Antonov's trial, Agca appeared to be totally deranged. If that was not an act, he was clearly capable of undertaking delusional missions. So it is possible, though by no means certain, that he himself decided to eliminate a person he described as a "crusader."

A lesson here is that a lone assassin may find reason to falsely implicate others in a putative conspiracy. For example, James Earl Ray, who confessed to the 1968 murder of Dr. Martin Luther King, Jr. in 1969, asserted in an unsuccessful attempt to win a new trial eight years later that he had a co-conspirator named "Raoul" (even though a polygraph test financed by *Playboy* magazine showed that he had acted alone). In the attack on the pope, the Cold War interest in implicating Soviet intelligence in a papal assassination attempt provided Agca with an incentive, if only to break the boredom of prison, to implicate Antonov and other Bulgarian and Russian officials in the putative plot. Not all loners have help—even if they say they do.

PART TWO

SUICIDE, ACCIDENT, OR DISGUISED MURDER?

CHAPTER 7

THE MAYERLING INCIDENT

On January 30, 1889, two young lovers were found shot dead at a hunting lodge in Mayerling, Austria. One was Crown Prince Rudolf of Austria, the only son of Emperor Franz Josef I and the heir to the throne of the then-powerful Austro-Hungarian Empire; the other was Baroness Marie Vetseva, a beautiful seventeen-year-old aristocrat. Their deaths stirred the imagination of the world and over the next century and grew into a legend of a Romeo-and-Juliet-style suicide pact carried out because of the couple's unwillingness to be apart. It became the subject of the British ballet *Mayerling*, with music by Franz Liszt; the German opera *Mayerling: Requiem For Love*; the American operetta *Marinka*, with the hit song "One Touch of Venus"; the Hungarian musical *Rudolf*; the Japanese manga *Angel's Coffin*; the American television production *Mayerling* with Audrey Hepburn and Mel Ferrer as the star-crossed lovers; two Hollywood movies called *Mayerling*; and six other European movies. These romantic productions, however, lack any basis in fact.

The problem here is that little is known about the crime scene. All that is established is a sequence of events. In January 1889, the Austro-Hungarian Empire and its imperial family were in a state of crisis over the childless relationship of Crown Prince Rudolf and his wife, Princess Stephanie, the daughter of an important royal ally, King Leopold of Belgium. On January 29, 1889, Prince Rudolf departed from Vienna for a remote lodge in upper Austria with his teenage mistress Marie Vetseva, and a servant. On January 30, the imperial family was notified by local police that the prince and his mistress were dead. Their bodies had been discovered by a servant. The imperial family ordered the police to seal the crime scene and remove Vetseva's body from the scene. It was secretly buried on the grounds of a nearby monastery, where it would remain unexamined for more than half a century. All police reports of the crime were ordered expunged. On February 1, the Imperial Court issued an official statement saying that Prince Rudolf died from heart failure. No mention was made of the Baroness Marie Vetseva. Later that week, Prince Rudolf was buried in the imperial crypt after the pope gave dispensation for burial on holy ground. However, because of persistent rumors of murder, suicide, and a cover-up, the Vatican in 1889 appointed a special papal nuncio, or representative of the pope, to determine the basic facts to support the pope's dispensation, since suicide victims were not under normal circumstances permitted to be buried on holy ground. The results were filed away in the Vatican archives and kept secret for nearly ninety years.

What is now known about the double death emerged largely as a result of access to the Vatican's investigation, which was first made available to outside scholars in 1979. This investigation had revealed that both corpses were in the prince's bedroom, that the advanced state of rigor mortis of Marie Vetseva's body indicated that she had died many hours earlier than Prince Rudolf, that only a single shot was fired that night at Mayerling lodge, and that Prince Rudolf died instantly from a bullet wound. The several hours between their deaths ruled out a near-simultaneous suicide. Before any sort of thorough medical examination could be performed on Marie Vetseva's body, it was spirited away. In 1955, during the final days of the Russian occupation of Austria, her grave was accidently re-opened by Russian troops. Given the opportunity to re-inter it, family members agreed to allow a doctor to examine Vetseva's skeleton. An Austrian physician, Dr. Gerd Holler, examined her bones and skull and found no penetration holes or other damage consistent with a bullet wound. This belated examination was consistent with the police report, which said that only one shot had been fired in the lodge. If accurate, the examination means that Vetseva had died by means other than a gunshot several hours before the prince's death. Dr. Holler, who became a relentless investigator of the incident, succeeded three decades later in getting the Vatican to open its archives.

The mystery surrounding Vetseva's death has led to a surfeit of speculative theories, the most romantic of which is the double suicide. According to this theory, the prince and baroness, unable to pursue their love affair because of intrigues of the court, killed themselves in a suicide pact. Presumably, she first killed herself, and then, after several hours, he followed suit. A second theory proposed in a number of books on the subject is that Prince Rudolf and Marie Vetseva were murdered together. The murder theory received support from Empress Zita, the widow of the last emperor. Shortly before her death, the empress claimed in an 1988 interview that the prince and his lover were killed as part of a political plot and that their murders were disguised as a double suicide. Finally, there is the theory that Prince Rudolf killed Marie Vetseva in a heated dispute and, several hours later, killed himself because he was unable to cope with the consequences of his crime.

To borrow from Lord Acton, if political power corrupts a crime investigation, absolute power, such at that held by the Austro-Hungarian emperor, corrupts the evidence absolutely. The best evidence we have is the secret report of the Vatican discovered by Dr. Holler. It contains no suspicion of police perjuring themselves or forging reports. If true, this would rule out the double-murder theory since police, servants, and other witnesses told the papal nuncio that no one else broke into the house. The medical report would also rule out a double suicide because of the long gap between Marie Vetseva's and Prince Rudolf's deaths. Nor does it seem plausible that seventeen-year-old Marie, who came from a religious family, intended to commit suicide, which was a serious sin. As there was no suicide note, I believe that the simplest scenario that fits the evidence is that Prince Rudolf first killed his lover and then himself.

Importantly, the Mayerling case shows that the possibility of solving a murder mystery does not perish with the death of the witnesses and destruction of evidence. So long as a body can be exhumed, forensic tools can be employed to cast a new light on a crime.

CHAPTER 8

WHO KILLED GOD'S BANKER?

I.

On June 11, 1982, Roberto Calvi, the chairman of the Banco Ambrosiano, left Italy. He had with him a black briefcase that an assistant had seen him stuff with documents from his safe. The disappearance of "God's banker," as he was known in the Italian media because of the massive investments he made for the Vatican, set in motion an international manhunt. One week later, his body was found hanging under Blackfriars Bridge in London with an orange noose around his neck and his feet submerged in the swirling waters of the Thames. The black bag was gone. Also missing was $1.2 billion from Banco Ambrosiano's subsidiaries in the Bahamas, Nicaragua, Peru, and Luxembourg. The Vatican bank was missing a half-billion dollars in the form of loans to anonymous corporations owned by unknown parties.

Blackfriars Bridge, which had been built across the River Thames in 1769, had been undergoing extensive repairs, and scaffolding had been erected alongside it. To get up and down the scaffolding, iron ladders had been installed; Calvi's body was found hanging from this abutting scaffolding. When the London river police cut down the body on the morning of June 19, 1982, they did not know immediately that it was the missing Italian banker. The Italian passport on the corpse identified him as "Gian Roberto Calvino." It was a bogus passport, it turned out, that he had used to get into Britain. The police ruled out robbery, as "Calvino" still wore a very expensive Patek Philippe watch on his wrist and had about $14,000 in Swiss francs, British pounds, and Italian lire in his wallet. They also found seven large pieces of masonry stuffed in his pants. Even after he was identified, Scotland Yard, the Italian financial police, and Interpol were all perplexed as to how this banker from Milan came to be dangling at the end of a rope over the Thames in London. Did he commit suicide, or was he murdered? The coroner's jury rendered a verdict of probable suicide on July 23, 1982, but that verdict was overturned on March 29, 1983, and a second coroner's jury in London, unable to decide whether it was murder or suicide, rendered an open verdict.

I was also baffled by the circumstances of the hanging of God's banker. I had come to London in 1983 on assignment from *Vanity Fair* to investigate his death, not realizing at the time that the twists and turns in my own investigation would span the next three decades.

I went to see Professor Frederick Keith Simpson, one of England's most experienced and brilliant pathologists, who had conduced the autopsy. It had established that there was no river water in Calvi's lungs, so he had not drowned. The cause of death was asphyxia, or loss of oxygen. There was a V-shaped wound on his neck, consistent with suicide by hanging, and there were no marks on his arms to indicate that he had been restrained, no puncture marks on his body to indicate that he had been injected with a drug, and no traces of suspicious chemicals or drugs in his stomach (other than the residue of a sleeping pill he had taken the previous night). In short, there was no medical evidence of foul play.

The time of the death was fixed by his Patek Philippe watch, which, though valued at over $100,000, was not waterproof. It stopped at 1:52 a.m. While the watch could have stopped for reasons other than water damage, the water marks on the face of it, when taken together with the dropping level of the tide that night at Blackfriars Bridge, established the latest time at which his body could have been suspended from the scaffolding. After 2:30 a.m., the level of the water in the Thames at Blackfriars Bridge would not have been high enough to have reached Calvi's wrist, so he must have been hanging before then. But he could not have hanged himself before 1:00 a.m. because the river level then would have been above his mouth, and there was no river water in his body. So, if he committed suicide, it could only have been between 1:00 and 2:30 a.m. Making the problem more vexing, during these hours there was a low tide, and the distance to the water would most likely have broken his neck. Yet the pathologist had determined that Calvi's neck had not suffered the kind of injury that would have occurred in such a free-fall. In fact, he could have not have dropped more than two feet before his fall was broken by the water. To get that near to the water, after tying the rope, he would have had to climb twelve feet down a nearly vertical iron ladder, and then, with seven pieces of masonry in his clothes, step across a two-and-one-half-foot gap onto the scaffolding's rusty poles, which were arranged like monkey bars in a children's playground. Next he would have to tie the rope and shimmy down to the next level of the scaffolding in the darkness. The medical examination had found none of the signs, including splinters, cuts, or abrasions on his hands, or rust and tears in his grey suit, that such a descent would be expected to have produced. Whereas climbing up and down ladders and scaffolding might present no problem for a young man in the peak of health, Calvi was sixty-two years old and overweight, and he suffered from vertigo. Even in the absence of any murder signatures on Calvi's corpse, I found it difficult to accept that he killed himself without help.

I next went to Rome to speak to Italian investigators.

What was clear from their investigation was that Calvi had co-conspirators in getting to London. Italian authorities had established that he had used three false identities, eight separate private-plane flights around Europe, a speedboat, four different cars, and fourteen temporary residences in getting into Britain. He had gone from Rome to Venice by plane, then to Trieste by car, where someone smuggled him in a speedboat to Yugoslavia. From there, a car had driven him to a mountain retreat in Austria, and then, on June 15, disguised as a Fiat executive, he had flown from a small airport in Austria to London in a leased jet. The facilitator of this incredibly complex escape was Flavio Carboni, a well-connected Sardinian businessman. Calvi had previously used Carboni to fix problems, and when he learned he was about to be arrested for bank fraud, he asked Carboni to arrange his escape from Italy. To this end, he had given him access to about $19 million in numbered accounts. Carboni then employed Silvano Vittor, a cigarette smuggler, to be Calvi's bodyguard and driver. He also had two strikingly beautiful Austrian sisters, Manuela and Michaela Klienszig, help arrange the logistics.

Once in London, Carboni and the Klienszig sisters stayed at a deluxe hotel, but Calvi and Vittor checked into an inexpensive suite at a second-rate residential hotel, the Chelsea Cloisters. Calvi used the alias "Calvino." It was the last place any witness saw him on June 18. When policed searched the suite the next day, Vittor was gone. All police found in the suite was Calvi's personal belongings, including his toilet kit and sleeping pills, neatly packed inside two locked suitcases, as if they were waiting to be picked up by someone. His black attaché case was missing, however. Despite an intense search, Scotland Yard could not find a single hotel employee, taxi driver, or other witness to Calvi's movements that night (or, for that matter, in the three days he had been in London prior to his death). During these London days, he was "the invisible man,"

EDWARD JAY EPSTEIN

as Police Deputy Superintendent White told me. "We don't even know how he got from his hotel, four and one half miles away, to Blackfriars Bridge. And we do not know how Calvi's body got onto the end of that rope."

Although the coroner's jury did not find direct evidence of murder, Carlo Calvi, Calvi's only son, was convinced, as he told me, "my father did not commit suicide." He was also determined to prove it to the insurer Unione Italiana, which could avoid a $10-million payment if the death was in fact by suicide. In 1989, he hired Kroll Associates, one of the world's leading private-detective agencies, to reinvestigate the case. Kroll, with Carlo Calvi's permission, gave me access to their meticulous reconstruction of the crime. After locating, authenticating, and reassembling the original scaffolding that Calvi had been hanged from, Kroll's forensic experts conducted a reenactment in which a movie stuntman was retained as a stand-in for Calvi. He was roughly the same size and weight, and he walked all the possible routes along the scaffolding poles that Calvi would have to walk if he had indeed tied the rope and hanged himself. The stand-in wore exact copies of the handmade loafers Calvi wore that night. These shoes were then put in water for the same time that Calvi's shoes had been submerged, and then microscopically examined by a former London police laboratory chemist. On every route, the chemist found that the soles of the stand-in's shoes had picked up yellow paint smears that matched those on the scaffolding poles. Given Calvi's weight, and the pressure of the shoe on the narrow pole, he concluded that such telltale traces were unavoidable. Yet, when he microscopically examined the soles of the shoes Calvi had actually worn, he found no traces of yellow paint on the soles. Since there was no way Calvi could have hanged himself except by walking on the scaffolding, this investigation concluded that "Someone else had to have tied him to the scaffolding and killed him."

The reconstruction convinced me that this was indeed a murder, but the final proof came in December 1998, when a Rome court authorized the exhumation of Calvi's corpse, which had been buried for sixteen years. His bones and other remains were reexamined by a panel of forensic experts, who concluded that the injuries to his neck were inconsistent with self-hanging, and that therefore he had most likely been murdered. If so, it was a murder disguised to look like a suicide.

But who killed Calvi?

II.

It was not difficult to find a motive for silencing Calvi. For those who ruled the world of money, Calvi's death in June 1982 closed a Pandora's box of troubles. Not only was $1.2 billion of Calvi's bank's money missing, but through a subsidiary in Luxembourg, Calvi had been acting for the sovereign state of the Vatican. His departure from Italy on June 11, 1982, had caused a panic. It reached Italy's top monetary authorities while they were aboard a military jet en route to Brussels to face the grim prospect of a devaluation of the lira—the fifth in three years. Whatever might happen to the lira in Brussels that day, the concern of these men was now focused on the missing banker. The collapse of Calvi's bank, the second-largest private bank in Italy, was now practically unavoidable, and this, in turn, could seriously undermine the credibility of the entire Italian banking system. One of the officials on the plane, Mario Sarcinelli, the director general of the Treasury Ministry, also had a special interest in the Calvi case. It had almost destroyed his career three years earlier, when, as the deputy director of the Bank of Italy, he had begun an investigation into the Banco Ambrosiano. Before he could complete it, police arrived at the palatial headquarters of the Bank of Italy in Rome and arrested him on what he called "trumped up charges." He was accused of withholding information and confined to a dungeon in the Regina Coeli prison in Rome. Finally, after ten days, he was freed on condition that he leave the Bank of Italy, and this ended Sarcinelli's investigation.

Two other specially chartered jets took to the air on June 11. The first of these planes had been chartered in Luxembourg to go to Milan. It carried secret documents that up to this time had been seen only by Calvi and his top deputy. They were hand-delivered to Michel Leemans, Calvi's trusted deputy at the investment banking unit of Banco Ambrosiano, who subsequently told me that the documents identified the true owner of a group of anonymous companies that held the mystery block of Banco Ambrosiano stock that had stymied Sarcinelli's investigators four years earlier.

The other chartered plane was an Alitalia Boeing 727 carrying Pope John Paul II to Geneva, Switzerland. Accompanying the pope on this flight was Archbishop Paul Casimir Marcinkus, the president of the Vatican's bank, which was called the Istituto per le Opere di Religione (Institute for Religious Works). For the past week, Calvi's deputies at the Banco Ambrosiano had been desperately trying to reach Marcinkus because Calvi had made him a director of the Banco Ambrosiano subsidiary in the Bahamas that had served as a staging post for the international operations of the Banco Ambrosiano. The son of an immigrant window-washer, Marcinkus had come to the Vatican in 1950 as a twenty-eight-year-old student priest and had never left. He quickly rose through the ranks of the bureaucracy to become the right hand of first Pope Paul and then Pope John Paul II. Three months before Calvi's disappearance, the pope had stood by Marcinkus' side at a meeting of the fifteen Cardinals on the Commission for Vatican Finances. When questions were raised about the Vatican's faltering income and rising deficits, the pope had held his hand up to Marcinkus and replied

"If you have any problems—ask [him], he'll know how to solve them." The cardinals also had no doubts about Marcinkus' loyalty to the pope: he had, as one cardinal remarked, "the fidelity of a Saint Bernard."

When Marcinkus returned with the pope from Geneva, according to Leemans, he immediately asked for a meeting with Leemans, who was now in charge of the faltering Banco Ambrosiano. Leemans said that he then showed Marcinkus two documents that he had been sent from Luxembourg on the chartered jet. Marcinkus, according to Leemans, acknowledged that they were "letters of patronage," signed by his deputy and initialed by him. They clearly identified the Vatican Bank as the owner of the key anonymous companies through which the Vatican had incurred huge debts. Leemans explained that the Banco Ambrosiano Group would be forced into bankruptcy in a matter of hours unless these debts were repaid by the Vatican.

Leemans said that the archbishop replied that the Vatican recognized no debt to the Banco Ambrosiano. He dismissed the letters of patronage as legally meaningless because he held a trump card—a "counter-letter," signed by Calvi, which released the Vatican from any responsibility proceeding from his initialing of the "letters of patronage." As far as he was concerned, initialing these letters was merely a personal mistake on his part. "I did it purely as an act of friendship to Calvi," he told Leemans. "I realize that I will have to pay personally for that error of judgment."

Leemans could not accept this explanation at face value. He did not believe that these letters of patronage, which involved the Vatican in a debt exceeding one billion dollars, had been simply dashed out by Marcinkus as a token of friendship. Moreover, before these letters had been issued, Marcinkus had sent his deputy to Lugano, Switzerland, to see secret records held in a bank vault—a vault to which the Vatican held one key and the Banco Ambrosiano the other. These records confirmed that the Vatican's bank was listed as the owner of record of the companies in question. They also showed that these companies held as their main asset over 10 percent of the shares of the Banco Ambrosiano. If that were true, Leemans reasoned, the archbishop had an interest in issuing the letters that went beyond personal friendship with Calvi.

But the Vatican was a sovereign state that did not have to answer to any authority other than the pope. It could only be sued in a court in the Vatican with the permission of the pope. If Marcinkus stood his ground and insisted that the letters, and whatever other evidence turned up, proceeded from his personal errors and naivety, the Vatican could not be held legally responsible for the huge debt. Seeing that there was no practical way around the stonewall erected by Marcinkus, Leemans suggested that they work together to prevent the collapse of the Banco Ambrosiano with all the attendant public revelations. Specifically, he proposed raising a loan on the world market for the Vatican bank that would be used to save the Banco Ambrosiano.

The archbishop, calculating that the interest for such a loan would amount to more than a hundred million dollars per year, according to Leemans, said, "We just don't have that kind of money."

As soon as he left the gates of the Vatican, Leemans placed a telephone call to Milan that interrupted the tense Board of Directors meeting of the Banco Ambrosiano. "Call in Grandmother," Leemans said, which was the prearranged signal to ask the Bank of Italy to take over the bank. It was the last meeting that the Board of Directors ever held. Trading in its shares was immediately suspended. The eight-six-year-old bank, founded by priests in Milan, had expired.

While the stunned employees of the bank milled around, a grey-haired woman plummeted from the executive office on the top floor to her death on the pavement below. Amidst the commotion, the acting president interrupted a press briefing to announce, "Calvi's secretary just killed herself." Graziela Corrocher not only had been Calvi's secretary since he had become head of the bank; she was the only other person at the bank who knew his full calendar of appointments and meetings. She left behind a note scrawled in red that cursed Calvi.

Later that evening at an office on the Avenue des Citronniers in Monte Carlo, the employee on duty received a phone call ordering him to immediately close down what had been the European headquarters of Banco Ambrosiano Overseas in the Bahamas. His eleven years of night duty in this lonely room had consisted mainly of typing cryptic telephone messages from Milan into a telex machine, which had been specially constructed so that, unlike standard machines, it did not produce any copy of its messages on paper. There was also no paper trail of the work done here which, unbeknownst to him or the other employee of this branch office, had resulted in transferring more than $1.2 billion borrowed by the Banco Ambrosiano and its subsidiaries from banks around the world to anonymous corporations in Panama and Liechtenstein.

III.

By this time, the corpse of Calvi had been cut down from under Blackfriars Bridge in London, and the Italian counsel in London had cabled Rome, "They have our banker." This ended the search for Calvi, but there was a greater mystery: the whereabouts of the money.

The trail of the money, which began at the Banco Ambrosiano in Milan and then passed through its subsidiary in Monte Carlo, led to Panama. The money had been transferred there, and at other offshore banking centers, to anonymous corporations. Although records indicated that they were owned by the Vatican, the Vatican denied that it controlled their financial activities. Indeed, the precise relationship between these shadowy companies and the Vatican was known by no more than three persons at the Banco Ambrosiano. They were Carlo Canesi, who had made the original arrangements with the Vatican in the late 1960s; Calvi, who was his assistant and successor; and possibly Graziela Corrocher, the personal secretary for both men. And all three of them were now dead. Nor could any documents be found, except for the two ambiguous "letters of patronage" in the bank's records, which were disputed by the Vatican. The problem was that Calvi had left Italy with a black attaché case full of key documents, but it had not been recovered in London.

If the answer to the mystery could not be found in Milan or London, it might be found in the Vatican, a technically sovereign state occupying some 108 acres in the heart of Rome. In 1983, through banking contacts I had made while writing an unrelated article for the *Institutional Investor*, I arranged an interview with the one person likely to know about the Calvi affair, Archbishop Marcinkus. Although it had been unprecedented for an archbishop of the Vatican Curia to sit on the board of directors of a private bank, Marcinkus had traveled to the Bahamas for bank meetings. He explained at our first meeting that he had done so to educate himself in banking because "extraordinary times called for extraordinary measures." He was a giant of a man, standing six feet four inches tall, with huge hands that toyed with objects as he spoke. Since he was an American, there was no need for a translator. Early in the interview, he pointed out that despite its priceless works of art, and its valuable property in Italy in the form of churches, the Vatican had a financial problem that dated back over two centuries.

At the beginning of the nineteenth century, it had been

sufficiently weak that Napoleon was able to kidnap the pope and keep him prisoner in France for seven years. Even after the Papal States were restored to the Vatican by the Treaty of Vienna in 1815, the cost of financing its wartime debt so exceeded its paltry income that it was only saved from bankruptcy when the French government assumed part of the Vatican debt. Finally, in 1870, in the process of unifying Italy, King Emmanuel seized Rome and all the remaining territory of the Papal States and left the pope, Pius IX, barricaded in his palace, a prisoner in the Vatican. Although the new Italian parliament passed a law offering modest compensation for all the papal territories that had been expropriated, Pope Pius IX refused, saying "I need money badly but what do you bring me, a part of what you stole from me." That statement defined the Vatican position for the next six decades, as it negotiated with a succession of Italian governments with neither sovereign status nor money.

The pope's only source of income during this period was an annual collection from Catholics around the world called Peter's Pence, which had been revived from the times of the Crusades. But Peter's Pence rarely exceeded a million dollars in a year and, unable to borrow further to pay expenses, the pope had to curtail Vatican services as essential as the Sacred Roman Rota. Indeed, by 1922 the Vatican was so impoverished that it borrowed $100,000 from a local Roman bank to pay for the funeral of Pope Benedict XV.

Finally, on February 29, 1929, Pope Pius XI came to terms with the government of Benito Mussolini. In the agreement, called the Lateran Treaty, the pope recognized that the Papal States, including Rome, were now part of Italy. In return, Mussolini accepted that a small parcel of land surrounding St. Peter's, called Vatican City, henceforth would be completely independent of the laws of Italy, and the pope would be completely sovereign over this tiny territory. In addition, Mussolini awarded the Vatican compensation for the papal property seized in 1870 of $52.4 million in the form of long-term Italian bonds, paying 5-percent interest each year, and $39.7 million in cash.

Although the Vatican became financially solvent for the first time in over a century, it had now been officially reduced from a kingdom occupying most of central Italy to a token city-state in a patch of Rome. To make it autonomous in fact as well as in law, the pope immediately expended part of the cash from the settlement on constructing a railroad station, a telephone exchange, administration buildings, a courthouse, radio transmitters, a jail, printing presses, barracks for the Swiss Guard, and an electric power plant.

None of this left the Vatican with much money. Aside from the Peter's Pence collection and the sale of Vatican coins, postage stamps, and museum admissions—all of which dwindled during the world depressions of the 1930s—the only income that the Vatican could count on was the approximately $2.5 million per year in interest from its government bonds, a sum that shrank with the declining value of the Italian currency. As the situation grew more desperate, the pope assigned the remainder of what the Vatican received in compensation to an investment unit called "Special Administration," designed to use the Vatican's unique sovereign standing to trade in the foreign-exchange markets. He retained Bernardino Nogara, a banker who was an expert in international finance, to run it. To protect the Vatican against further devaluations in the lira, Nogara bought gold, dollars, and other foreign currency, and then borrowed against them. He also engaged in complex arbitrage operations that increased the Vatican's patrimony by more than 50 percent in ten years, while also providing the income necessary to pay the Vatican's deficit. So the Vatican finally found a means of economic salvation: taking advantage of its sovereign exemption from regulation to trade.

World War II again put the Vatican in serious jeopardy.

Surrounded by Fascist Italy, and threatened with annihilation by the Communists who were battling to take over Italy, Pope Pius XII briefly considered moving the Vatican to America. In 1942, as an immediate expedient for safeguarding its funds during the war, the pope authorized the creation of a private bank within the walls of the Vatican, whose true function was obscured by its name, "The Institute for Religious Works." The Vatican official charged with superintending this bank was Giovanni Battista Montini, a priest from a prominent banking family in northern Italy, who had served in the Vatican's Secretariat of State for twenty years. Montini organized the bank not only as a safe haven for the Vatican's own money but also as a channel through which Catholic dioceses, missions, orders, and other entities could invest their funds. Even after Montini left the Secretariat to become the Archbishop of Milan in 1954, he continued to oversee the operations of the bank as part of a three-man commission. When he became pope in 1963, taking the name Paul VI, he made the bank a key instrument of expanding Vatican financial power.

The immediate problem confronting Pope Paul VI was a new Italian law requiring foreign investors, including the Vatican, to pay a 30-percent tax on dividends. Since this tax, if paid, would further squeeze Vatican income to the point at which it would have to curtail services that it considered essential, it refused to pay the tax on the grounds that it violated the Lateran Treaty of 1929. While the stalemate continued, Pope Paul VI found a remedy that would not only avoid the issue of direct Italian taxation but also eliminate much of the pejorative publicity about its investments in Italy. The Vatican bank would transfer most of its investments to anonymous companies in Liechtenstein, Panama, and other secretive offshore centers. These companies would be separated from the Vatican by many layers of banks and other intermediaries. This move would also be invisible to Italian tax collectors, since no worldly authority, not even the Italian government, had the right to inspect Vatican records. To effect this change, the Vatican required the help of banks that could, with utter secrecy, set up these anonymous accounts for it and assist in transferring its assets to them.

The bank in Milan that Pope Paul VI initially turned to for help was the small and, as its name implied, extremely private, Banca Privata Finanziata. It was run by a highly successful financier named Michele Sindona, who was expert at maneuvering funds offshore.

The liaison with Sindona eventually grew dangerous. His banking empire became entangled in criminal investigations, and some of the banks he controlled went bankrupt. As concerns mounted in 1969, Sindona was summoned to the Apostolic Palace in the Vatican for a meeting with Pope Paul VI; Cardinal Alberto di Jorio, the President of the Vatican Bank; and Cardinal Sergio Guerri, the head of the commission responsible for the administration of the Vatican city-state. Sindona was then told that although he would be allowed to complete the current transactions that he was undertaking for the Vatican, he would then have to step aside. Marcinkus was the man the pope put in charge of replacing Sindona's Banca Privata Finanziata. At the time, Marcinkus was only a forty-nine-year-old American priest, with, as he put it, "not the slightest knowledge about banking." Marcinkus first served Pope Paul VI as an English translator on his trips to America and then as his personal bodyguard. His mission now, as he saw it, was to untangle Sindona's convoluted machinations, and to find a new bank to replace Sindona's. The bank he found was the venerable Banco Ambrosiano, which was named after the patron saint of Milan, and located on Via Clerica in that city.

There was much that he liked about the Banco Ambrosiano. It had been originally founded and owned by priests in Milan in 1896. For decades, this bank was headed by Franco

Ratti, the nephew of Pope Pius XI, and then by Duke Gallerati Scotti, a trusted friend of Pope Paul VI's from Milan. Aside from the personal connections, the Vatican then owned the largest single block of stock in the Banco Ambrosiano. Its new chairman, Carlo Canesi, and its general manager, Roberto Calvi, also seemed eminently trustworthy to Marcinkus. But Pope Paul VI wanted to be absolutely sure of the relationship, so Marcinkus with, as he put it, "the pope's seal of approval," arranged for the Vatican bank to sell the Banco Ambrosiano the controlling interest it held in the Banca Cattolica del Veneto, a Venice bank with more than 100 branches. Aside from the official price of $30 million, the Vatican bank also got a secret side payment of $6.2 million. This money, channeled into the Vatican's subsidiaries in Liechtenstein, was then used by Calvi to buy for the Vatican enough additional shares in the Banco Ambrosiano to give it control of his bank.

Calvi, the son of a bank clerk, who would succeed Canesi as chairman, consolidated the Vatican's anonymous holding companies under a wholly owned subsidiary in the Bahamas, called the Cisalpine Overseas Bank (Nassau). This entity, based in Nassau and controlled from a small office in Monte Carlo, became the center of a dizzying daisy-chain of money transfers and borrowing. With the pope's approval, Marcinkus became president of the Vatican bank, and he served on the board of this subsidiary in the Bahamas.

Initially, Marcinkus continued, Calvi was able to generate huge profits for the Vatican, but there was still a problem with Sindona. In November 1977, Sindona, who had been arrested in New York for making false statements in his attempt to take over an American bank, demanded that Calvi pay him nearly $10 million. Sindona claimed that he was owed this money as a "commission" and needed it for his legal expenses in America. When Calvi refused, Sindona carried out a threat to ruin Calvi.

On November 13, 1977, employees of the Banco Ambrosiano

were stunned to find the walls of the surrounding buildings of Milan's financial center plastered with giant white, yellow, and blue posters revealing in great detail the ultra-secret transactions of the bank. The event, which became known in Italy as the day of the "tazebas," or Chinese banners, since the excess of colorful posters made the financial district of Milan look like Beijing, had been organized by Sindona. Since he had been privy to the secret transfers, the wall posters had revealed the numbered accounts in Switzerland through which passed the secret side payments that had been used by Calvi and the Vatican bank to get control of the Banco Ambrosiano. In addition, they contained three questions which, if correctly answered, would expose the sham transactions between the Vatican bank and the Banco Ambrosiano. Calvi ordered that the posters be ripped down, but it was too late, since Sindona had also sent an anonymous letter to the Bank of Italy detailing the transactions. The Bank of Italy, the central bank of Italy, had no choice but to launch an investigation.

To make matters worse for both Calvi and Marcinkus, the court-appointed liquidator of Sindona's banks, Mario Ambrosoli, reported that in Sindona's records he had found coded evidence of a $6.5-million illegal payoff to an "American bishop and Milanese banker." The press suggested that the bishop was Marcinkus and the banker, Calvi. Before Ambrosoli could go further in unraveling the code, Ambrosoli was shot dead at point-blank range in front of his home by two unidentified men. While his evidence may have been problematic, his silencing further amplified the furor over the posters.

Marcinkus' position was further weakened by a series of "unfortunate events," as he put it. First, Pope Paul VI, his main supporter, died in August 1978. Shortly afterward, his successor, Pope John Paul, also abruptly died. Then the election of the first non-Italian pope in seven centuries, John Paul II, left the Curia in disarray. In addition, Luigi Mennini, who was then the chief aide to Marcinkus at the Vatican bank, was arrested in Italy for currency manipulation. As the pressure built, the new pope appointed a commission of fifteen cardinals to study the finances of the Vatican.

Calvi was also making threats, according to Marcinkus. In May 1981, Calvi was arrested for violating Italy's foreign-exchange regulations and convicted. He was then taken to the medieval Lodi prison and put into a cell with four terrorists, who kept him awake day and night talking and playing a radio. Calvi warned Marcinkus, "This trial is called IOR," the Italian initials of the Vatican bank. (According to Calvi's son, Carlos Calvi, Marcinkus sent a message back, "Our problems are your problems too.") Calvi then attempted suicide by slashing his wrists and swallowing an overdose of barbiturates. Then on July 20, 1981, after spending two months in Lodi, Calvi was released on bail while the appeal of his four-year sentence was processed, and he resumed work as head of the Banco Ambrosiano.

But the Bank of Italy was pressing to see the books of the bank's overseas subsidiaries, and so Calvi continued to ask Marcinkus to help. But Marcinkus could not acknowledge the debt of the anonymous companies, since doing so would bankrupt the Holy See. When Marcinkus turned him down, Calvi turned to records in the vault of the Banco Ambrosiano's banking subsidiary in Switzerland that he claimed would establish the Vatican's ownership of the subsidiaries. The chief accountant of the Vatican bank, Pellegrino de Strobel, was then dispatched to Switzerland to view the secret records. Since they appeared to substantiate Calvi's claim, the fatal deal was made: Marcinkus' deputy acknowledged that the Vatican bank controlled the eight anonymous companies, and Calvi provided the Vatican bank with the letter releasing the Vatican from any liability arising from the activities of these anonymous companies. The problem now confronting Marcinkus was that key documents pertaining to this arrangement had vanished along with Calvi.

As it turned out, Calvi could speak from the grave. In the summer of 1982, a special committee of inquiry in Parliament eerily heard Calvi's posthumous recollections on tape. Flavio Carboni, the Sardinian who had help organized Calvi's escape from Italy, had kept a microphone concealed behind his lapel during his final conversations with Calvi. These tapes had been seized when Carboni was arrested in Switzerland. On them, Calvi rambled on for no less than ten hours. At one point, Calvi recounted a conversation he had had with Marcinkus, claiming to have warned him "Be careful . . . if it comes out that you gave money to Solidarity, there won't be one stone of the Vatican left standing." (He was referring to the Polish labor union movement that helped undermine the Soviet Union's control of Poland.)

Marcinkus stonewalled Italian regulators, stating that Calvi was the sole author of the machinations. Italian authorities then issued subpoenas, but they were returned unopened on the basis that the Vatican was not subject to the laws of Italy. Finally, on August 6, 1982, the minister of finance, Beniamino Andreatta, ordered the Banco Ambrosiano liquidated and all its assets turned over to a new consortium of banks. The Vatican's controlling block of stock in the bank was worthless. The missing $1.2 billion was never recovered.

Why had the Vatican engaged in these massive transactions? "You can't run the church on Hail Marys alone," Archbishop Marcinkus told me. As for the details of the transfers, he said the pope had entrusted two lay bankers with this task: Sindona, with whom the Pope had met personally, and Calvi. "They and they alone know," he concluded. Calvi was dead, but Sindona was in prison in the United States.

I went to see Sindona in Otisville Federal Prison in upstate New York in April 1984. Born in Patti, Sicily, in 1920 and educated by Jesuit priests, Sindona had become one of the most successful financiers in Europe and the principal financial advisor to the Vatican by the time he was forty-three. Then, in March 1979, he was indicted by a U.S. federal grand jury on charges of fraud proceeding from his 1972 takeover of the Franklin National Bank. Although released on bond, he was required to remain in New York. Sindona instead staged his own kidnapping and fled in disguise to Italy. When arrested three months later, he was tried, convicted, and sentenced to twenty-five years in prison.

When I met him in the Otisville prison visiting room, the grey-haired financier appeared frail and nervous. After asking me to buy him a vanilla ice cream, we began the one-hour interview. He came right to the point, saying that he had only done what Pope Paul VI had instructed him to do: shift the Vatican's Italian assets to tax-free offshore havens. When I asked him about the formerly anonymous entities, some of which had been found to have the code-names "Suprafin," "Zitropo," and "Manic," he said that they themselves were merely vehicles to hide the transfers of money. It was, as he described it, purely a money laundering scheme, which he said was "legal" because the Vatican was sovereign. With the help of Calvi, the money had been deposited in dozens of letter-box companies, which then borrowed against them from the Banco Ambrosiano and sent the proceeds to other offshore entities.

If so, why couldn't the funds be recovered? Sindona answered that the Vatican, again with Calvi's help, had used these funds to make "questionable investments." As an example, he cited the Vatican's attempt to buy control of Rizzoli, which owned Italy's largest newspaper, the *Corriere della Sera.* "I don't know how much was lost," he said; by that time, Sindona said, he was no longer advising the Vatican.

He claimed to know nothing about Calvi's death, but added, as I was leaving the room, that he might have a similar fate if he was ever sent back to Italy. It was the last time I saw Sindona. On September 25, 1984, he was extradited to Italy, and on March 18, 1986, he died in a prison in Rome from a dose of cyanide in his coffee, a death ruled a suicide.

IV.

When Calvi was arrested the year before his death in Milan, it was on a questionable technicality about an incident that had occurred a decade earlier. His bank had arranged legal currency transfers in 1971 that were held by a magistrate to violate a retroactive 1976 foreign-exchange law. Along with Calvi, six other former and present executives of the Banco Ambrosiano were arrested. Mass arrests of bankers by magistrates on technical offenses had by the 1980s become common in Italy. Because Calvi spent two months in Lodi prison, on getting out, he was determined to pay whatever was needed to be paid to get political protection against future imprisonment. "It is a question of surviving in a climate that is becoming like a religious war," he said in a newspaper interview. "It is an atmosphere that favors every sort of barbarism."

The person who offered Calvi such protection in this "religious war" was Licio Gelli. A mattress-spring manufacturer and poet from Arezzo, Gelli claimed to run a powerful web of influence in the form of a Masonic lodge in Rome called Propagandi Due, or P-2. This secret society, according to a sixty-four-volume investigation by a commission of the Italian Parliament, included forty-three members of Parliament, forty-eight generals, the heads of Italy's intelligence service, the top magistrates in the judiciary system, the civil servants running various state-owned enterprises (including the energy company ENI), key bank regulators, and leading businessmen.

The report concluded that P-2 was a veritable "state within

---

a state." The commission had come to these conclusions largely based on the files of Gelli and his close associates, but most of those named in them denied any such membership in Gelli's secret lodge. Nor did P-2 ever hold meetings or conduct ordinary Masonic business, as is prescribed by Freemasonry. Whether any of powerful individuals were actually members of P-2 or whether the lists were part of a con game staged by Gelli, as long as people believed it existed, P-2 provided a highly profitable clearing house for businessmen interested in buying influence or protection from government officials. For these transactions, Gelli acted as the go-between, deal-maker, and record-keeper. Gelli extracted a heavy price from Calvi for arranging political protection, which, as it turns out, was never provided.

In accordance with Gelli's instructions, Calvi transferred $21 million to a South American bank. Calvi later told three magistrates investigating the P-2 lodge that Gelli was funneling the money through intermediaries to top officials of Italy's Socialist Party, who presumably would intervene with bank regulators on the behalf of the Banco Ambrosiano. There were also much larger diversions that he elected not to tell the magistrates about. In 1982, Juerg Heer, the executive director of the credit section of Zurich's powerful Rothschild Bank, witnessed some extraordinary transfers from Calvi's Luxembourg subsidiary to a Gelli-controlled corporate shell in Panama called Bellatrix. According to Heer, these loans, which amounted to $142 million, were temporarily deposited by Bellatrix at the Rothschild Bank, and then were used by Bellatrix to buy shares in Rizzoli at ten times their market value from Gelli and his associates. By this trick, almost 90 percent of the $142 million of the Banco Ambrosiano loan went into the pockets of Gelli and his associates, according to Heer. This diversion became so blatant by the spring of 1982 that the Rothschild Bank director assisting Bellatrix warned Heer, "We have to find a solution or

I will end up in Lake Zurich." The solution Heer found was to temporarily put the Bellatrix money into two different accounts at the bank. One was called Zirka; the other Reciota. They both supposedly were controlled by an independent fiduciary agent. Nevertheless, the money was released into other numbered accounts controlled by Gelli and then disappeared. All that Calvi's Luxembourg subsidiary had as collateral was the Rizzoli shares, which were now worth only a small fraction of the money it had loaned. Making matters worse for Calvi, Italian law had been changed in 1982 and now blocked the transfer of these Rizzoli shares to the bank's Luxembourg subsidiary. So Calvi informed Gelli that the Rizzoli deal had not been consummated and that the $142 million loaned to the Gelli entities still belonged to his bank. According to Calvi's personal assistant, as late as June 1982, Calvi counted on this diverted money as a "reserve fund," and part of Calvi's purpose in secretly slipping out of Italy in 1982 was to get the Bank Rothschild in Zurich to return the Bellatrix money from the numbered accounts. It was a destination he never reached.

The only further instructions Heer received in Zurich came from one of Gelli's associates shortly after Calvi's body was identified. According to Heer, he was requested to carry out a "secret operation." It involved some $5 million in cash packed in a suitcase that was delivered to him at the Rothschild Bank. The money supposedly had come from one of Gelli's numbered accounts in Geneva. Heer also received, along with the suitcase, one-half of a $100 bill. Following Gelli's associate's instructions, he gave the suitcase to two strangers who later arrived at the bank with the matching half of the bill, and who left with the suitcase in an armored limousine.

Less than three months later, on September 13, 1982, Gelli was arrested in Switzerland after making a $55-million withdrawal from the same numbered account in Geneva. The subsequent investigation uncovered records showing that this money had come from the money Calvi had diverted through Bellatrix, confirming Heer's account of the Rothschild transactions. (Heer was subsequently sued by the Rothschild Bank for exceeding his authority in arranging these loans, and, as a result, imprisoned for two months.)

Gelli then escaped from the Champ-Dollon Prison outside of Geneva and went to Argentina. In Italy, Gelli was sentenced in absentia to eight years for financing terrorism in Florence, and another fourteen months for money-laundering in San Remo. In 1987, Gelli surrendered in Chile and was sentenced to two months in prison in Switzerland. In February 1988, he was extradited back to Italy, accompanied by two armored cars and one hundred soldiers, to face trial in Bologna for slander. Although an appeals court threw out his conviction for slander, in 1992 he was convicted and sentenced to eighteen years and six months for fraud in connection with the diversion of money from Calvi's Banco Ambrosiano. Before he could be imprisoned, he fled to France. By the time he was found on the Riviera, he was over eighty, and under Italian law, too old to be imprisoned in Italy. Finally, in 2005, at the age of eighty-six, he was implicated in the murder of Calvi, but acquitted in a subsequent trial.

Behind every great crime, to paraphrase Balzac, there is a multitude of theories in Italy. In the case of the hanging of God's banker, almost all the theories proceed from a single motive: silencing Calvi. Various theories thus point to all the financial, political, and criminal interests for whom Calvi was laundering money, a list that includes offshore bankers, Gelli's P-2 lodge, and the Vatican. In almost all of these theories, the Mafia, or some offshoot of it, organizes the actual murder. The umbrella theory, at least in the realm of fiction, can be found in Francis Ford Coppola's 1990 movie *The Godfather Part III*. It depicts the hanging of a Calvi-like banker under Blackfriars Bridge in London as the work of Mafia killers who carried out this murder on the orders of the Godfather, who did so as a favor to corrupt figures in the Vatican. In the realm of reality, Italian magistrates advanced a similar theory in court based almost entirely the testimony of "pentiti," or ex-Mafia turncoats who, despite their oath of silence, agreed to cooperate with government investigations. One such turncoat was Francesco Marino Mannoia, a former member of the Sicilian Mafia who had been involved in heroin trafficking and at least seventeen murders before his conversion to government witness. In July 1991, he claimed to have hearsay information about the Calvi case, saying that he had heard from others that Francesco Di-Carlo, another imprisoned Mafia hitman, had killed Calvi on orders from a Mafia boss Giuseppe Calo. For his part, DiCarlo, who was imprisoned in Britain for drug trafficking, denied the allegation. Instead, he told the magistrates that although he had been asked to "punish" the banker for squandering Mafia assets, he had refused the order. Then he offered his own hearsay evidence, saying that he had heard that two mafiosi from Naples had killed Calvi, but both men he mentioned were themselves dead.

The obvious problem with pentiti hearsay evidence is that it cannot be tested by confronting its source. Nor can the pentiti themselves be assumed to be telling the truth, since they have powerful incentives, including their freedom, money, and even vengeance, to invent unverifiable stories that assist high-profile prosecutions. On June 6, 2007, after 20 months of hearing such evidence in a prison in Rome, presiding judge Mario Lucio d'Andria dismissed the charges proceeding from this ex-Mafia testimony on the basis that there was "insufficient evidence" to continue.

My assessment, based on my interviews with some of the principal figures involved in the scandal, is more modest. The most obvious suspects in my view are the people responsible for Calvi's protection on the night he was killed, Flavio Carboni, and his associates in London. Carboni, it will be recalled, organized Calvi's escape, his travel plans, his forged documents, his bodyguard, and his hotel room at the Chelsea Cloisters. He had also accompanied Calvi in the private plane to London and was in constant touch with him by phone. So he had opportunity.

Carboni had also supplied Calvi's lone bodyguard, Vittor, who left Calvi unprotected that night. At about 5:00 p.m. Carboni phoned Calvi from the London Hilton, where he was staying, and told him to pack his bags since he had arranged for him to move to a flat, which was untrue. According to Vittor, Carboni arrived at the Chelsea Cloisters in a taxi that evening, and met Vittor at the front desk, but didn't go up to see Calvi, who was waiting for him to move him. Since Calvi was relying on Carboni to hide him, he presumably would have followed whatever instructions Carboni provided, such as getting into a car or even a onto bridge to await a boat. If so, whether or not he used them, Carboni had the means to get Calvi to Blackfriars Bridge without using force.

Carboni also showed what might be construed as consciousness of guilt. Using a pseudonym, he left England by going to Scotland, where he had a chartered jet waiting to fly him to Switzerland. (Vittor, also using a pseudonym, took an early-morning commercial flight to Austria.)

Carboni also had a motive: money. He had in his Swiss bank account in Zurich $11 million that he had gotten from Calvi and which Calvi, if he had lived, might have used for his own purposes. More important, Calvi's death also provided Carboni with the contents of Calvi's black attaché case. The last time Vittor saw Calvi, he had the bag, but, after his vanishing, the bag disappeared. The value of its contents became clear only six years later. An Italian police raid on a smuggling suspect turned up copies of two letters apparently sent by registered mail to Cardinal Agostino Casaroli, who then was a high-ranking Vatican official. The letters said that the smuggler had advanced to Carboni $1 million to get from him incriminating documents written by Calvi. I learned about this remarkable effort to extort money from the Vatican from Judge Almerighi, a self-styled Sherlock Holmes among investigating magistrates, who prided himself on his deductive logic. Since these documents had come from Calvi's missing black bag, and he was investigating the Calvi affair, they were brought to his attention. When I interviewed Judge Almerighi in Rome, he told me that the Vatican acknowledged to him that a Vatican bishop had written checks for $2 million to Carboni on the Instituto per le Opere di Religione, the Vatican's bank. The magistrate also uncovered a memo in which a Vatican official discussed paying $40 million to Carboni for other Calvi documents from the black bag. He concluded that these sensitive documents were being used, as he put it to me, "to blackmail the pope." In tracing the scheme back to June 20, 1982, Almerighi also found a witness who claimed to have seen Carboni give an envelope to a Vatican official the day after Calvi died. If Carboni believed that the Vatican would pay to keep secret the documents Calvi had in his black bag, Calvi might have appeared to be worth a great deal more dead than alive.

One clue that caught Almerighi's attention was the fact that Calvi had shaved off the moustache that he had worn his entire adult life on the day he was last seen in London by Vittor. "We know he had packed his bags and was waiting for a car that evening: he had an escape plan," Almerighi told me. "Shaving the moustache would be necessary if he was told he was getting a new identity." His reasoning was that Calvi was carefully following Carboni's instructions when he was delivered into the hands of a contract killer at the bridge. His view of the case, which was presented at trial, was that Carboni took Calvi's black bag and then betrayed him. Carboni had been first arrested in 1982, then released. In 1997, he was brought to trial, along with others, for the murder of Calvi, but he was acquitted in 2005. As a result, three decades later, the hanging of Calvi remains an unsolved crime.

But where murder intersects with high finance, follow the money. The obstacles to this approach in the case of God's banker's are not only that the money trail runs through an elaborate maze of offshore corporations but that the individuals who set up these accounts, including Calvi, Sindona, and Canesi, were dead, and that others who had knowledge of the pathways, such as Marcinkus, were protected by the sovereign secrecy of the Vatican. Even so, there was a thread that could be followed: the documents that Calvi had in his black bag when he fled Italy, and which vanished from his hotel room in London.

CHAPTER 9
THE DEATH OF DAG HAMMARSKJÖLD

In 1961, in the heat of a bloody war of secession in the heart of Africa, UN Secretary General Dag Hammarskjöld tried to mediate between the Republic of the Congo, which had just won its independence from Belgium, and Congo's breakaway mineral-rich province of Katanga, whose self-proclaimed president, Moise Tshombe, and his mercenary forces were secretly financed by the giant mining corporation, Union Minerale. At stake were billions of dollars in annual mineral revenues. To end the conflict, Hammarskjöld arranged a secret meeting in Rhodesia. On September 17, 1961, he took off in a UN-chartered DC-6 airliner from Leopoldville, the capital of the Republic of the Congo, on a 1,000-mile flight to Ndola in Rhodesia. Because of the danger that Union Minerale mercenaries might try to interfere with the mission, a decoy plane was sent ahead and no flight plan was filed. On board, Hammarskjöld was accompanied by only a small staff to maintain secrecy. The captain also maintained radio silence until the plane reached the Rhodesian border at 11:35 p.m. Only then did he notify the control tower at the Ndola airport that the UN plane would land there in less than thirty minutes. This was the last communication with the aircraft. Just after midnight, a large flash of light was seen in the sky near the airport. The next afternoon, the plane's wreckage was found some nine miles from the airport. So were the fifteen badly burned bodies of the members of Hammarskjöld's party and the crew. The only survivor was Hammarskjöld's security chief, Harold Julien, who died five days later in a hospital.

Even though the death of the UN Secretary General was no minor matter, investigators could not resolve whether he died by accident or design. The 180-man search party scoured a six-square-kilometer area but found few clues. The plane was not equipped with either a black box or a cockpit recorder. Swedish, British, and American experts were called in to examine the few pieces of the jigsaw puzzle that were recovered, and they found no signs of structural defects in the plane itself. The altimeters were determined by a U.S. lab to have been in working order at the time of the crash, so there was no technical reason for the pilots to have misjudged their altitude. Nor was there was evidence of fire aboard the plane before the crash. The Rhodesian Board of Investigation ruled the crash a probable accident but said it could not rule out the possibility of sabotage because major parts of the plane were not recovered and several witnesses testified that it had been left unguarded at the Leopoldville airport prior to the flight.

The United Nations then appointed its own Commission of Investigation, but since it relied heavily on the Rhodesian inquiry, its results were also inconclusive. One problem for the UN investigators was that they found out that the corpses of two of Hammarskjöld's Swedish bodyguards had multiple bullet wounds, and bodyguards do not ordinarily get shot in a plane crash. In this case, however, the Rhodesian medical examiners posited that the bullet wounds had been the result of exploding ammunition. The plane did carry ammunition that could have been ignited when the plane burned in the fire after the crash, but ballistics expert Major C. F. Westell found that exploding ammunition would not replicate their actual bullet wounds. He stated, "I can certainly describe as sheer nonsense the statement that cartridges of machine guns or pistols detonated in a fire can penetrate a human body." Adding further to

POLITICAL PLANE CRASHES

DATE	CRASH SITE	VICTIM
SEPTEMBER 7, 1940	Paraguay	Paraguayan dictator President José Félix Estigarribia
JULY 4, 1943	Gibraltar	Polish resistance leader Władysław Sikorski
MARCH 17, 1957	Cebu, Philippines	Philippines President Ramon Magsaysay
SEPTEMBER 18, 1957	Zambia	UN Secretary General Dag Hammarskjöld
APRIL 13, 1966	Iraq	Iraqi President Abdul Salam Arif
APRIL 27, 1969	Mongolia	Chinese Vice Premier Lin Biao
DECEMBER 4, 1980	Portugal	Portuguese Prime Minister Francisco de Sá Carne
MAY 24, 1981	Ecuador	Ecuadorian President Jaime Roldós Aguilera
JULY 31, 1981	Panama	Panamanian dictator Omar Torrijos
OCTOBER 19, 1986	Mozambique	Mozambique President Samora Machel
AUGUST 17, 1988	Pakistan	Pakistani President Zia-ul-haq
APRIL 6, 1994	Rwanda	Rwanda President Juvénal Habyarimana and Burunda President Cyprien Ntaryamira
FEBRUARY 26, 2004	Bosnia	Macadonia President Boris Trajkovski
OCTOBER 19, 2006	Nigeria	Sultan of Sokoto, head of Nigerian Supreme Council for Islamic Affairs
APRIL 10, 2010	Russia	Polish President Lech Kaczyński

the mystery, General Bjorn Egge, who was the first UN official to see Hammarskjöld's body, said in a newspaper interview in 2005 that he had seen a large hole in Hammarskjöld's forehead (and that it had been airbrushed out of the photographs). Since Hammarskjöld was not seated near the ammunition in the rear of the plane, a bullet wound in him would suggest that he had been shot.

Then, in 1998, after the apartheid government fell in South Africa, new evidence emerged from the archives of South Africa's intelligence archive. According to Archbishop Desmond Tutu, the Nobel laureate who headed South Africa's Truth and Reconciliation Commission, documents in the files indicated that a bomb had been planted in the plane's landing gear. One such report implicated both the CIA and Britain's MI-5 in the sabotage, though this could not be verified. The British Foreign Office, in denying its validity, suggested that it may have been planted in the files as disinformation. In any case, without any forensic means of establishing the facts surrounding Hammarskjöld's death, the case could not be settled by a questionable intelligence record. It thus remains an unresolved mystery.

The most innocent theory is that the crash was caused by pilot error. According to it, the pilot, though experienced, was fatigued by the tense flight, and in his approach he misjudged the distance to the airport. A second theory is that the plane was sabotaged by those opposed to Hammarskjöld's efforts to get Tshombe to end the secession of Katanga. There is also a theory that someone aboard the plane tried to hijack it, and a gunfight broke out. This scenario would account for the guards' bullet wounds. Finally, there is the theory that a plane piloted by a mercenary tried to intercept the UN plane after it broke radio silence, and caused the crash. In 2011, A. Susan Williams, a research fellow at the University of London, argued in her book *Who Killed Hammarskjöld?* that there was an explosion before the plane fell from the sky, as the only survivor of the crash, Harold Julien, had testified, and that U.S. intelligence had intercepted a message from the cockpit in which the pilot says "I've hit it."

My assessment is that the crash involved more than pilot error. The problem with both the hijacker and interception theories is that the pilot was in radio contact with the control tower in the last half-hour and, if there had been a battle on the plane or an attack by another aircraft, he certainly would have reported it over the radio or sounded a mayday alert, as he did not suffer bullet wounds. Before the plane was reported missing, several witnesses reported to police a bright flash in the sky. Such an explosion high in the sky could scatter parts of the plane far from where the wreckage was found and account for why they were not found by the search party. Such an explosion would also discount the pilot error theory. So the most compelling explanation is sabotage, possibly an explosive device planted on the plane before it departed and triggered by the lowering of the landing gear. In this scenario, the bullet wounds remain a problem. They could have been the result of a gunman finding the wreckage before the search party and completing the job, or from a guard on the plane discharging his weapon in panic after the explosion. But unless some of the missing pieces of wreckage turn up after a half-century, we will never know the answer.

The lesson here is that an assassination disguised as a plane crash, if not a perfect crime, makes it difficult to definitively identify the culprit by conventional forensic methods. The successful explosion of an aircraft leaves no crime scene and no witnesses.

CHAPTER 10
THE STRANGE DEATH OF MARILYN MONROE

By 1962, Marilyn Monroe had become a living legend. Unlike the pageant of iconic blond bombshells that preceded her as sex symbols for movie audiences, her appeal went far beyond anything that Hollywood's publicity machine could create. Born Norma Jeane Mortenson in 1926 and brought up in orphanages and foster homes, she transcended the boundaries of the entertainment universe, and through her intimate association with President John F. Kennedy, Attorney General Robert F. Kennedy, and other members of the Kennedy clan, she gained entry to the corridors of power before her death.

She died on August 4, 1962, in her home in Los Angeles after a day of frantic phone calls to members of the Kennedy family. The exact time is unknown. The Los Angeles police received an urgent phone call at 4:25 a.m. on Sunday, August 5, 1962, from her psychoanalyst, Ralph Greenson, informing them that Marilyn Monroe had committed suicide. When they arrived at her Brentwood home, they were met by Dr. Greenson, Dr. Hyman Engelberg, her physician, and her live-in housekeeper, Eunice Murray. Murray said she had been concerned because the light was on in Monroe's bedroom at 3:00 a.m., and Monroe did not answer when called. Murray had called Dr. Engelberg, who, with her, had discovered her dead.

In her bedroom, the police found Monroe's nude body

lying face down on her bed. Next to her body, they saw several nearly empty bottles of the barbiturate Nembutal. They did not see any glass in the room that she might have used to take the capsules (though one would turn up later), and there was no running water in the room that Monroe could have used to swallow the pills. Murray told the police that she had cleaned the room and done the laundry after finding the body, saying that she wanted to make sure everything was neat and tidy before the police arrived. Later, an empty glass turned up in the room, but the police insisted that it was not there when they initially searched the room.

The police estimated from the advanced state of rigor mortis that Monroe had died between 9:30 and 11:30 p.m. on Saturday night. So there was a gap of near five to seven hours before the police were notified. After examining the body, the coroner determined that Monroe had died from a fatal mixture of at least thirty-eight capsules of Nembutal and chloral hydrate, a hypnotic sedative (also used illegally in bars as a "knockout drug"). One problem was that if she had swallowed thirty-eight yellow Nembutal capsules, they would have left crystals, yellow dye, and other residue in her digestive system, but the coroner could find no traces of them in her stomach or her intestines. Could she have been injected with the drug? That possibility was ruled out because the coroner could find no injection marks, bruises, or other signs that the drugs had been intravenously delivered. The final possibility he considered was that the drugs had been administered rectally. But there was no enema bag found in her home. The coroner, Dr. Thomas Noguchi, later attempted to obtain a further toxicological analysis of her liver, kidneys, and other organs, but he was told that they had been destroyed. Even though it was not clear how she took the lethal mixture, he concluded that her death was a "probable suicide."

Yet, whether or not she committed suicide, contradictory

accounts of how and when her death was discovered leave open the possibility of a cover-up. Eunice Murray said that Monroe retired to her bedroom at about 8:00 p.m. on Saturday and that she did not see her again, or notice that anything was amiss, until about 3:00 a.m. on Sunday morning, when Monroe didn't respond to Murray's repeated calls. Only then did she call Monroe's doctor. But Murray's son-in-law, Norman Jeffries, who was working as a handyman in the Monroe house and was there that evening, said that between 9:30 and 10:00 p.m. he heard a panicked commotion in the house. He said three men then arrived and ordered both him and Murray to leave the house. He identified one of those three men as Attorney General Robert Kennedy. (Neighbor Elizabeth Pollard described a similar scene to police, saying that she saw Robert Kennedy and two other men approaching the house that night, although she placed this visit earlier than did Jeffries.) When Jeffries and his mother-in-law returned to Monroe's house, it was about 10:30 p.m. He then saw Monroe's lifeless body on the bed, and shortly after the doctor and others began to arrive.

Jeffries' story would help fill in the five-hour gap and also explain how several of Monroe's associates had been informed, as they claimed they were, on Saturday night about her death. One problem with the story is that Robert Kennedy, who had been at the nearby Beverly Hills Hotel, had an alibi for Saturday night. He had checked out of the hotel and flown to San Francisco on Saturday afternoon. Although no flight record could be found, he was registered at the St. Francis Hotel on Saurday night. If so, Kennedy could not have been one of the three men whom Jeffries and Pollard saw that night—at least not at 9:30 p.m. The two had only ever seen Kennedy on television, so they both might have mistaken someone else for him. As other neighbors also saw unidentified individuals arriving and leaving well before midnight—one even claiming to have seen an ambulance—a mystery remains as to who these were, and why they ordered Jeffries and Murray out of the house for an hour.

There is no shortage of theories about the death of Marilyn Monroe, including suicide, accident, and disguised murder. The coroner's theory is probable suicide. Then there is the theory advanced on Court TV that her death was an accident. According to this investigation by Rachael Bell for Court TV's *Crime Library*, her psychoanalyst might have given her a chloral hydrate enema to help her sleep, and then her internist, unaware of the other medical interventions, could have given her a prescription for the barbiturate Nembutal, and the interaction of the Nembutal and chloral hydrate then proved lethal. Finally, there is the murder theory advanced by Norman Mailer in his 1973 best-seller *Marilyn*. Mailer suggests that Monroe was murdered by U.S. intelligence operatives because of the threat she posed to the Kennedy clan, and that the murder was disguised to look like a suicide. While Mailer provides no evidence to support the murder theory, thirty-three years later the FBI released a report in its files written by a former FBI agent (whose name was deleted) saying that at the time of her death Monroe was threatening to reveal the extramarital relationship she had had with Robert Kennedy and that Kennedy's intermediaries may have encouraged her to carry out a suicide threat to protect Kennedy's political career.

The driving force behind these theories is not the evidence. It is both Marilyn Monroe's status as a media sex symbol and her putative liaisons with Robert and John F. Kennedy. My assessment is that Marilyn Monroe killed herself, and there may also have been an unnecessary cover-up.

As for the drug overdose, Monroe had a long history of overdosing on drugs. According to the witnesses who had been in contact with her on the night of her death, she was prone to taking drugs to help her sleep. I believe that on the night of August 4, 1962, either by accident or design, she took, or allowed to be administered to her, all the drugs found in her body. As in all drug-overdose deaths, it is possible that her drug dosages were purposely altered to cause her to unintentionally swallow a lethal dose, but in this case there is no credible evidence to support such a murder scenario. The belated and uncorroborated reports in FBI files are not credible, in my view, and likely were placed in the files by Kennedy's political enemies.

The cover-up is another story. Even if there was no involvement by President Kennedy, Attorney General Kennedy, or any member of the Kennedy entourage in the death of Marilyn Monroe, their political operatives may have taken actions, with or without higher approval, to protect the Kennedys' reputations. So, as has been alleged, items may have been removed that might have linked the troubled Hollywood star to high-profile individuals, such as President Kennedy, Attorney General Kennedy, and their brother-in-law Peter Lawford.

The lesson here is that a cover-up does not necessarily require an underlying crime. It can be done simply as a prophylactic to protect the reputation of parties not involved in the crime. Such prophylactic cover-ups often occur in high-profile cases. Immediately after the JFK assassination in 1963, for example, the FBI ordered agent James Hosty to burn a threatening letter he had received from Lee Harvey Oswald prior to the assassination, not because the FBI was in any way involved in the crime, but because its director, J. Edgar Hoover, was concerned that the letter could be used to tarnish the reputation of the FBI. As a result, a potentially crucial piece of evidence was intentionally destroyed by the agency then investigating the crime. In the Marilyn Monroe case there is persuasive evidence that the death scene was altered. This was presumably done during the five-to-seven-hour gap before the police were called in, and, if the witness Jeffries is believed, when the housekeeper and he were ordered to leave. This intervention left ample time to remove any items of evidence that compromised those with whom Monroe had had romantic liaisons. Even if the prophylactic cover-up was done with the best intentions, the contradictions it produced in witnesses' testimony cast a permanent aura of mystery over the death of an international celebrity.

CHAPTER 11
THE CRASH OF ENRICO MATTEI

Enrico Mattei, an extraordinarily ambitious Italian civil servant, had become by 1962 the arch-nemesis of the international oil cartel. He gained his power in postwar Italy by reorganizing a state entity called Ente Nazionale Idrocarburini, or ENI, which in 1948 had a chain of gas stations and a few natural-gas wells, into a huge conglomerate that supplied most of Italy with its fuel. To feed ENI's refineries in southern Italy, Mattei attempted to make deals in the Middle East that undermined the near-monopoly of the cartel, and its three controlling partners, Exxon (then called Standard Oil of New Jersey), BP (then called Anglo-Iranian Oil), and Royal Dutch Shell. To get a concession in Iran, whose oil up to then went to the cartel for a small royalty, he offered Shah Reza Pahlavi of Iran a much richer cut: a 50-50 partnership on newly discovered oil. The Shah agreed, but ENI failed to find any new oil in Iran. Then, in 1961, at the height of the Cold War, Mattei turned to the only other major source of oil not controlled by the cartel, the Soviet Union. He not only offered to pay them hard currency for oil but to build a pipeline through Eastern Europe so it could be delivered to Italy. This move was viewed with such deep concern by the new administration of President John F. Kennedy that the administration pressured American companies to cut off the steel exports that Mattei needed for the pipeline. The cartel was also concerned enough to use its leverage over the Italian politicians it was secretly financing, including those in Italy's ruling Christian Democracy Party, to get the government to derail the Soviet oil agreement. After Exxon offered to supply ENI with Libyan oil on condition that it terminate the deal, Mattei asked for a personal meeting with President Kennedy. It was scheduled for November 1962. But on October 27 of that year, at a critical point in Mattei's negotiations with both the Soviet Union and the United States, he was killed when his company plane crashed in Northern Italy.

The circumstances of the crash were as follows: The Morane-Saulnier MS-760 plane had taken off from Catania, Sicily, around midday en route to Milan. Only three people were aboard the small jet: Mattei; the pilot Irnerio Bertuzzi; and William McHale, an American reporter who was interviewing Mattei. All three men died when the plane fell from the sky and crashed in a blazing fire near the village of Bascape.

The official inquiry was headed by Giulio Andreotti, the defense minister and political strongman of the Christian Democracy party. In 1962, the forensics for determining the cause of air crashes was heavily dependent on recovering the plane's flight instruments, as there were no black boxes or flight recorders on small planes. In this case, however, key pieces of the plane's instruments had been inexplicably destroyed at the scene. The flight gauges, for example, had been dissolved in acid. So, without any direct evidence of an explosion, the investigation was stymied. After determining from weather reports that there had been thunderstorms in the area, it was ruled that the crash was a "probable accident" caused by bad weather.

Even with this official finding, there was considerable suspicion in Italy that more was involved than a thunderstorm, and the Mattei crash became the subject of countless journalistic investigations. In 1995, the remains of Mattei and his pilot were exhumed by court order and reexamined by a panel of experts. Even though thirty-three years had elapsed, there were now more accurate forensic tools. And through them, the panel found tiny bits of metal in the crash victims' bones. They further determined that these fragments had been deformed by an enormous pressure before the fiery crash, and they concluded that there was an explosion inside the plane. This new analysis suggested that Mattei had been the victim of an assassination. In light of the international intrigue surrounding Mattei at the time of his death, numerous conspiracy theories have been advanced as to who was behind the assassination. To begin with, there is the contract-killing theory. According to Tomasso Buscetti, an ex-Mafia "pentito" who also provided leads in the Roberto Calvi case, the Sicilian Mafia was given the contract to kill Mattei on behalf of American oil interests and had one of its men put a bomb aboard the plane in Catania. Even though Buscetti's allegation was unsubstantiated, it led to the 1995 exhumation of the bodies. (Buscetti claimed that the Andreotti investigation was merely a cover-up.) Next, there is a "French Connection" theory. According to Philippe Thyraud de Vosjoli, a former agent of the French secret service SDECE, Mattei's plane was sabotaged by a SDECE operative code-named Laurent, who placed high explosives on board that would be triggered by its landing gear. And finally, the CIA theory: that CIA operatives sabotaged Mattei's plane to prevent him from building the pipeline to the Soviet Union.

The fact that a small plane crashed in 1962 in bad weather is not in itself suspicious, but if there was an explosive device aboard it, there can be little doubt that Mattei was murdered. My assessment is that this was the work of an intelligence service. In an exhaustive review of the forensic evidence in 2009, Italian academics Donato Firrao and Graziano Ubertalli concluded that "a small charge bomb had been planted behind the dashboard from the exterior of the plane." This job was most likely done by the agent of an experienced intelligence service. In this context, I find the account of Philippe de Vosjoli credible. I spent two days interviewing de Vosjoli in Lighthouse Point, Florida, in 1980, and I believe he was in a position to know about SDECE's covert operations. He recalled that French intelligence had mounted a similar attack on March 29, 1959, on a plane carrying Barthélemy Boganda, the prime minister of a French territory that is now the Central African Republic. Boganda's plane exploded in midair about 100 miles west of the airport at Bangui. According to de Vosjoli, a miniature explosive was used by French intelligence operatives to make the assassination appear to be an accident. De Vosjoli said the same technique was repeated by French intelligence in 1962 to eliminate Mattei. Even though de Vosjoli had no evidence to back his theory, his description of the explosive device is consistent with the findings of the 1997 forensic analysis and, in my view, gives further weight to his story that French intelligence had a hand in the downing of Mattei's aircraft.

In 1962, before forensic investigative techniques for determining the cause of plane crashes had been fully perfected, the theory that Mattei's plane crashed because of bad weather was perfectly plausible. In 1995, more highly developed forensics changed the scientific verdict from a likely accident to a likely murder.

CHAPTER 12

THE DISAPPEARANCE OF LIN BIAO

In the fall of 1971, Marshal Lin Biao, the designated successor of Mao Zedong to rule China, suddenly disappeared from view. The annual National Day celebration, in which he was expected to appear on the podium in his customary place next to Mao, and which had been held every year since the Communists took power in 1948, was abruptly canceled, and Lin Biao was not mentioned in any newspaper or television broadcast for nearly two years. During this period, only the top leadership learned that he was dead. Mao explained that Marshal Lin, who had been his comrade-in-arms and Communist China's most decorated hero, was a traitor who had been planning to assassinate him and then stage a coup d'état that September. After the putative plot was uncovered, Mao had the entire military command secretly purged and ordered Lin arrested. According to Mao, Lin then attempted to defect to the Soviet Union, which was now China's enemy, but his military aircraft ran out of fuel and crashed in Mongolia, killing Lin Biao and all aboard the fleeing plane. So, in this official account, released to the public in 1973, Lin died in an accidental plane crash.

The basic facts emerged only gradually. On September 13, 1971, a British-made Trident airliner, powered by three jet engines, took off from Shanhaiguan Airbase in eastern China, flew less than 1,000 miles into Mongolia, a vassal state of the Soviet Union, and then crashed into the grasslands near the town of Ondorkhaan. Aboard the doomed aircraft were Lin

Biao, his entire family, and a half-dozen of his top aides. No one survived the crash. The weather was clear that day, the plane was well within its range of 2,000 miles at the time of the crash, and the officer at the plane's controls, Colonel Pan Jungyin, who was a deputy commander of the Chinese air force, was one of China's most experienced pilots.

Mongolia, which was not an ally of China's in 1971, conducted only a perfunctory investigation. It established that the plane had not run out of fuel. Indeed, there was so much excess fuel in the pods that it fed a blazing fire that incinerated most of the plane, including all of its flight instruments. No autopsies were conducted on the badly charred bodies, which were buried in a shallow mass grave near the crash site. Because the plane was well beyond the range of China's primitive surface-to-air missiles, the investigators ruled out the possibility that the aircraft had been downed by a Chinese missile. And as there was no other aircraft detected in this area, they concluded that the crash was an accident caused by pilot error.

Moscow, apparently not satisfied that it was an accident, subsequently sent in a KGB team to exhume the remains. The results of this investigation were kept secret but, according to a KGB defector who claimed that he had had access to the investigation, Soviet pathologists determined that some of the passengers aboard the plane died before it crashed and burned.

U.S. intelligence was also suspicious of the circumstances surrounding the crash. The NSA was closely monitoring communication, radar, and other signals in China as part of the preparations for President Richard Nixon's trip to China. Through its signal intercepts on September 13, 1971, it learned that China had grounded all military plane flights just before Lin's flight took off and that the flights only resumed after his plane crashed. This extraordinary shutdown suggests that a decision was made by Mao to allow the flight. At no point did Mao seem concerned that the plane would make it to the Soviet

Union. When Mao was told by his premier Chou En-Lai that Lin's plane was about to take off, he calmly recited to Chou an ancient Chinese proverb that began "Rain must fall." According to Dr. Li Zhisui, Mao's personal physician, who wrote his memoirs after he emigrated to the United States, after the plane crashed Mao was greatly relieved to hear that there were no survivors. But if Mao wanted Lin Biao dead, could he have depended on a random accident to bring about this outcome? All that is known for certain is that the counter-coup that Mao feared never took place.

The vacuum left by the suppression of virtually all the evidence concerning the crash has been filled by numerous theories. Even the official finding that the crash was caused by pilot error is no more than a theory. An alternative theory is that the plane was sabotaged. According to this theory, Lin Biao was encouraged to leave China with his wife, son, and military aides, but a time or pressure-activated bomb was planted aboard their plane. There is also the staged crash theory advanced by Stanislav Lunev, who had served as a high-ranking intelligence officer on the Russian General Staff. According to Lunev, Lin Biao and his party had been executed and their corpses then placed on the plane and that after flying the corpse-filled aircraft towards the Mongolian border, the Chinese pilot set the controls on auto-pilot, and parachuted out. Lunev does not explain what purpose would be served by such an elaborate staging of an accident.

My assessment is that Lin Biao's jet did not accidently fall from the sky. The weather was clear, the plane was at its cruising altitude, there was no evidence of a fuel shortage, and there were no distress calls. A more plausible explanation is that Mao had intervened to make certain that Marshal Lin never reached Moscow alive, and that a timed explosive had been planted aboard the plane. This bomb would account for why the plane was allowed to take off, why Chinese fighters did not attempt to intercept it, and why Mao told Chou that "The rain must fall." Quite possibly, the explosion was planned to occur over Chinese territory, where the cover-up could be managed, but because of the lack of headwinds, the plane made it to Mongolia. In any case, I believe that the plane crashed because of Chinese sabotage.

The obvious lesson here is that a regime in a closed society can control the shape and timing of the information about a crime. Even though the information in this case concerned a political leader as prominent as Marshal Lin Biao, the regime managed to suppress any mention of it in public for two years. To be sure, this crime occurred more than four decades ago, but the regime in China still retains that same power over information, as is illustrated by the murder of Neil Heywood in Chongqing, China, on November 14, 2011. Heywood, who was a British consultant to Bo Xilai, then a powerful member of the China's ruling politburo, was found dead in his hotel room. His death was officially attributed to his alcohol consumption, even though a secret police report showed that he had been poisoned by potassium cyanide. His body was cremated before an autopsy could be performed. The natural-death verdict went unchallenged for three months, and it would have remained largely forgotten if not for the defection of Wang Lijun, the local police chief and vice-mayor, to the U.S. Embassy in February 2012. After Wang revealed that Heywood was murdered by Gu Kailai, the wife of Bo Xilai, the Chinese regime decided to reveal the murder. It purged Bo Xilai, and, after extracting a confession from Gu, convicted her of the murder. Yet it still controlled all the evidence, and it may have used the portions of it that it elected to release, as it did in the Lin Biao case, to justify political changes.

CHAPTER 13
THE ELIMINATION OF GENERAL ZIA

The death of President Muhammad Zia-ul-Haq of Pakistan and his top deputies in August 1988 altered the face of the country's politics in Pakistan in a way in which no simple coup d'état could have done. Pakistan is the only country named after an acronym: "P" stands for Punjab, "A" for Afghanistan, and the "K" for Kashmiri. It once reflected the dream of a trans-Asia Islamic state; only the "P" actually became part of Pakistan when it was carved out of British India in 1947 as a haven for Muslims. General Zia was mindful of this dream when he organized a military coup in 1977 and seized power. Zia moved almost immediately to placate the mullahs in his country by pursuing a policy of "Islamization" and reinstating the law of the Koran. In an extraordinary balancing act, he also strove to build an ultra-modern military machine, complete with nuclear arms, and also to use his intelligence service, the ISI, to wage war against the Soviet occupiers of Afghanistan and the Indian army in Kashmiri. This great game, and his regime, came to an abrupt end on August 17, 1988.

I went to Pakistan in the winter of 1989 on a *Vanity Fair* assignment to investigate Zia's death. Soon after I arrived in Islamabad, I found that the Pakistani officials I had made arrangements to interview were no longer available to me, either on or off the record. One aide to the foreign minister said that the subject of the "tragic accident," as he termed the plane crash that had killed General Zia, was now off limits. Since the

Pakistan government was stonewalling, I turned for assistance to the only other source I could find: the children of the generals killed in the crash. My assumption that they had a motive to discover what was behind the death of their fathers proved correct. A number of these young men, including the sons of General Zia and General Akhtar Abdur Rahman (who for ten years had headed Pakistan's equivalent of the CIA, the Inter-Services Intelligence agency, or ISI), most of whom were in their mid-twenties, not only proved enormously eager to help but, through the medium of their fathers' military aides, had access to key officials, including the airport security officers at the control towers who had actually taped the final conversation from Zia's plane, and the medical officers who had superintended the disposal of the bodies after the crash. With their help, I was able to gradually piece together the story.

On August 17, General Zia boarded Pak One, an American-built Hercules C-130 transport plane, at the military air base outside of Bahawalpur, Pakistan. He had reluctantly gone to Bahawalpur that morning, on his first trip aboard Pak One since May 29, to witness a demonstration of the new American Abrams tank. The plane took off at 3:46 p.m., precisely on schedule for the trip back to the capital city of Islamabad. Seated next to Zia in the air-conditioned VIP capsule was General Akhtar Abdur Rahman, then Chairman of the Joint Chiefs of Staff and, after Zia, the second most powerful man in Pakistan. Among the other passengers were General Mohamed Afzal, Zia's chief of the General Staff; eight other Pakistan generals; Zia's top aides; and two American guests: Ambassador Arnold L. Raphel, and General Herbert M. Wassom, the head of the U.S. military-aid mission to Pakistan.

Shortly after takeoff, only eighteen miles from the airport, on a bright clear day, the giant aircraft lurched up and down three times in the sky, as if were on an invisible roller coaster, and then plunged straight into the desert and exploded in a fireball. All thirty persons on board, including four crew members, were dead. Within hours, army tanks sealed off public buildings and television stations, signifying a change in power. But the mystery remained: What caused the plane to crash?

Since it involved an American-built plane, and the CIA had been partners with Zia in the war against Soviet forces in Afghanistan, the United States obtained permission for U.S. forensic experts to carry out the investigation for Pakistan's board of inquiry. But Pakistan limited the number of U.S. experts to seven Air Force accident investigators and specifically excluded any criminal, counterterrorist, or sabotage experts. The team, headed by Colonel Daniel E. Sowada, issued a 365-page red-bound report, which I obtained from a source at the Pentagon. The team had worked to eliminate what was not possible, following the precept that once the impossible is eliminated, what remains, no matter how improbable, is the truth. First, they ruled out the possibility that the plane had blown up in midair. If it had exploded in this manner, the pieces of the plane, which had different shapes and therefore different resistance to wind, would have been strewn over a wide area—but that had not happened. By reassembling the plane in a giant jigsaw puzzle and scrutinizing with magnifying glasses the edges of each broken piece, they established that the plane was in one piece when it had hit the ground. They thus concluded that structural failure—i.e. the breaking-up of the plane in flight—was not the cause. Next, they eliminated the possibility of a missile attack. If the plane had been hit by a missile, intense heat would have melted the aluminum panels and, as the plane dived, the wind would have left telltale streaks in the molten metal. But there were no streaks on the panels, and no missile part or other ordnance had been found in the area.

They further ruled out the possibility that there was an onboard fire while the plane was in the air since, if there had been one, the passengers would have breathed in soot before they died. Yet, the single autopsy performed, which was on the American general seated in the VIP capsule, showed that there was no soot in his trachea, indicating that he had died before, not after, the fire ignited by the crash.

If it was not a missile or fire, another possibility was power failure. If that had happened, the propellers would not have been turning at their full torque when the plane crashed, which would have affected the way that their blades had broken off and curled on impact. But by examining the degree of curling on each broken propeller blade, the investigators determined that in fact the propellers were spinning at full speed when the plane hit the ground.

Next they turned to the fuel. They ruled out the possibility of contaminated fuel by taking samples of the diesel fuel from the refueling truck, and by analyzing the residues still left in the fuel pumps in the plane, which they determined had been operating normally at the time of the crash. They also ruled out any problem with the electric power on the plane because both electric clocks on board had stopped at the exact moment of impact. The final possibility for a mechanical failure was that the controls became inoperable. But the Hercules C-130 had not one but three redundant control system. The two sets of hydraulic controls were backed up, in case of leaks of fluid in both of them, by a mechanical system of cables. If any one of them worked, the pilots would have been able to fly the plane. By comparing the position of the controls with the mechanisms in the hydraulic valves and the stabilizers in the tail of the plane (which are moved through this system when the pilot moves the steering wheel), they established that the control system was working when the plane crashed. This was confirmed by a computer simulation of the flight performed by Lockheed, the builder of the C-130. They also ruled out the possibility that the controls had temporarily jammed by a microscopic examination of the mechanical parts to see if there were any signs of jamming or binding.

That left the possibility of pilot error. But the crash had occurred after a routine and safe takeoff in perfectly clear day-time weather, and the hand-picked pilots were fully experienced with the C-130 and had medical checkups before the flight. Since the plane was not in any critical phase of flight, such as takeoff or landing, where poor judgment on the part of the pilots could have resulted in the mishap, the investigators ruled out pilot error as a possible cause. Since they precluded both a mechanical failure and pilot error, a conclusion of assassination was all but inescapable.

Based on this investigation, Pakistan's board of inquiry concluded that the cause of the crash of Pak One was a criminal act "leading to the loss of control of the aircraft." It suggested that the pilots must have been incapacitated, but this was as far as it could go, since there was no black box or cockpit recorder on Pak One and no autopsies had been done on the remains of the pilots.

What had happened to the pilots during the final minutes of the flight? When I went to Pakistan in February 1989, I attempted to answer that question by finding other planes in the area that might have intercepted radio reports from Pak One. There were three other planes in the area tuned to the same frequency for communications—a turbojet carrying General Aslam Beg, the Army's vice chief of staff, which was waiting on the runway at Bahawalpur airport to take off next; Pak 379, which was the backup C-130 in case anything went wrong to delay Pak One; and a Cessna security plane that took off before Pak One to scout for terrorists. With the assistance of the families of the military leaders killed in the crash, I managed to locate the pilots of these planes—all of whom were well acquainted with the flight crew of Pak One and its procedures—who could listen to the conversation between Pak One and the control tower in Bahawalpur. They independently described the same sequence of events. First, Pak One reported its estimated time of arrival in the capital. Then, when the control tower asked its position, it failed to respond. At the same time Pak 379 was trying unsuccessfully to get in touch with Pak One to verify its arrival time. All they heard from Pak One was "Stand by," but no message followed. When this silence persisted, the control tower became progressively more frantic in its efforts to contact Zia's pilot, Wing Commander Mash'hood. Three or four minutes passed. Then, a faint voice in Pak One called out "Mash'hood, Mash'hood." One of the pilots overhearing this conversation recognized the voice. It was Zia's military secretary, Brigadier Najib Ahmed, who apparently, from the low volume of his voice, was in the back of the flight deck (where a door connected to the VIP capsule). If the radio was switched on and was picking up background sounds, it was the next-best thing to a cockpit flight recorder. Under these circumstances, the long silence between "Stand by" and the faint calls to Mash'hood, like the dog that didn't bark, was the relevant fact. Why wouldn't Mash'hood or any of the three other members of the flight crew have spoken if they were in trouble? The pilots aboard the other planes, who were fully familiar with Mash'hood, and the procedures he was trained in, explained that if Pak One's crew was conscious and in trouble, they would not in any circumstances have remained silent for this period of time. If there had been difficulties with controls, Mash'hood would have instantly given the emergency "Mayday" signal so help would be dispatched to the scene. Even if he had for some reason chosen not to communicate with the control tower, he would have been heard shouting orders to his crew to prepare for an emergency landing. And if there had been an attempt at a hijacking in the cockpit or a scuffle between the pilots, it would also be overheard. In retrospect, the pilots of the other aircraft had only one explanation for the prolonged silence: Mash'hood and the other pilots were unconscious while the thumb switch that operated the microphone had been kept opened by the clenched hand of a pilot.

The account of the eyewitnesses at the crash site dovetailed with the radio silence. They had seen the plane slowly pitching up and down. According to a C-130 expert to whom I spoke at Lockheed, a C-130 characteristically goes into a pattern known as a "phugoid" when no pilot is flying it. First, the unattended plane dives toward the ground then the mechanism in the tail automatically overcorrects for this downward motion, causing the plane to head momentarily upward. This pattern would continue, each swing becoming more pronounced until the plane crashed. Analyzing the weight on the plane, and how it had been loaded, this expert calculated that the plane would have made three roller-coaster turns before crashing, which is exactly what the witnesses had reported. He concluded from this pattern that had the pilots been conscious, they would have corrected the "phugoid"—or at least, would have made an effort, which would have been reflected in the settings of the controls. Since this had not happened, only one possibility remained: the pilots were paralyzed, unconscious, or dead.

Meanwhile, an analysis of chemicals found in the plane's wreckage, performed by the laboratory of the Bureau of Alcohol, Firearms, and Tobacco in Washington, D.C., found foreign traces of pentaerythritol tetranitrate (PNET), a secondary high explosive commonly used by saboteurs as a detonator, as well as antimony and sulfur, which, in the compound antimony sulfide, is used in fuses to set off such a device. Using these same chemicals, Pakistan ordnance experts reconstructed a low-level explosive detonator that could have been used to burst a flask the size of a soda can. These tests showed that it was possible that such a device could have been used to dispense an odorless poison gas that incapacitated the pilots. Indeed, the

ATF lab also found phosphorous residue in the cockpit, which could have come from poison gas.

The problem in pursuing this lead was that no medical examinations or autopsies were performed on the bodies of the pilots and other members of the flight crew. Doctors at the military hospital in Bahawalpur reported that parts of the victims' bodies had been brought there in plastic body bags from the crash site on the night of August 17, and stored there, so that autopsies could be performed by a team of American and Pakistani pathologists. But before the pathologists had arrived, the hospital received orders to return these plastic bags to the coffins for burial. The commanding officer ordered the medical preparations to cease and the bodies to be turned over for immediate burial. The official explanation given in the report is that Islamic law requires burial within twenty-four hours. But this could not have been the real reason, since the bodies were not returned to their families for burial until two days after the crash, as relatives confirmed to me. Nor were the families ever asked permission for autopsy examinations. And, as I learned from a doctor for the Pakistan Air Force, Islamic law notwithstanding, autopsies are routinely done on pilots in cases of air crashes. This intervention made it impossible to determine whether a nerve gas or other toxic agent had paralyzed the crew.

These orders to literally bury the evidence came directly from the Army, which was now under the authority of General Beg, who, after having his turbojet pilot circle over the burning wreckage of Pak One, flew immediately back to Islamabad, to assume command. For their part, Pakistani military authorities concentrated their investigation on the possibility that Shiite fanatics were responsible for the crash. The copilot of Pak One, Wing Commander Sajid, was a Shiite (as are more than ten percent of Pakistan's Muslims), as was one of the pilots of the backup C-130. This pilot, though he protested his innocence, was kept in custody for more than two months and roughly interrogated about whether Wing Commander Sajid had discussed a suicide mission. Finally, the Army abandoned this effort after the Air Force demonstrated that it would have been physically impossible for the copilot alone to have caused a C-130 to crash in the way it did.

The government then appointed a commission headed by Justice Shafiur Rehman, a well-respected judge on the Supreme Court, to establish the cause of the crash. Five years later, in 1993, it issued a secret report concluding that the Army had so effectively obstructed the investigation that the perpetrators behind the crash could not be brought to justice. The one un-counted casualty of Pak One was thus the truth.

There is, to be sure, an abundance of theories based on who had a motive to kill General Zia. Not unlike the plot of Agatha Christie's *Murder on the Orient Express*, in which, if one looked hard enough, everyone aboard the train had a motive for the murder, many parties, with the means to sabotage a plane, had a motive to eliminate Zia.

First, there is the CIA. According to this theory, the CIA had become concerned that Zia was diverting a large share of the weapons it supplied to the ISI to an extreme Mujahideen group led by Gulbuddin Hekmatyar. Not only was this group anti-American, but its strategy appeared to be aimed at divid-ing the rest of the Afghan resistance so that it could take over in Kabul—with Zia's support.

Second, there is the Bhutto family. Zia had, after all, usurped power from President Zulfikar Ali Bhutto. He had also allowed Bhutto to be hanged like a common criminal in 1979 on what Bhutto's family viewed as a trumped-up charge. In addition, Zia outlawed Bhutto's political party, the Pakistan People's Party; imprisoned his wife (even though she was suffering from lung cancer) and his daughter, Benazir Bhutto; and had both his sons, who were in exile abroad, convicted of high crimes in absentia. The eldest son, Shah Nawaz, was then murdered in France in 1986, and the younger son, Mir Murtaza, driven into hiding. Demanding vengeance, Mir Murtaza Bhutto headed an anti-Zia group called Al Zulfikar ("the sword"), which operated out of Afghanistan and Syria. One of its operations was to hijack a Pakistan International Airlines Boeing 727 with 100 passengers aboard. Another involved attempting to blow Pak One out of the sky with Zia aboard it by firing a Soviet-built SAM 7 missile at it. In all, Mir Murtaza claimed he was behind five attempts to assassinate Zia. Initially, his group also had taken credit for the successful destruction of Pak One in a phone call to the BBC, but it subsequently retracted this claim. In any case, there was no doubt that he was well motivated. (Mir Murtaza was killed in a shootout with police in Karachi in 1996.)

A third theory is that the KGB killed Zia. Moscow also had a motive, since Zia was behind covert attacks on Soviet troops not only in Afghanistan but in the Soviet Union itself. Earlier that August, the Soviet Union had temporarily suspended its troop withdrawals from Afghanistan because it alleged that Zia had violated the Geneva Accords, which had been signed in May. A spokesman for the foreign ministry in Moscow said only a week before the crash that Zia's "obstructionist policy cannot be tolerated." Moscow officials even took the extraordinary step of calling in the American Ambassador to Moscow, Jack Matlock, and informing him that it intended "to teach Zia a lesson." It certainly had the means in place in Pakistan to make this threat credible, having trained, subsidized, and effectively run the Afghan intelligence service, WAD, which operated in Pakistan. In 1988, according to a State Department report, such covert operations had killed and wounded more than 1,400 people in Pakistan.

A fourth theory was that India was the culprit. Less than two weeks before the crash, the Indian prime minister, Rajiv Gandhi, had warned Pakistan that it would have cause "to regret its behavior" in covertly supplying weapons to Sikh terrorists in India. Not only had the Sikhs assassinated Indira Gandhi, Rajiv's mother, when she was prime minister, they now had more than 2,000 armed guerrillas located mainly around the Pakistan border, and Zia had been supplying them with AK-47 assault rifles, rocket launchers, and sanctuaries inside Pakistan. Accordingly, India had a motive to get rid of Zia. It also had the means, having organized a special covert-action unit that went by the initials R.A.W, to recruit agents inside Pakistan.

A fifth theory was that Shiites were behind Zia's death. Zia's Sunni regime had been repressing the Shiite minority, and, according to this theory, the Shiites struck back by recruiting the Shiite copilot of Zia's plane, Wing Commander Sajid. This was why Pakistani military authorities arrested the Shiite pilot of the backup C-130, who was a close friend of Sajid, and interrogated him for more than two months. (Even under torture, he insisted that, as far as he knew, Sajid was a loyal pilot who would not commit suicide.) The problem here was that in order to crash the plane Sajid would have had to overpower the rest of the four-man flight crew, but no such struggle had been heard over the radio.

Finally, there is the Army coup theory. Zia had told his close associates that he planned to purge and reorganize the army, and this threat, according to this theory, would provide a motive for a preemptive move against Zia. Among the few top generals not aboard Pak One was General Aslam Beg, the Army's vice chief of staff. He waved good-bye to Zia from the runway, and then, after the crash, flew immediately to Islamabad to take control, ordering army units to cordon off official residences, government buildings, and other strategic locations in the capital.

My assessment is that Zia and all thirty people aboard Pak One, were victims of sabotage. After going to Islamabad and

Lahore to investigate in 1989, I was allowed to read the red-cover secret U.S. report on the accident by a U.S. Defense Department official, who asked to remain anonymous. This report reinforced my conclusion that the pilots and flight crew were incapacitated by a quick-acting nerve gas, such as "VX," which is odorless, easily transportable in liquid form, and, when vaporized by a small explosion, would cause paralysis and loss of speech within thirty seconds. VX gas would leave precisely the residue of phosphorous that was found in the chemical analysis of debris from the cockpit. A soda-sized can of VX could have been planted in the air vent of the pilot's compartment and triggered by a pressure sensor to activate on takeoff.

But who did it? All the suspected parties—including Mir Murtazi Bhutto's terrorists—had the capability of obtaining VX or a similar nerve gas, and any of them could have recruited an agent to plant a gas bomb on Pak One, since it had been grounded at the airstrip at Bahawalpur in violation of the prescribed procedure of flying it to the larger airport at Multan, where it could be properly guarded. During its four-hour grounding at Bahawalpur, workers reportedly entered Pak One without being searched in order to work on adjusting its cargo door. One of them could have planted a device. So all the suspects had the means to sabotage the plane. But only one of these parties, the Pakistan military, had the power to stop the planned autopsies, seize the telephone records of calls made to Zia and Rahman just prior to the crash, transfer the military personnel at Bahawalpur who might have witnessed the crime, stifle interrogations of police, and keep the FBI out of the picture. In short, only the Pakistan generals who assumed control that day had the power to create a cover-up that followed the crash. They also had a motive for making it look like something more legitimate than a coup d'état.

In addition, the Pakistan military was the only agency capable of assuring that both President Zia and his second-in-command, General Rahman, were on the plane together. And unless both of these men could be eliminated simultaneously, no regime change could be certain. According to General Rahman's family, whom I interviewed at length in Lahore, General Rahman had not wanted to go to the tank demonstration, but he was told that Zia needed his counsel on an "urgent matter." So, under pressure from a general on Beg's staff, he changed his plans and flew with Zia. But that counsel turned out to be untrue. Not only was Zia surprised to see Rahman on the plane, but, as General Rahman related in a phone call from Bahawalpur to his son just before his death, Zia told him that there was no "urgent matter" requiring his presence on the plane.

Zia's eldest son, Ijaz ul-Haq, also believed that his father had been manipulated by the military into going to the tank demonstration. He told me that his father was in the midst of making major changes in the military hierarchy and saw no point in going to this tank demonstration. He then received "continued calls" from General Mahmud Durrani, who was on Beg's staff, pressing him to be at the demonstration. The general said that the "Americans would consider it a slight" if he missed this event. So, despite his misgivings, he agreed to go. But according to U.S. Ambassador Robert Bigger Oakley, who in August 1988 had been the assistant to the president for Pakistan on the National Security Council, neither the U.S. embassy nor the military mission had pressed for Zia's attendance. He also told me that Ambassador Raphel, his predecessor, made a snap decision twenty-four hours beforehand to fly on Pak One when he learned, to his surprise, that Zia would be aboard the plane. If so, Zia, like Rahman, had been misled by his advisors.

The level of orchestration necessary to bring about this regime change, both before the crash and in effecting the cover-up after the crash, persuades me that this was an inside job by a Pakistani military cabal. The journalistic lesson in the Zia case is that even when a government officially embargoes a subject, such as the Pakistan government did in this case, in a relatively porous country such as Pakistan, it is possible to get answers from low-level civil servants, such as air tower controllers, mortuary officers, and police officials.

CHAPTER 14

THE SUBMERGED SPY

On September 24, 1978, the *Brillig*, a thirty-one-foot sloop, was found off the western shore of Chesapeake Bay. No one was aboard the vessel. Its owner, and last known passenger, was John Arthur Paisley, a fifty-five-year-old former deputy director of the CIA's Office of Strategic Research, who had worked on ultra-secret assessments of the CIA, such as "B Team," a unit of the president's foreign intelligence advisory board. In his last known communication from the boat, Paisley informed a friend, Mike Yohn, over the ship-to-shore radio that he had an important report to write. Aboard the *Brillig*, which Paisley had named from the "Jabberwocky" poem in Lewis Carroll's book *Through the Looking Glass*, was a telephone directory from the CIA and other documents.

Then, on September 26, 1978, Paisley's body bobbed up in the nearby Patuxent River. Strapped to the body, which had been disfigured beyond recognition by its immersion, were diving weights weighing thirty-eight pounds. The autopsy established that the cause of death was a gunshot wound behind the left ear. There were also rope burns on the neck. But since there was no evidence of anyone else aboard the *Brillig*, the death was ruled a suicide by Calvert County, Maryland coroner, Dr. George Weems. Since no weapon had been found on the ship, and there was no blood or brain tissue anywhere on deck, the theory of the Maryland State Police was that Paisley must have strapped thirty-eight pounds of weight on his chest,

APPARENT SUICIDES OF INTELLIGENCE OPERATIVES

DATE	VICTIM	CAUSE OF DEATH
FEBRUARY 10, 1941	General Walter Krivitsky *Soviet intelligence defector*	Shot by pistol
NOVEMBER 28, 1953	Frank Olson *liaison with CIA technical* *division*	Leapt from window after being given LSD
JULY 20, 1963	Jack Dunlap *CIA liaison with NSA* *and a double agent for the* *Soviet Union*	Carbon monoxide poisoning
OCTOBER 29, 1965	Frank Wisner *CIA executive*	Shot with shotgun
OCTOBER 8, 1968	Major-General Horst Wendland *deputy head of the BND*	Shot by pistol
OCTOBER 8, 1968	Admiral Hermann Ludke *NATO liaison*	Shot by rifle
OCTOBER 15, 1968	Hans-Heinrich Schenk *German Ministry official*	Hanged by rope
OCTOBER 16, 1968	Edeltraud Grapentin *German Ministry official*	Sleeping pills overdose
OCTOBER 18, 1968	Colonel Johannes Grimm *German Defense Agency*	Shot by pistol
OCTOBER 23, 1968	Gerald Bohm *German Ministry official*	Drowned in river
SEPTEMBER 26, 1978	John Paisley *CIA official*	Drowned
APRIL 29, 1983	Waldo Dubberstei *Defense Intelligence official* *(and suspected double* *agent)*	Shot with shotgun

positioned himself in the water next to the boat, and then shot himself.

This verdict raised eyebrows among his former colleagues at the CIA, since it was well known that Paisley was right-handed, so to shoot himself behind his left ear would be difficult. As a result of the unconvincing verdict, a number of theories have emerged to account for the death. First, there is the coroner's theory that Paisley shot himself. Despite the convolutions he would have had to go through, it is possible that he shot himself behind the left ear while holding onto the boat.

Second, there is the "man-who-never-was" theory. In this version, the corpse that floated to the surface was not that of Paisley but a corpse dressed in his clothing. The basis for this theory, which has been advanced by investigative journalist Joseph Trento among others, is that the CIA's office of security had focused its search for a possible mole in Paisley's unit just before his retirement from the CIA in 1974. In this view, Paisley faked his own death to avoid being exposed as a KGB mole. The theory proceeds from the fact that the badly decomposed corpse had been cremated without being positively identified by any of Paisley's family members. In addition, the skin on his fingers had been peeled back several layers, making fingerprint identification less than certain.

Finally, there is the theory that Paisley was killed by an unknown party. In these circumstances, murder is the only plausible alternative to suicide.

My assessment is that this was a case of a murder that did not go as planned. The evidence is that the corpse was Paisley's. Not only was there one matching fingerprint, but Paisley's own dentist identified the dental work (even though this identification had to be done from memory, since the dental X-rays had been lost when the dentist had moved offices). The suicide theory is not credible to me, because the fact that no weapon was found at the scene is not consistent with suicide. Nor are the rope burns on the corpse's neck or the bullet hole behind the left ear. It is also implausible that a man bent on suicide would both shoot and, by wearing weights, drown himself.

A far simpler explanation is that he was shot elsewhere, execution-style, behind the left ear, after he made the call to his friend. His body was then weighted down, possibly with even more weight than was found strapped to his chest, and then dropped in the water, with the expectation that the weights would keep the body from surfacing. The motive may well have been intelligence-related in light of the CIA documents on the boat. Graham Greene's 1978 novel *The Human Factor*, which concerns the problem of eliminating a suspected mole in an intelligence service, may be illuminating here. In Greene's spy story, a secret service discovers a mole but assesses that a court trial could compromise its secret operation. So it elects to use a non-judicial remedy by poisoning the mole with afla-toxin, which disguises the murder as an accidental death as the result of ingesting moldy peanuts. While this is fiction, in-telligence services did have this capability in the late 1970s. If Paisley had been involved in some sort of double-game of spy-ing, it is possible that one side disposed of him in a way that, if the body had not surfaced, would make the murder appear to be a disappearance as the result of a boating accident. In any case, as a large part of the evidence has been lost or destroyed, including even the fingerprint sample in CIA records, Paisley's death remains an unsolved crime.

The intrigue that surrounds an intelligence operative in life does not necessarily end with his demise, even if his death is declared an apparent suicide or accidental death. This is es-pecially true if the death is violent and there are no witnesses. For example, the demise of CIA liaison Frank Olson, who fell or was defenestrated from a tenth-floor window at the Hotel Pennsylvania on November 28, 1953, remained the subject of such intense speculation that more than four decades later, after the body was exhumed and a second autopsy was performed, the district attorney in New York ordered a belated homicide investigation, though no charges were ever brought. Since spies are occupationally engaged in a life of deception, in which their biography is often rearranged into a legend to suit the requisites of national security, their deaths are not always accepted as what they appear to be.

PART THREE
COLD CASE FILE

CHAPTER 15
JACK THE RIPPER

Jack the Ripper may be the most celebrated serial killer in history. Not only has he been the subject of books, movies, television reenactments, and even an opera, but his name is commonly used by tabloid journalists as convenient shorthand to describe a depraved serial killer. The real mystery is whether "Jack The Ripper" actually existed or if he was a composite character used by the rising tabloid media to link a number of unrelated murders to sell newspapers and increase circulation. Prior to the emergence of Jack the Ripper in Victorian London in 1888, there had been a large number of attacks on prostitutes on the unlit streets and in the alleys of the Whitechapel district of London. Since there was much ethnic violence in these slums, the police paid little attention to the attacks. But the new tabloids—so named because the content was compressed like a pharmaceutical tablet into four pages—were in the midst of a take-no-prisoner circulation war for survival. The newest of them, *The Star*, which was close to going bankrupt, saw an opportunity in the prostitute murders. Since there was little interest in individual murders of prostitutes, it linked three together and attributed the killings to single serial murderer. The demonic name it gave him came from a letter of unknown provenance claiming authorship of the murders that was signed "Jack the Ripper." The letter came through the mail on September 28, 1888, to the main provider of stories to *The Star*, the Central News Agency. The "Jack the Ripper" name caught the public's imagination and reversed *The Star*'s faltering circulation. To compete with it, the other tabloids had to outdo it in reporting Jack the Ripper's deeds, and in less than six months, eleven separate deaths were attributed to the sinister killer.

What happened outside this circulation war is less clear. There was only one witness to the prostitute attacks, Emma Elizabeth Smith. Although fatally wounded by stabbing, she lived long enough to describe her attackers to the police. She said it was a gang of a few men and a teenager. This narrative of a gang contradicted the press's version of a solitary "Jack the Ripper." Such gang assaults were not uncommon in 1888. No other victim lived to identify her attacker, nor were there any other witnesses to the attacks. No weapons, clothing, or other telltale clues were found at any of the crime scenes. The police only had bodies, blood, and gore to go on. Without such forensic tools as fingerprint, hair, fiber, blood, or DNA analysis, it was not possible to tie the crimes to a single killer.

The police had only one means of linking any of the prostitute murders: a unique modus operandi. In a number of the crimes there were common features: necks were slashed, torsos were cut open, and organs removed. The problem here is that tabloids published enough of the gory anatomical details that another killer or killers could have imitated this modus operandi so that their crimes would be blamed on "Jack the Ripper." In any case, the modus operandi did not fit all eleven cases in police files. In the first two cases, the murdered prostitutes, Emma Elizabeth Smith and Martha Tabram, were stabbed, not slashed. They next four victims, Mary Ann Nichols, Annie Chapman, Catherine Eddowes, and Mary Jane Kelly, were slashed and had organs removed. In one case, that of Elizabeth Stride, the victim was slashed but the organs were not removed. According to Sir Melville Macnaghten, the assistant commissioner of the London Metropolitan Police, only five victims fit the pattern. He speculated that in the case of Elizabeth Stride, the murderer might have been interrupted by the sound of approaching footsteps. He wrote in his official report, "the Whitechapel murderer had five victims—and five victims only." Dr. Percy Clark, the assistant to the examining pathologist, who closely examined all these victims, reduced the number further, saying that only three of the victims conformed to the same modus operandi. (Andrew Cook, a historian who reexamined all the police reports for his 2009 book *Jack the Ripper: Case Closed*, went even further, concluding that all the killings were unconnected.) In any case, according to the medical examiner and police closest to the case, most of the murders were not committed by the same predator. Indeed, according to those closest to the investigation, the killer's profile only fits three of the murder cases.

But what of the letter and postcard, both in the same handwriting, signed "Jack the Ripper"? They created the tabloids' killer. When the letter was forwarded to Scotland Yard, which had received dozens of other letters claiming credit for the killings, its Criminal Investigation Department handling the case concluded that the letter was a hoax. It further suspected that it was forged by someone inside the Central News Agency. That suspicion was based on the finding that on previous occasions the Central News Agency had fabricated stories to increase their clients' circulation. In his memoirs, Sir Robert Anderson of Scotland Yard stated bluntly, "the 'Jack-the-Ripper's' letter which is preserved in the Police Museum at Scotland Yard, is the creation of an enterprising London journalist." Sir Melville Macnaghten also gave his appraisal of the "Jack the Ripper" letter, writing in his autobiography, "I have always thought I could discern the stained forefinger of the journalist—indeed, a year later, I had shrewd suspicions as to the actual author." (His suspect was Thomas J. Bulling, a deputy editor at the Central News Agency.)

If the letter was indeed a journalistic invention, it succeeded in creating international interest in the case, as the Central News Agency syndicated the story in two dozen countries, and in burnishing the specter of Jack the Ripper in the popular imagination for generations to come. It also helped spawn a wealth of theories about the case. These theories ran the gamut, enlisting ethnic groups, such as the Jewish butchers who worked in nearby slaughterhouses, and members of the British royal family. One author, Thomas Stowell, published an article in 1970 in *The Criminologist* theorizing that Prince Albert Victor, second in line to succession to the British throne, may have been the Jack the Ripper because he was driven insane by syphilis.

My assessment is that the concept of "Jack the Ripper" and much of the speculative finger-pointing surrounding the case is a construct of the media. The only pieces of evidence as to the existence of Jack the Ripper are a letter and postcard sent to news media, and the circumstances surrounding them strongly suggest to me that they were fabrications of one or more journalists interested in increasing circulation.

The theories that attempt to tie famous names to the case in more recent books proceed from nothing more than speculation based on what may have been possible. And it is possible to speculate that virtually any person in London was the serial killer. Indeed, even when counter-evidence emerged, such as that Prince Albert had an alibi on the night of some of the murders, it has been disregarded. All we really know for certain 124 years later is that four—or possibly five—prostitutes were killed and brutalized in a similar way in London in 1888. Since two of these murders occurred after the massive newspaper publicity began, they might have been the work of a copycat killer. We do not know even how many different murderers are responsible.

Without forensic tools to process a crime scene—techniques

that are now taken for granted in popular television programs such as *CSI* and *Law & Order*—it was often impossible for police to factually establish the identities of the perpetrators in crimes to which there were no witnesses. Fingerprint classification, such as the Henry Classification System in Britain and the Bertillon system in the United States, was not used by police until the turn of the twentieth century. Hair, fiber, and ballistics identification, which depended on the availability of the modern comparative microscope, was not employed until the late 1920s. DNA typing was not used as a forensic tool until the late 1980s. In 1888, when London police found the bodies of dead prostitutes, they had no means of identifying who was present at the various crime scenes, and therefore could only use guesswork to determine how many of these crimes were linked to a single killer. As a result, the press was free to merge together a number of unsolved crimes as the work of a serial killer.

CHAPTER 16

THE HARRY OAKES MURDER

Sir Harry Oakes was the richest man in the British colony of the Bahamas in 1943. Born in 1874 in America, he made his fortune buying gold mines in Canada, and he got his title from King George VI for money he gave to the King's namesake hospital in Britain. In the Bahamas, where he took up residency to avoid taxes, he owned a large share of the British colony's economy by 1943, including its airport, bus services, commercial real estate, and golf course. He also became a central part of its social life through his close association with the Duke of Windsor, the former King Edward VIII of England, who had been sent to the Bahamas as its governor in 1940 after his pro-Nazi sympathies made him a political vulnerability in Britain. On the night of July 7, 1943, in the midst of a tropical storm, Oakes was murdered in his home in Cable Beach and his battered and burned body covered in white feathers. Since his entire family had moved to his summer estate in Bar Harbor, Maine, the only other person staying in the house was his friend Harold Christie, a Bahamian real estate speculator and a business associate of Oakes. Christie reported the crime at 8:00 the next morning. The police found Oakes' half-charred body in bed in front of a blood-stained lacquered screen. Since the unburnt parts of his body were smeared with inflammable gasoline, they theorized that the perpetrator had set the fire to cover up the murder but that the sudden rainstorm had put it out. With the crime revealed, the Duke of Windsor attempted to stifle any public discussion of it by using his imperial powers in the Crown colony to invoke full press censorship in the Bahamas, but even he could not stop the murder of a man as rich as Oakes from growing into an international scandal.

Meanwhile, Bahamian authorities, unable to get assistance from Scotland Yard because of the exigencies of World War II, could not cope with the pressures put on them by the Duke of Windsor to speedily conclude the investigation. They were baffled by the upward flow of blood on Oakes' corpse, which indicated that it had been moved onto the bed while he was still bleeding, but their only eyewitness, Christie, who was in room next door at the time of the murder, insisted that he had not heard any suspicious noises in the house. This left the police unsure where Oakes met his end. To confuse matters further, there was a serious question of how Oakes had died, indeed so serious that the authorities had to recall in midair the plane carrying Oakes' body to its burial place in Maine. Whereas a hastily done autopsy concluded that Oakes' fatal head injuries had been caused by a blow from a blunt instrument, X-rays of Oakes' right mastoid bones showed four puncture wounds, indicating that he had been killed by a sharp, pointed weapon. Additional photographs taken of the peripatetic corpse did not resolve the discrepancy, nor was any murder weapon found, blunt or sharp. Aside from Christie, the only other possible witnesses at the house, two night watchmen, could not be found.

Meanwhile, the Duke of Windsor brought in from America a Miami homicide detective, Edward Melchen, who had worked as the Duke's personal aide when he visited Florida, and his associate, Captain James Barker, with a mandate to quickly bring the investigation to a conclusion. Even though they had no authority in the Bahamas, he reportedly asked them to confirm that it was a suicide (despite the fact that forensic evidence showed Oakes had been hit from behind). Instead, less than thirty-six hours later, the Miami detectives announced that it was a murder, and they then claimed that they had recovered a partial fingerprint from the bloody lacquer screen, missed by the Bahamian police, that identified the murderer. The print matched that of Alfred de Marigny, a yachtsman who had married Oakes' eighteen-year-old daughter Nancy the year before. On the basis of this fingerprint, he was indicted, a rope was ordered for his execution, and the Duke of Windsor left the country so he could not be called as a witness at the murder trial, which began on October 18, 1943. In the cross-examination, however, the testimony of the American detectives was impeached, and it turned out that the fingerprint could not have come from the bloody screen because it did not match the lines in the screen, and may have been lifted from the water glass that de Marigny had drank from when questioned. De Marigny was acquitted in less than two hours.

The investigation was never reopened, even after de Marigny claimed to have located a key witness, one of the watchmen on duty at the Oakes' home on the night of the murder. According to de Marigny, the watchman said he saw two men arrive in a car around midnight, and enter the house, and, soon afterward, flames in Oakes' bedroom window. He was then paid 100 pounds sterling to leave the island. De Marigny's wife also hired a private detective, Raymond Schindler, who reexamined the crime scene and found that it had been so thoroughly scrubbed down that, even before the trial, any fingerprints, hairs, fibers, or other clues had been obliterated. "The authorities told me that was done 'so as not to confuse the issue,'" Schindler wrote to Scotland Yard. He added that Government House, which was the seat of British rule in the Bahamas, had "stopped the reopening of the investigation."

The consignment of the murder to limbo left the door open to other speculation. The theory advanced by de Marigny is that Oakes was killed by thugs because of his illegal activities.

According to de Marigny, he had been involved with the Duke of Windsor and with Oakes' houseguest Christie, who was a rum smuggler during Prohibition, in a scheme to illicitly smuggle currency out of the Bahamas. According to this theory, the Duke of Windsor organized the cover-up because his partner in these shady dealings, Christie, could be implicated in the murder. The British government then cooperated in the cover-up by recalling the Duke of Windsor to prevent any further tarnishing of his royal reputation.

Another theory advanced is that Meyer Lansky, a well-known American organized crime figure, sent the killers that night. In his book *King X*, Marshall Houts claims that the Duke of Windsor had approved Lansky's expansion of casino gambling into the Bahamas, but that Oakes was blocking it. According to Houts' reconstruction, Lansky's men killed Oakes at another location and had Christie take his body back to his home.

Finally, there is the theory that Oakes' lawyer, Walter Foskett, was behind the murder. On June 10, 1959, the FBI forwarded Scotland Yard a report based on information from Fred Maloof, an art dealer from Maryland, who said that Foskett had embezzled money from Oakes in an art sale he had arranged and, just days before his death, Oakes threatened to expose Foskett. If so, Foskett had a motive to silence him.

My assessment proceeds from the forensic evidence showing that the body had to have been moved onto the bed and then set aflame. The perpetrator clearly had an interest in making the scene appear to be an accident instead of a murder, which suggests that rather than thugs, someone involved with Oakes carried out the crime. The circumstances also indicate that someone inside the house was complicit in allowing access. The only person in the house that night was Christie. His claim that he did not hear the bludgeoning, the moving of Oakes' body, or the fire is not credible. If he had been involved in illegal businesses with Oakes, as de Marigny alleges, he had a motive to maintain silence about what happened that night.

Perhaps the most important lesson of the Oakes case is that frame-ups do not only occur in fiction. If the political stakes are high enough, as they were in the Harry Oakes case, an innocent person can be framed for murder.

CHAPTER 17

THE BLACK DAHLIA

The mutilated body of a nude woman, severed at the waist, was found on January 15, 1947, in Los Angeles. Taking a page from the playbook of Jack the Ripper, a reporter from William Randolph Hearst's *Los Angeles Herald Express* tagged the unknown female "The Black Dahlia," a name that conjured up in the press images of a slinky adventurer. The hunt for the Black Dahlia's killer so intoxicated the public imagination over the next five years that no fewer than thirty men falsely confessed or falsely identified relatives as the sadistic murderer. Six decades later, the fictive sex life of the victim became the subject of Brian De Palma's 2006 movie *The Black Dahlia*.

The facts are more prosaic. Initially, after body parts were found in a vacant lot near Norton Avenue, the police did not even know the identity of the corpse. Only when the body was reassembled could police learn that the victim was a young, diminutive woman—five feet, five inches tall and weighing 115 pounds—with blue eyes and brown hair. There was no blood surrounding the body, and the crime scene had been so badly trampled by journalists, police, and bystanders that it yielded no usable footprints, fingerprints, hair, fibers, or other clues.

According to the autopsy, the cause of death was blood loss combined with a concussion of the brain. The bleeding proceeded from ear-to-ear facial lacerations. She also had deep rope burns on both her wrists and ankles, indicating that she had been tied spread-eagle and then tortured. The lack of blood suggested that the killer had murdered her elsewhere, drained away her blood, cleaned the body parts, transported them to the vacant lot, and then posed them with her arms at right angles above her head.

Her fingerprints were sent to the FBI in Washington, which matched them to the prints of twenty-two-year-old Elizabeth Short, whose fingerprints were on file because she had worked as a clerk at an army base and had been arrested for under-age drinking in Florida. Police then established that she had worked on and off as a waitress in Los Angeles. According to witnesses at the boarding house where she had resided, Short had been missing for about six days before her body was discovered. Soon after the Black Dahlia was identified, the editor of the *Los Angeles Examiner*, another Hearst newspaper, reported that he had received a phone call from the "Black Dahlia Avenger," who claimed to be the killer and demanded that the *Examiner* provide more publicity for the crime. As proof of his bona fides, he mailed the *Examiner* a number of Short's putative possessions, including an address book, a birth certificate, business cards, and photographs. Since an empty handbag had been found in a garbage bin a short distance from the body, either the "Black Avenger" was the killer or a publicity-seeker who had found Short's handbag and, after removing the contents, discarded it. In any case, inscribed on the address book was the name "Mark Hansen." When questioned, Hansen, a Hollywood nightclub owner, told police that Short had lived in his home for about six months from May to October 1946. She had shared a room with his girlfriend, Ann Toth, who was a friend of Short. Toth provided a number of suspects, including Hansen. The prime suspect was Robert Manley, who was with Short in a motel on January 9, making him the last person known to have seen her alive. Manley was briefly arrested, but after he passed a polygraph test, he was released. Despite one of the largest and longest investigations in the history of Los

Angeles, the police were unable to connect any of the suspects to the murder or, for that matter, even locate the place in which Short was mutilated. As a result, no one was ever indicted for the murder of Elizabeth Short.

The theories of who did it fall into two basic categories: acquaintances and strangers. As for the former, Manley remained a prime candidate among theorists for a decade. Since he had been with Short a week before she was murdered, he had the opportunity. He also had serious psychiatric problems, as it later developed, including hearing imaginary voices. In 1954, his wife committed him to a psychiatric hospital and agreed to have him questioned under sodium pentothal—a drug that the CIA experimented with as a truth serum. On the drug Manley maintained that he was innocent of Short's murder, and he was released. He died in 1986. Other theories focus on various other men she knew or might have known in Hollywood, but they have no grounding in evidence. The stranger theories suggest that she was picked up by a sadistic drifter or a Jack-the-Ripper-style serial killer. Captain Jack Donahoe of the Los Angeles police, for example, developed the theory that Short's murder was "likely connected" to a series of sadistic murders in Chicago (for which William Heirens was convicted). He based this on his own analysis of the "Black Dahlia Avenger's" handwriting and the fact that one victim in Chicago was named Suzanne Degnan and Short's body was found only three blocks from Degnan Boulevard. Another such theory is that Short was killed by the so-called Cleveland Torso Killer, who killed and dismembered women in Cleveland between 1934 and 1938, although the Los Angeles police could not find any similarity in the modus operandi of the killers.

My assessment is that Captain Donahoe, though wrong about the Chicago linkage, was right that a serial predator was at work. Media attention, even when it is as unrelenting as in the Black Dahlia case, can confuse rather than clarify a crime investigation. All the evidence points to a killer who had pre-pared a discreet place to imprison, torture, and mutilate his victim and was able to carry out this gruesome deed without leaving a trace. The long police investigation shows that none of the men she dated, including Manley and Hansen, had such a facility. I believe Short was the victim of a random predator.

CHAPTER 18

THE PURSUIT OF DR. SAM SHEPPARD

The brutal murder of Marilyn Sheppard in her bedroom in 1956, and the arrest of her husband, Dr. Samuel Sheppard, captivated the public's attention: Did a stranger break into the Sheppard home and batter his wife to death, as Dr. Sheppard claimed, or did Sheppard himself commit the murder, as the prosecution claimed? The trial so stirred the popular imagination that it inspired one of television's longest-running weekly series, *The Fugitive*, as well as movie of the same name.

A husband killing his own wife is a familiar crime to police. When a wife is murdered at home, suspicion commonly falls on the husband. If the husband has no verifiable alibi, and there are no witnesses, police tend to classify the crime as a possible domestic homicide. Nor is such a scenario a difficult case for prosecutors to make in court. A husband living at home has both opportunity and a presumed motive to "terminate the marriage." The problem for investigators is eliminating the possibility that an intruder entered the home and committed the murder.

The Marilyn Sheppard murder occurred on the Fourth of July holiday weekend in the lakefront suburb of Bayview, Ohio, just outside of Cleveland. At 6:00 a.m. on July 4, 1956, police were summoned to the home of Dr. Samuel Holmes Sheppard, one of Cleveland's most prominent orthopedic doctors. When they arrived, they found Sheppard's wife Marilyn dead in the upstairs bedroom. Her half-naked body had been beaten so savagely and her face slashed so many times that she was barely recognizable. The entire room, including the walls, floor, and closet doors, had been splattered with blood. No murder weapon was found at the scene, but downstairs police found signs of an apparent robbery. Dr. Sheppard's medical bag had been overturned with its contents strewn on the floor. Dr. Sheppard's sports trophies were smashed. Desk drawers had been pulled open. Yet, according to Dr. Sheppard, nothing was missing. So police considered it a possibility that the robbery had been faked to cover up the murder.

The time of Marilyn's death was established as approximately 4:30 a.m. Asked to account for his movements, Sheppard said that after a dinner party that night he fell asleep on a day bed in the downstairs den. He was awakened by his wife's scream and, rushing upstairs, saw an unknown person. When he got to her bedroom, he was knocked out from behind. When he regained consciousness, still woozy, he took Marilyn's pulse and found that she was dead. At that moment, he said that he heard someone leaving by the back door. He ran after him along the Lake Erie shore and caught up with a "bushy-haired" person. But he was then knocked out again.

Police almost immediately doubted his story because there were no signs of forced entry. Instead, they assumed it was a domestic homicide. Since they believed that Dr. Sheppard was the only other person in the house, they made little more than a perfunctory effort to recover fingerprints, blood samples, hair, and fiber evidence. If it were a domestic homicide, collecting such evidence would serve no purpose other than to prove that Sam and Marilyn Sheppard shared the home. The police at the scene were so convinced that this was a domestic homicide that detectives dispatched to the hospital to question Sheppard were instructed to get a full confession. One detective, playing the "bad cop," told him: "I don't know about my partner, but

I think you killed your wife." Despite such tactics, Sheppard steadfastly insisted he was innocent and was himself a victim of the same assailant who murdered his wife.

Nevertheless, on July 29, 1954, Sheppard was arrested for the murder. The trial, which began in October 1954, became a media circus. Few trials in American history had generated as much lurid coverage. The prosecution spent weeks bringing out the erotic details of Sheppard's three-year tryst with Susan Hayes, a nurse at his hospital, to establish that he had already betrayed his wife. His defense lawyers focused on gory crime-scene evidence. They produced expert witnesses who testified that Marilyn's broken teeth indicated that she had bitten her attacker in the struggle. But Sheppard had no open wounds. The defense also produced a report by one of America's most eminent neurosurgeons, Dr. Charles Elkin, who examined Sheppard after the murder and found that he had suffered a cervical concussion and nerve injury, that he had weak nerve reflexes that were impossible for him to fake, and that his injuries could not have been self-inflicted. Two other witnesses found by his private investigators testified that they had seen a bushy-haired man near the Sheppard home on the day of the crime. Sheppard, taking the stand in his own defense, described his fight with a "bushy-haired intruder." The jury did not believe Sheppard's story and, on December 21, 1954, brought in a verdict of second-degree murder, and he was later sentenced to life imprisonment.

Sheppard spent nearly ten years in prison before the U.S. Supreme Court overturned his conviction on the grounds he was denied due process. When he was retried in 1966, he was quickly acquitted.

As a free man, he never returned to medicine. Instead he wrote a book, wrestled professionally under the name "The Killer," became an alcoholic, and died of liver disease in 1970, at the age of forty-six.

The mystery did not die with him. His son reopened the case in 1998 on the basis of new DNA evidence, which did not exist at the time of the crime. The new DNA tests showed traces of blood on Sheppard's clothes that was neither his nor his wife's. The same blood was also found on a closet door only a few feet away from where Marilyn was murdered.

There are three principal theories of the murder. The police theory is that Dr. Sheppard murdered his wife, staged a fake robbery, invented the bushy-haired man, and inflicted his injuries on himself. Next, there is the handyman theory, in which Richard George Eberling, who worked in the Sheppard house, is alleged to have murdered Marilyn Sheppard. Eberling had his own house-cleaning company, which serviced the Sheppard home. This gave him access to the home on the night of the murder. He also had reportedly stolen items from some of the houses he cleaned, which might have provided a motive, since a ring belonging to Marilyn was found in his possession. He indeed admitted entering the Sheppard home on the day of the murder, saying he had cut himself and was seeking bandages. In 1984, he was convicted (along with another man) of murdering Ethel May Durkin in Lakeville, Ohio, so he was capable of homicide. DNA tests on him proved inconclusive, and he died in prison in 1998. Finally, there is the "neighbor theory." Its main proponent is F. Lee Bailey, who was Sheppard's attorney in his retrial. Bailey contends that there is evidence that Marilyn Sheppard was having an affair with her neighbor, and that the neighbor's jealous wife might have killed her.

My assessment is that the new DNA evidence supports Dr. Sheppard's story that there was a third person in the house. If blood was left during the attack, it means that some unidentified person was in the bedroom or had access to the home. If the bushy-haired intruder was capable of knocking Sheppard out twice, it was unlikely to be the neighbor's wife. Since there were no signs of forced entry, the intruder almost surely had easy access to the house. In my view, the person who had these qualifications, Richard Eberling, was the killer.

The lesson here is the powerful role played in police investigation by a phenomenon called "confirmation bias." In social psychology, it is defined as the tendency of people to favor information that confirms their beliefs over information that undercuts their beliefs. In the Sheppard case, the hypothesis of the police was that the husband had killed his wife. The investigation then focused on inconsistencies in his story that tended to confirm their hypothesis, while rejecting contrary evidence, such as that of an intruder. The consequence was a miscarriage of justice.

CHAPTER 19

THE KILLING OF JONBENET RAMSEY

In 1996, the reported kidnapping of JonBenet Ramsey, a six-year-old star in the world of child beauty pageants, set off a monthlong media feeding frenzy reminiscent of the 1932 Lindbergh kidnapping. In both cases, a high-profile child was taken from its bed while the parents were at home, and was then found dead. And in both cases, police could find no signs of forced entry, identifiable fingerprints, or credible witnesses to the putative intruder except for a handwritten ransom note. With Lindbergh, who was a national hero, the police focused on the intruder, but in the Ramsey case, the police focused on the family.

The JonBenet Ramsey investigation began on the morning of December 26, 1996, after her father, John Ramsey, reported her missing from her home in Boulder, Colorado. He told police that the last time the child star was seen by anyone in the family was when he carried her to bed at 10:00 on Christmas night. He showed them a handwritten ransom note that he had found in the house that said that JonBenet had been abducted by a "group" representing a "foreign faction." It demanded that $118,000, the exact size of John Ramsey's annual bonus, be delivered to the kidnappers. At 1:05 p.m. that day, before the ransom money could be paid, Ramsey found his daughter's body covered in a white blanket in the wine cellar.

The medical examination established that her wrists had been tied above her head, and her mouth covered by duct tape, and that she had been garroted by a nylon cord. From the advanced state of rigor mortis, the time of death was between 10:00 p.m. on December 25 and 6:00 a.m. on December 26. The autopsy determined that she was killed by either strangulation or a skull-fracturing blow to the head, and that there were indications that she had been sexually assaulted.

The only solid clue for the investigators was the ransom note. Forensic experts found that the three sheets of paper used in it, as well as the pen with which it was written, came from a table near the kitchen in the Ramsey home. This meant that someone inside the house had taken the time to write a lengthy letter before or after the strangling of JonBenet.

Police found a footprint made by a hiking boot in dust and a palm print on the door of the wine cellar that could have come from an outsider, but they could not date them to the night of the kidnapping. They also found a pubic hair in the blanket in which JonBenet was wrapped that could not be matched to any family member, but it also could have been left in the blanket at an earlier time or resulted from the accidental contamination of the crime scene, which was not initially sealed off. So, even with modern DNA tests, there was no certain evidence of an intruder.

The investigators were also unable to find an escape route. There was an opened basement window, but there were no footprints in the snow outside the window. So the investigation homed in on the activities of the three family members who were in the house—John Ramsey; JonBenet's mother, Patsy; and JonBenet's brother, Burke. Despite an intensive effort, however, the police were unable to match the handwriting samples of any family member to the ransom note, or to find any other evidence implicating them.

Meanwhile, the family hired lawyers to protect their interests and file lawsuits against the media outlets that were reporting police "leaks." So the investigation ground to a halt.

It took nearly twelve years for the district attorney's office to officially exonerate the family members on the basis of the DNA. Even though the investigation officially resumed, the Boulder police chief observed, "Some cases never get solved." There were a number of false confessions, such as that of John Mark Karr in 2006, but none of these confessors matched the DNA profile established by the FBI.

The theories fall into either the domestic-violence category or the unknown-intruder category. The former theories raise the suspicion, which is common when a murder occurs in a household and there are no witnesses, that the ransom note was fabricated to cover the involvement of a Ramsey family member in the death of JonBenet. It was alleged that Patsy Ramsey may have altered her handwriting to avoid it being matched to the note, but this is hardly evidence. The intruder theories posited that some outsider who knew the layout of the Ramsey house, possibly a neighbor, business associate, or relative, murdered JonBenet as an act of revenge or anger against her parents and wrote the ransom note to divert police attention. Finally, there is the sexual-predator theory. Because JonBenet appeared in beauty pageants, there is the possibility that a sexual predator stalked her, cased the house, broke in somehow, and assaulted her.

My assessment is that the abduction and murder were committed by an outsider. As the district attorney explained: "The match of male DNA on two separate items of clothing worn by the victim at the time of the murder makes it clear to us that an unknown male handled these items." This lack of a match convinces me that someone broke into the house. It turns out that there were thirty-eight registered sex offenders within a two-mile radius of the Ramsey home, and, with the attention that JonBenet received as a child star, it is likely that the unknown DNA came from a sexual predator. If he was a known sex offender, he may well have left the note not to collect a ransom but to mislead the police investigation.

DNA is a double-edged sword. It can prove the innocence of an outsider, as it did in the case of the bogus confessor John Mark Karr, but its presence cannot serve as evidence for insiders, such as the Ramsey family members, whose DNA would be expected to be found in the house. While DNA analysis provides a substantial advance over fingerprints in identifying individuals at a crime scene, it still requires a positive match to a person who is not expected to be at the scene of the crime.

CHAPTER 20

THE ZODIAC

A series of attacks on young couples in Northern California in the late 1960s terrified the public after a serial killer, called "The Zodiac," taunted newspapers with coded letters, a signature symbol of a circle bisected by one horizontal and one vertical line, and bloody artifacts from his crimes. Even though the murders themselves stopped in 1970, Zodiac letters extended the journalistic fascination with the case.

The first two victims were high school students, Betty Lou Jensen and David Faraday. Both were shot to death on a secluded lover's lane in the town of Benicia at about 11:00 p.m. on December 20, 1968. Police found no motive, witnesses, or clues.

A similar incident occurred on July 4, 1969, in the parking lot of a park in Vallejo, California. Michael Renault Mageau, nineteen, and Darlene Elizabeth Ferrin, twenty-two, were shot by an unknown man. Ferrin died, but Mageau survived.

Up until August, these attacks had not been connected by police. But on August 1, 1969, letters were sent to the *Vallejo Times-Herald*, the *San Francisco Chronicle*, and the *San Francisco Examiner* that linked the attacks. Each letter contained one-third of a 408-symbol cryptogram, which, the writer claimed, revealed the identity of the killer. He not only challenged these newspapers to investigate his murders but warned that unless each paper printed his letter on their front page he would shoot "a dozen people over the weekend." The

Chronicle immediately published its third of the cryptogram, and there were no murders that weekend. But the press had now become deeply involved in the killer's activities. Two amateur cryptographers, Donald and Bettye Harden, managed to crack the code on August 8, but it contained no names or clues, other than to say that the killer was collecting "slaves" for the afterlife.

The next letter received by the *San Francisco Examiner* provided non-public details about the two previous attacks. It was signed "The Zodiac," which, as with the "Jack the Ripper" case, provided the media with a vivid name for their headlines.

The next killing came on September 27, 1969, near Lake Berryessa in Napa Valley. This time the killer wore a Zodiac costume, consisting of a black hood, clip-on sunglasses, and a bib with the same cross-hair Zodiac symbol that was in the letters. When he appeared in the park, he carried a gun in one hand and held pieces of a clothesline in the other. He then approached Bryan Hartnell and Cecilia Shepard and ordered Shepard to tie up Hartnell. He then stabbed them both repeatedly, leaving them in a pool of blood. He then drew his Zodiac symbol on Hartnell's car door. Shepard died from her wounds, but Hartnell survived to tell the story.

The final murder attributed to the Zodiac was in San Francisco on October 11, 1969. According to three teenage witnesses who watched the attack, a taxicab stopped and the passenger shot the driver, Paul Lee Stine, to death. The passenger then calmly cut off part of his victim's bloodstained shirt and fled the scene on foot.

Police speculated that this murder was committed by the Zodiac merely to get bloody swatches from Stine's shirt. He sent these swatches with his next round of letters to newspapers in which he demanded that a lawyer meet him. He named two of America's most celebrated defense lawyers, F. Lee Bailey and Melvin Belli, and said that either would be acceptable to him and that they should await his call on the Jim Dunbar television show. Belli came on the show in front of a television audience in Daly City, California. Although Belli followed the Zodiac's directions, the Zodiac did not show up. However, Belli himself later received in the mail a swatch from Stine's shirt with a letter asking for his professional help. That was the last Belli heard from the Zodiac, and the last bloody swatch to appear. Letters of unknown provenance continued to be received by newspapers with coded messages, but none could be deciphered. The Zodiac, or the letter-writers claiming his identity, eventually took credit for no less than thirty-seven murders. This led to a new journalistic enterprise: mining the police cold case files for similar killings over the past decade. Although this pursuit continued for a decade, none of the unsolved cases could be tied by evidence to the Zodiac. The police were also stymied by their inability to match evidence at the four crime scenes, or to match the crime scenes to the letters. Even when DNA analysis became available in the 1990s, investigators were unable to match DNA found in the saliva on the stamps on the letters to any crime scene or suspect.

The only suspect identified by a victim was Arthur Leigh Allen, a convicted child molester. At the time of the Zodiac murders, he was in his mid-thirties, lived with his parents, and was a gun collector. In 1991, Michael Mageau, the first survivor, identified Allen from a picture on his 1968 driver's license as the man who shot him. Allen also worked only a few miles from where victim Darlene Ferrin was killed, and he wore a Zodiac-brand watch (with the same symbol found in the letters). However, Allen's fingerprints did not match those taken from the fourth crime scene, Stine's taxicab. Nor did Allen's DNA match the DNA found on the envelopes of the letters, when DNA testing became available. And Sherwood Morrill, head of the Questioned Documents Section of California's Criminal Identification and Investigation Bureau, could not match the handwriting in the Zodiac letters to Allen. So no charges were ever filed. With no other eyewitness identifications, and no murder weapon, the trail was cold.

Based on the lack of any matching evidence at the different crime scenes or in the letters, I assess that a single person could not have both attacked all the victims and written all the letters deemed authentic by the police. It is possible that the letter-writer was not the killer, but he must have had access to the police files, since the early letters contained unpublished details of the first two attacks. One possibility is that the letter-writer was a police investigator who wanted to link the crimes and justify a hunt for a serial killer, or a journalist who learned these details from his or her investigation. In my view, a copycat killer or killers attacked both the couple in Napa Valley and the taxi-driver, Paul Lee Stine, and the police's departments chief suspect, Allen, may indeed have been the killer in the first two attacks. If so, he was wrongly exonerated when police found his fingerprints and DNA did not match DNA and fingerprints found in Stine's taxicab.

An investigation can become the prisoner of its own flawed assumption. In the Zodiac case, police assumed they were dealing with a single perpetrator. The police therefore wrongly ruled out their chief suspect, because his fingerprints and DNA did not match evidence collected at one of the crime scenes. Yet, the later attacks were possibly the work of a copycat killer who adopted the Zodiac's modus operandi. If that is true, by remaining locked into the assumption of a lone killer who was also sending letters, the police sacrificed solving a key part of the larger mystery.

CHAPTER 21

THE VANISHING OF JIMMY HOFFA

James Riddle Hoffa, one of America's best-known labor leaders, vanished without a trace in 1975. The son of a coal miner, he had built the International Brotherhood of Teamsters into the largest, richest, and most politically powerful union in the United States. He had also famously made an enemy of Robert F. Kennedy in 1959 when he was called before the Senate sub-committee investigating organized crime, known as the McClellan Rackets Committee, for which Kennedy was the general counsel. Since Hoffa's union's pension fund had financed the building of much of the casino economy of Las Vegas, Kennedy relentlessly questioned Hoffa about the union leadership's involvement with mobsters. Hoffa answered by mocking Kennedy. The enmity between Hoffa and Kennedy intensified in 1961 when his older brother John F. Kennedy became president, and appointed him attorney general. One of Robert Kennedy's first acts was to create a "Get Hoffa" task force at the Justice Department. He ordered no-holds-barred surveillance and wiretaps on Hoffa and minute scrutiny of all his past activities. As a result, Hoffa was convicted of jury tampering and fraud, and, in 1967, sent to prison. Even after his conviction and jailing, Hoffa was reelected president of the Teamsters. Finally, in 1971, his sentence was commuted by President Richard M. Nixon after Hoffa agreed to officially resign the Teamster presidency. The FBI remained involved in the case, investigating Hoffa's behind-the-scenes influence

VANISHINGS

DATE	VICTIM	LAST SEEN
SEPTEMBER 29, 1913	Rudolf Diesel *inventor*	Aboard the *Dresden*, English Channel, December 26, 1913
AFTER **DECEMBER 26, 1913**	Ambrose Bierce *writer*	Chihuahua, Mexico
AUGUST 6, 1930	Joseph Force Crater *Judge*	Billy Haas Chophouse, New York
MARCH 26, 1967	Jim Thompson *Silk magnate*	Church service at Cameron Highlands, Malaysia
DECEMBER 17, 1967	Harold Holt *Prime Minister of* *Australia*	Cheviot Beach, Australia
NOVEMBER 8, 1974	Richard John Bingham *7th Earl of Lucan*	In car in Sussex, England
JUNE 22, 1983	Emanuela Orlandi *daughter of Vatican* *Bank executive*	Boarding bus to Vatican City, Italy
JULY 31, 1975	James Hoffa *labor leader*	Red Fox Restaurant, Bloomfield, Michigan
MARCH 31, 1985	Vladimir Alexandrov *Soviet scientist*	Nuclear Winter Confer- ence, Madrid, Spain
AUGUST 13, 2003	David Sneddon *American hiker*	Shangri-la, China
MARCH 8, 2007	Robert Levinson *private investigator* *and former FBI agent*	Kish Island, Iran
MARCH 22, 2011	Rebecca Coriam *Disney employee*	Lounge of the ship *Disney Wonder*, off coast of Mexico

to maintain control over the Teamsters, and Hoffa remained under surveillance until his death.

On July 30, 1975, Hoffa went to a limousine-service office in Pontiac, Michigan, where he had told a friend he was meeting with Tony Giacalone, reputedly an organized crime figure in Detroit, and Tony Provenzano, a New Jersey Teamster official. His calendar had the notation "TG—2 p.m.—Red Fox," which apparently referred to his meeting with Tony Giacalone at the Red Fox restaurant in Bloomfield Hills, Michigan.

Hoffa arrived at the Red Fox shortly before 2:00 p.m., but no one met him, according to witnesses. At 2:15 p.m., Hoffa telephoned his wife from a call box and said "I wonder where the hell Tony is." He said he was still waiting. He never returned home. When police investigators, called by his wife, went to the restaurant, they found Hoffa's car but not Hoffa. The subsequent investigation found no signs of a struggle, no weapon, and no witnesses to his departure. Both Tony Giacalone and Tony Provenzano, when questioned, categorically denied that they had had any plan to meet Hoffa. They both also had alibis: Giacalone had spent the afternoon in a steam room at the Southfield Athletic Club on the outskirts of Detroit; Provenzano had been at a local Teamsters meeting in Hoboken, New Jersey.

The FBI launched one of the largest investigations in its history to find out what had happened to Jimmy Hoffa. It lasted longer than a quarter of a century and is summed up in 1,879 pages of FBI files recently released on a CD-ROM. At one point, they checked out every meat-packing plant in the Detroit area looking for frozen body parts, but found none from Hoffa. After a source on the TV show *A Current Affair* claimed to be a Mafia hitman who witnessed Hoffa's killing, the FBI spent months investigating and polygraphing him before determining that his story was a fabrication. On various tips, the FBI excavated graves, construction sites, and garbage dumps without ever finding Hoffa's body—or proof that he was dead. As late as September 28, 2012, the FBI tested soil in a driveway in a suburb of Detroit for DNA traces of Hoffa but found none. No one has ever been charged with Hoffa's murder.

The consensus theory in law-enforcement circles is that Hoffa was murdered at the behest of Mafia leaders out of concern that he would regain control of the Teamsters. A fifty-six-page report prepared by the FBI in January 1976 states that it is probable that Hoffa was murdered by organized crime figures to prevent him from regaining control over the union's pension fund. A second theory is that Tony Provenzano had him killed as part of an internal power struggle for control of the Teamsters. Proponents of this theory point out that Hoffa had become a problem for Provenzano, and that there was a history of other enemies of Provenzano disappearing. Three years earlier, a man allegedly involved in counterfeiting money with Provenzano had disappeared. So did Tony Castellito, the treasurer of Provenzano's local union chapter. Finally, there is the theory that Hoffa was killed by his own adopted son, Charles O'Brien. Through DNA analysis in the 1990s, investigators found a hair that matched Hoffa's DNA in a Mercury that had been driven by O'Brien. Witnesses told the FBI that O'Brien had strongly opposed Hoffa's plan to run in the Teamsters election in 1975. But O'Brien had an alibi: at the time of Hoffa's disappearance witnesses saw him cutting a forty-pound frozen salmon into steaks at the home of a Teamsters official.

My assessment is that the absence of evidence is itself a clue to who abducted Hoffa. The disappearance was so professionally accomplished that a twenty-five-year investigation failed to turn up a body, signs of a struggle, witnesses, or any forensic evidence (DNA evidence could not have been foreseen in 1975), and the obvious suspects also had convenient alibis. This organization indicates that Hoffa's elimination was a well-planned operation carried out by criminals who were experienced in murder and who also had the influence among Hoffa's associates to assure that he would go to a prearranged meeting. This persuades me that the FBI was correct in attributing his disappearance to organized crime.

It is difficult, if not impossible, to solve a murder if the corpse vanishes and does not resurface. This is especially true if there are no witnesses. There is no body and no crime scene.

PART FOUR
CRIMES OF STATE

CHAPTER 22

DEATH IN UKRAINE: THE CASE OF THE HEADLESS JOURNALIST

I.

A journalist is decapitated in Ukraine. The president of Ukraine is implicated in the murder by secret tape recordings. The Minister of the Interior supposedly commits suicide by shooting himself in the head, using two shots. The Minister's two top deputies are eliminated as witnesses, the first by a fatal heart attack, the second as the result of a coma that leaves him brain-dead. The government itself is destabilized by the release of the secret recordings of the president, which are posted on a website financed by a Russian billionaire exiled in London. Intertwined in the case of the headless journalist are four separate types of political crime: murder, cover-up, espionage, and coup d'état.

The murder took place in 2000 outside Ukraine's capital city, Kiev. The victim was Georgiy Gongadze, the thirty-one-year-old Georgian-born editor who co-founded *Ukrayinska Pravda* ("Ukrainian Truth"), a website created earlier that year, which conducted relentless attacks on Leonid Kuchma, who in 1996, after serving as prime minister, had been elected president. Ukraine, Europe's second-largest country, was still politically fragile, having only become independent of Russia nine years earlier.

Gongadze was not the first Ukrainian journalist to disappear or die under suspicious circumstances during the Kuchma regime, but his death was immediately considered suspicious because he had published an open letter complaining of harassment by the domestic security service, known by its Russian initials as the SBU, shortly before his disappearance. When he was reported missing on September 17, 2000, a large crowd, led by journalists carrying placards with Gongadze's photograph on them, occupied Kiev's main square. These demonstrations grew to more than 100,000 protesters, effectively paralyzing the government of Ukraine.

Then, on November 3, 2000, a headless body was found in a shallow grave in a forest forty-three miles from Kiev. What remained of the corpse had been badly disfigured by dioxin, which pathologists concluded may have been poured on the victim while he was still alive. The corpse then inexplicably vanished from the custody of the local police and only later re-emerged in a morgue in Kiev, along with some of Gongadze's personal effects. A subsequent DNA analysis performed by a U.S. military lab determined with 99.6 percent certainty that it was the remains of Gongadze. Witness testimony also established that he had been kidnapped from Kiev, after dining with a female friend on September 16, 2000.

Initially, police attributed the murder to common criminals, eventually arresting a suspect, who died in custody, but on November 28, Oleksandr Moroz, the leader of the main opposition party, made public the contents of stolen tape recordings that purported to be the secret deliberations of Kuchma and his cabinet. In one of these tapes, a voice sounding like President Kuchma can be heard discussing Gongadze. It said "Throw him out! Give him to the Chechens!" This sensational disclosure undermined the regime of President Kuchma and eventually made him a suspect in Gongadze's murder.

The "Cassette Scandal," as it was called, convulsed the

nation for the next five years. It proceeded from a two-year espionage operation allegedly run by Major Mykola Melnychenko, a KGB-trained counterintelligence officer, who served as Kuchma's electronic security chief. Supposedly, more than 200 hours of secret discussions in the inner sanctum of Kuchma's government had been recorded from early 1998 to September 16, 2000, by Major Melnychenko on a store-bought Toshiba dictation machine. But before he could be questioned, Melnychenko left Ukraine with his family.

At first, the government declared the tapes to be crude forgeries, but members of the government recorded on the tapes identified their voices, and independent forensic examinations showed that the recordings had no obvious signs of being forged. The examinations did not rule out the possibility, however, that the tapes had been edited or doctored by using sophisticated techniques.

In 2005, after Kuchma was replaced as president and the so-called Orange Revolution swept away much of his regime, a new investigation of the murder of Gongadze resulted in the eventual arrest of three SBU agents who had been part of a surveillance team watching Gongadze. They were Valeriy Kostenko, Mykola Protasov, and Oleksandr Popovych. The legal process dragged on for another five years. After they were charged with murdering and decapitating him, they confessed and implicated their immediate superior, General Aleksiy Pukach, who they said had actually strangled Gongadze. General Pukach then disappeared, and remained a fugitive for more than four years, before being arrested in July 2009. As all the legal proceedings against him were conducted behind closed doors to preserve state secrets, I obtained his account through lawyers involved in the case. Pukach not only admitted his role in the crime, but he led investigators to the missing head, which he had buried near a tree. This admission solved the mystery of who had killed Gongadze: it was a political crime undertaken by the security apparatus of the government. But the real issue, as in all political crimes, is who was ultimately responsible.

The Prosecutor General stated that the orders were given by Interior Minister Yuri Kravchenko, for whom General Pukach worked. Kravchenko had also been a participant in the recorded conversations about Gongadze in the summer of 2000. But Kravchenko could no longer be questioned, since on March 4, 2005, he died of gunshot wounds in his home in Kiev. As he had left a note, authorities declared his death a suicide. Even so, many observers remained unconvinced that he had killed himself. The medical examination showed that Kravchenko had two gunshot wounds in his head. One bullet had struck him in his chin and the other in his temple. As Mykola Polishchuk, Ukraine's former health minister and an authority on firearm wounds, noted "The direction of the wound is uncharacteristic of a wound inflicted by the person himself, because it travels from bottom to top and from inside to outside. It is extremely difficult to believe that a person would be capable of injuring himself in this way."

The only remaining lead in the investigation came from one of the convicted SBU agents, General Pukach's driver, Olexsandr Popovych. He testified at his trial that a few weeks after Gongadze's decapitation, he had driven the general to a meeting at a restaurant with two of Kravchenko's top intelligence deputies, Major General Yuri Dagaev and Eduard Feres, and overheard them discussing the need to re-bury the headless corpse. But neither of these men could be questioned: in 2003, General Dagaev had died of an apparent heart attack at age fifty-three; Feres was in a vegetative coma, and he died in 2009.

Even so, on March 24, 2011, Ukrainian prosecutors moved against ex-President Kuchma. On the basis of what was supposedly said on the eleven-year-old recordings, they charged him with complicity in Gongadze's murder.

II.

I met with Kuchma in Kiev on December 9, 2011, at offices inside the foundation he created. Although he had retired as president in January 2005, he still preferred to be called "Mr. President." His red hair and youthful smile made him seem much younger than his seventy-three years. Although he spoke in Russian, with his lawyer acting as an English translator, he appeared to understand my questions, giving quick and focused answers.

He denied having any involvement in Gongadze's murder. He acknowledged that the voice on the tapes was his, but he said that the tapes had been doctored to incriminate him.

He cited two independent forensic examinations showing that whatever had been originally recorded had been digitally transferred to a computer file. It was an MP3 file, not the original cassette tape recordings, that was released. Because of the digital conversion, it was not possible to determine how many devices were used in making the recordings, or the extent to which it had been tampered with.

Kuchma was convinced that the penetration of Ukraine's inner sanctum was the work of a sophisticated intelligence operation. He said that his counterintelligence experts had reconstructed some of the recordings and come to the conclusion that the two-year espionage operation required the services of more than a single man. To capture all these recordings, according to this reconstruction, multiple microphones would have had to be implanted in walls and other places in which they would not be discovered by security sweeps.

In Kiev, I also interviewed the Ukrainian intelligence general who worked on this analysis. He agreed with Kuchma's assessment, saying "These hundreds of hours of recording could not have all been done by Melnychenko." He pointed out that there were two different teams that checked the room before

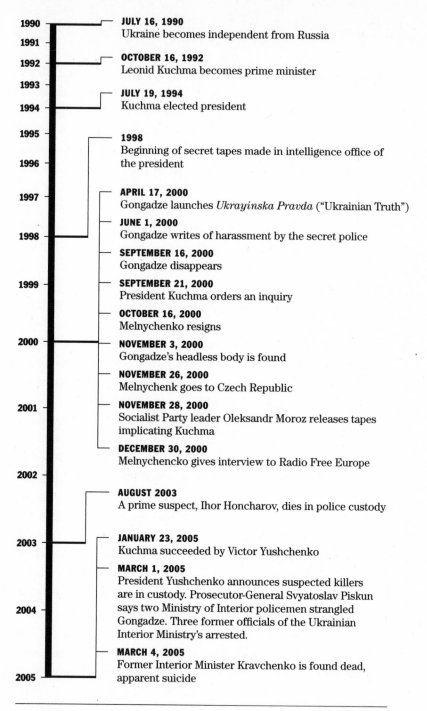

1990
1991

JULY 16, 1990
Ukraine becomes independent from Russia

1992

OCTOBER 16, 1992
Leonid Kuchma becomes prime minister

1993

JULY 19, 1994
Kuchma elected president

1994

1995

1998
Beginning of secret tapes made in intelligence office of
the president

1996

1997

APRIL 17, 2000
Gongadze launches *Ukrayinska Pravda* ("Ukrainian Truth")

JUNE 1, 2000
Gongadze writes of harassment by the secret police

1998

SEPTEMBER 16, 2000
Gongadze disappears

1999

SEPTEMBER 21, 2000
President Kuchma orders an inquiry

OCTOBER 16, 2000
Melnychenko resigns

2000

NOVEMBER 3, 2000
Gongadze's headless body is found

NOVEMBER 26, 2000
Melnychenk goes to Czech Republic

2001

NOVEMBER 28, 2000
Socialist Party leader Oleksandr Moroz releases tapes
implicating Kuchma

DECEMBER 30, 2000
Melnychencko gives interview to Radio Free Europe

2002

AUGUST 2003
A prime suspect, Ihor Honcharov, dies in police custody

2003

JANUARY 23, 2005
Kuchma succeeded by Victor Yushchenko

MARCH 1, 2005
President Yushchenko announces suspected killers
are in custody. Prosecutor-General Svyatoslav Piskun
says two Ministry of Interior policemen strangled
Gongadze. Three former officials of the Ukrainian
Interior Ministry's arrested.

2004

MARCH 4, 2005
Former Interior Minister Kravchenko is found dead,
apparent suicide

2005

EDWARD JAY EPSTEIN

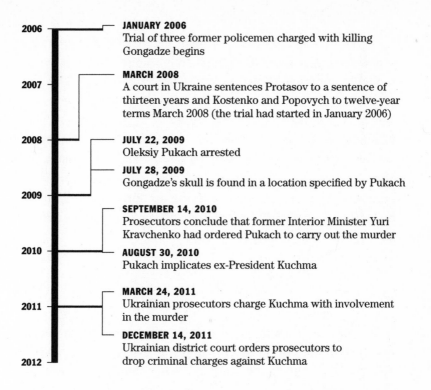

2006 — JANUARY 2006
Trial of three former policemen charged with killing
Gongadze begins

2007 — MARCH 2008
A court in Ukraine sentences Protasov to a sentence of
thirteen years and Kostenko and Popovych to twelve-year
terms March 2008 (the trial had started in January 2006)

2008 — JULY 22, 2009
Oleksiy Pukach arrested

JULY 28, 2009
Gongadze's skull is found in a location specified by Pukach

2009

SEPTEMBER 14, 2010
Prosecutors conclude that former Interior Minister Yuri
Kravchenko had ordered Pukach to carry out the murder

2010 — AUGUST 30, 2010
Pukach implicates ex-President Kuchma

2011 — MARCH 24, 2011
Ukrainian prosecutors charge Kuchma with involvement
in the murder

DECEMBER 14, 2011
Ukrainian district court orders prosecutors to
2012 — drop criminal charges against Kuchma

every cabinet meeting, one from the foreign intelligence service and the other, which Melnychenko headed, from Domestic Security. Indeed, one purpose of this redundancy was to allow the two intelligence organizations to keep an eye on each other. Under this arrangement, the general explained, Melnychenko could not have simply slipped a dictation machine under a sofa without it being detected. Nor could he have simply left the machine unattended for more than a day, since the batteries would have to be changed daily. "This operation required the sort of equipment that has been developed by espionage services like the KGB," he said. "Melnychenko's claim that he acted alone is merely a convenient cover for those responsible." If so, Melnychenko had been working for an intelligence service with the wherewithal to penetrate a president's lair, after which he had exposed the operation by releasing the recordings. When

I asked the general why an intelligence service would allow its secret sources and methods to be compromised in this way, he replied that perhaps it was not its decision.

Kuchma made it clear to me that he believed Melnychenko was part of a plot to drive him from power, and that whoever was behind the plot wanted to be certain that Melnychenko was not questioned: A few days before the tapes were released, Melnychenko received a bogus passport from an unknown party and fled Ukraine. The Ukraine authorities could do no more than indict him for the theft of state secrets and conspiracy, charges which still stand.

III.

In the absence of definitive evidence, there are two principal theories about who masterminded the murder of Gongadze. The first one holds that President Kuchma himself ordered the hit. The prosecutors advanced this theory on March 24, 2011, more than a decade after the crime, by charging Kuchma with complicity in the murder. By that time, the key witnesses in the chain of command to whom General Pukach supposedly reported, including the Minister of the Interior's two top aides and the Minister himself, were dead. The only evidence to support the Kuchma theory came from recordings, and neither the provenance nor the veracity of these tapes had been established. The theory also ran into a judicial stumbling block on December 14, 2011. The Ukraine high court ruled that even if the original cassettes could be obtained—and the tapes have still not been released—they could not be entered into evidence because they were the product of espionage against the state, which is a criminal act. This ruling, which is under appeal by the prosecutors, effectively invalidated the legal case against Kuchma.

The other main theory is that the murder was the work of a rogue SBU unit in the Interior Ministry under the command of Pukach. After all, this unit had the victim under close surveillance in September 2000 and, according to Gongadze's own report, was harassing him.

There are also other intriguing theories. One focuses on the possible involvement of Boris Berezovsky, a Russian oligarch in exile in London. Berezovsky, who himself was a fugitive from a Russian arrest warrant, had devoted a substantial part of his resources to attempting to overthrow Russian president Vladimir Putin. And, along with the CIA, Berezovsky benefited from the fruits of Melnychenko's penetration, including receiving "Compramata," or blackmail material, in the form of recorded conversations among high officials about money laundering and arms traffic, material that could be used for leverage against Russian and Ukrainian officials. Beginning in 2002, Berezovsky provided Melnychenko with financial support, including a $50,000 payment, through his Civil Liberties Foundation. Alexander Goldfarb, who worked for the foundation, personally delivered to Kiev a more extensive copy of the recordings than had been initially released. He told me that Berezovsky had provided $50 million to dissident elements in Ukraine who participated in what became known as the Orange Revolution. If so, Berezovsky was deeply involved in the power struggles in Ukraine.

Finally, there is a theory that the crime was organized by Kuchma's rivals in Ukraine to bring about his downfall. Yevhen Marchuk, who was Kuchma's main political opponent, had formerly headed the Ukrainian KGB and served on Ukraine's National Security and Defense Council. According to this view, he was in a position to recruit operatives, such as Pukach, and it was also Marchuk who used these tapes to undermine Kuchma.

IV.

We know that Gongadze was murdered by a Ministry of the Interior surveillance unit acting under the command of General Pukach. We also know that there was an elaborate cover-up. According to the trial testimony of Pukach's driver, the cover-up was handled by two top deputies, Dagaev and Feres, of Minister of the Interior Kravchenko. What we do not know is how much higher the cover-up went, because all these men at the top tier of the ministry—Kravchenko, Dagaev, and Feres—met their deaths before they could be questioned on the subject by prosecutors. A number of the key investigators, including Deputy Prosecutor Roman Shubin in September 2012, also met premature deaths. My assessment, based on my interviews in Ukraine in 2011, is that these deaths may well be part of the continuing cover-up.

This does not mean that either the president or his Minister of the Interior had been behind the murder of Gongadze. Nor is there credible evidence that either man had any advance knowledge of the murder. Pukach, whose men had Gongadze under close surveillance in 2000, was well aware that the journalist was not only a vocal opponent of the regime but was attempting to expose Pukach's surveillance unit. Under these circumstances, Pukach needed no higher authority to have Gongadze taken for a "walk in the wood," as the elimination of journalists was euphemistically called by the KGB. (Pukach had served in the KGB when Ukraine was part of the Soviet Union.) Gongadze was only one of a long list of Ukrainian journalists who vanished in this manner both before and after Ukraine got its independence. For his part, Pukach had little concern that Gongadze's disappearance would be fully investigated, because none of the previous deaths or disappearances of journalists had been solved. What he had not anticipated, and what made this crime different from previous eliminations of dissidents, was the unprecedented release of secret recordings of the president and his intelligence council. It was these recordings that made Gongadze's disappearance an international scandal.

This leads us to an even more intriguing mystery: Who was behind the release of these recordings? Based on my interviews with President Kuchma, Ukrainian intelligence officials, and forensic experts, it is clear to me that these recordings were the product of a large-scale espionage operation. It is not clear when in the 1990s this spying began, but given the sophisticated tradecraft of the operation, it may have been organized by the KGB before Ukraine achieved full independence. Russia, after all, had vital interests in Ukraine, including its shipment of gas to Europe and its principal naval base in the Crimea. I believe that, as often happens in such long-term espionage, the operation was discovered by parties in the Ukraine, and essentially hijacked. It is not clear why a portion of the recording was made public, but I am not convinced that Major Melnychenko was merely used to deliver the recordings to the public. In my investigation of his defection first to the Czech Republic and then to America, I was told by a top Czech official who handled his case that immediately after he arrived in Prague, the CIA made a very unusual request. After informing Czech authorities that there was a "contract" out on Melnychenko, it asked that the Czech secret service take extraordinary measures, including using a bulletproof car to transport him and round-the-clock counter-surveillance, to protect him until he could be transported to the United States. Since by this time the revelations of the tapes about Gongadze had been made public, the concern of whoever put out the assassination contract was not what was on the tapes that Melnychenko had already delivered but what he might know that was not on the released tapes. At that point, no one knew what he might have overheard while the tapes were being recorded.

Gaza. Because of his position in this triangular trade, he was ordinarily protected by a team of armed bodyguards. But they had not been allowed to accompany him to Dubai on January 19 because there was no room on the flight, according to a Hamas spokesman in Damascus. So, whether by design or accident, he was stripped of his protection on an international trip in which he was vulnerable to assassination.

The Dubai authorities pursued the investigation. When police looked more closely at the crime scene, they found that the electronic lock on the door of the room had been reprogrammed to allow others entry, possibly the work of a sophisticated hacker. Then a Dubai forensic lab retesting Mabhouh's body fluids discovered traces of succinylcholine. This is a quick-acting, depolarizing, paralytic drug that, by rendering Mabhouh incapable of resisting, could account for the lack of bruises on the body. If so, murder could not be ruled out.

In February 2010, Dubai's chief coroner, Fawzi Benomran, reversed his verdict of a natural death. Instead, describing the death as "one of the most challenging cases" in the history of the Emirate, he concluded that it was a disguised homicide "meant to look like death from natural causes during sleep." Such a sophisticated use of pharmacology and electronic hacking to conceal an assassination suggested that this was not the work of ordinary criminals.

Dubai investigators examined 645 hours of videos from surveillance cameras at the hotel and elsewhere. They saw that, after Mabhouh left his hotel room, four suspicious-looking individuals got out of the elevator on the second floor near his room. Several hours later, at 8:25 p.m., Mabhouh returned to his room, according to the electronic lock. Shortly afterward, the video showed the four men leaving the floor.

The police theorized that these men had surreptitiously entered Mabhouh's room while he was out, and that they incapacitated him with the paralytic drug on his return. They then induced a heart attack by suffocating him with a pillow and reprogrammed the electric lock to make it appear to have been locked from the inside.

With the aid of facial-recognition software, Dubai police then found twenty-six suspects who had been in Dubai at the time of Mabhouh's brief visit. What made them suspicious is that they had entered Dubai using fake or fraudulently obtained passports from countries not requiring a Dubai visa, including Great Britain, Ireland, France, Germany, and Australia.

All the passports turned out to be stolen identities with faked passport photos. The credit cards, airline tickets, and pre-paid phone cards that these suspects used were also in the names of their stolen identities. The new evidence made it likely that Mabhouh's death was the work of an intelligence service. Presumably, only an intelligence service possessed the resources to provide fake IDs and the ability get operatives out of Dubai without leaving clues about their actual identities. The only hint to their real identities was that eight of the fake identities had been stolen from people with dual Israeli citizenship. As Mossad, Israel's national intelligence agency, had previously used dual citizens' passports to fake identities, Dubai authorities assumed that the suspects were from Mossad.

Dahi Khalfan Tamim, the head of the Dubai police force, stated on a government-owned website that he is "99 percent, if not 100 percent, sure that Mossad is standing behind the murder." While this authoritative finger-pointing was largely accepted by the media, Dubai was not a wholly uninterested party in the Mabhouh affair. In 2010, Dubai was the principal transshipment point for the arms trade between Iran and Hamas in which Mabhouh had been deeply involved. As stated by Sherlock Holmes, "There is nothing more deceptive than an obvious fact." Surveillance videos show that twenty-six people were in Dubai that day with false identities, but they do not show them engaging in any other illegal activity. Employing false identities is not uncommon in Dubai for intelligence agents from countries such as Israel that do not have diplomatic relations with the United Arab Emirates. The practice is also used by people in clandestine businesses such as arms and drug trafficking. Mabhouh himself reportedly had five different passports. The twenty-six people with bogus identities may well have been there on undercover business, but it does not necessarily follow that they were all in Dubai on the same undercover business, or that any of them were working together or even on the same side.

If Mossad had agents in Dubai, as seems to be the case, they might have been there to monitor the activities of arms smugglers in Dubai. Other intelligence services, including those of America, Russia, Iran, Syria, and the Palestinian Authority, may have had similar missions in Dubai. After all, Iran maintains its largest offshore financing facility in Dubai, which is used by the Revolutionary Guard, among others, to support its traffic in covert weapons. Since Mabhouh and Hamas were major players in this game, his presence may have attracted the attention of any of these parties. Consider, for example, that two of the twenty-six Dubai suspects exited by boat to Iran, according to Dubai authorities. This is an unlikely escape route for Mossad agents. Or that two other individuals whom the Dubai police had named as suspects worked for the Palestinian Authority, an archenemy of Hamas. (They were arrested in Jordan and turned over to Dubai.) Or that a third person wanted for questioning returned to Damascus just prior to the killing. While it may have been obvious that Mabhouh was being watched, it is less clear how or why this surveillance turned into murder.

The missing piece of the jigsaw remains Mabhouh's mission to Dubai, one apparently important enough for him to travel there without his normal contingent of bodyguards. He stated that he was in transit en route to China, which was merely a cover story, since he had not made arrangements to continue on to China. Mabhouh arrived from the airport at his hotel shortly before 3:00 p.m. and, after changing his clothes, left for an unknown destination. He was gone for several hours. But even with state-of-the-art surveillance cameras in Dubai, and extensive interviews with all the taxi drivers at the hotel, authorities claim they cannot determine either his whereabouts during these hours or the identity of the person or persons he met. Without knowing what he was doing, and with the intelligence services successfully cloaking and withdrawing their operatives, it remains an unsolved assassination.

There is no shortage of theories as to who murdered Mabhouh. The prime suspect of the Dubai authorities is Mossad. Certainly, Israel, which had previously attempted to capture Mabhouh, had a motive. There is also no doubt that Mossad had the capabilities to infiltrate agents disguised as tourists, who could follow and kill Mabhouh.

Another theory is that this was an inside job by Syria, which wanted to more tightly control the militant wing of Hamas. Someone in Syria apparently was responsible for having Mabhouh's bodyguards bumped from the plane just before his flight to Dubai. As Syrian security agencies tightly control information concerning Hamas, it is unlikely that we will find out why Mabhouh was stripped of his protection. Without bodyguards, the assassin only needed to gain access to his room, and, if this was an inside job, Mabhouh may have himself been lulled into opening the door.

Iran might also have arranged his elimination because he was diverting arms shipments. This might explain the report that two of the suspects with false identities fled to Iran.

My assessment is that Mossad had motive, means, and opportunity. It may also have had sources in Syrian intelligence that assisted by providing data about Mabhouh's movements. If so, it seems plausible to me that Israel assassinated Mabhouh.

CHAPTER 24

THE BEIRUT ASSASSINATION

The crime occurred at 12:56 p.m. on Valentine's Day, 2005. Rafik Hariri, the former prime minister of Lebanon, was blown up, along with most of his armored convoy, in front of the Hotel St. George in Beirut. The bomb had been packed into a white Mitsubishi van that had been moved into position by a suicide driver one minute and fifty seconds earlier; the powerful explosion tore a seven-foot deep crater into the street and killed twenty-three people.

The assassination caused an international uproar, and the Lebanese government turned to the United Nations for help. The U.N. Security Council appointed Detlev Mehlis, a German judge renowned for his solvings of terrorist bombings, to head its investigation. Early in the U.N. investigation, clues seemed to point to a jihadist suicide bomber. Various Islamist terrorists had used similar Mitsubishi vans in a spate of other Beirut bombings. Elements in the bomb were traced back to military explosives used by al-Qaeda of Iraq. A convenient videotape sent to Al Jazeera television showed a lone suicide bomber named Abu Addas claiming that he acted on behalf of an unknown jihadist group. But the lone-assassin theory did not last long.

The U.N. investigative team, which included forensic experts in explosives, DNA, and telecommunications from ten countries, found convincing evidence that the assassination was a cleverly disguised, state-sponsored operation. The

Mitsubishi van had been stolen in Japan, shipped via the port of Dubai to the Syrian-controlled Bekka Valley, where it was modified to carry the bomb, and then, only days before the assassination, driven over a military-controlled highway to Beirut.

One participant in the planning of the attack was Zuhir Ibn Mohamed Said Saddik, a Syrian intelligence operative. Saddik told investigators that the putative bomber, Abu Addas, was a mere decoy who had been induced to go to Syria and make the bogus video and was then killed. He further alleged that the actual van driver had been recruited in Iraq under false pretenses, presumably so that if he defected or was captured, he would wrongly identify his recruiters as jihadists. Saddik said that the "special explosives" in the TNT had been intentionally planted there to mislead investigators in the direction of Iraq. Saddik was arrested for his role in the crime in 2005 and was released without reason the following year. He vanished in March 2008 from a Paris suburb.

Meanwhile, the U.N. team uncovered evidence that the actual conspirators had resources and capabilities—including wiretaps of Hariri's phones—that pointed to a state-level intelligence service. U.N. telecommunications analysts determined that eight new telephone numbers and ten mobile telephones had been used, along with the wiretapping, to follow Hariri's movements with split-second precision and move the van into place.

In addition, a former Syrian intelligence agent told investigators that he had driven a Syrian military officer on a reconnaissance mission past the Hotel St. George on the day before the bombing, and that the officer had told him that four Lebanese generals, in collaboration with General Rustam Ghazali, the head of Syrian intelligence in Lebanon, had provided "money, telephones, cars, walkie-talkies, pagers, weapons, and ID cards" to the alleged assassination team.

Judge Mehlis' report, issued in October 2005, concluded

that "there is probable cause to believe that the decision to assassinate former Prime Minister Rafik Hariri, could not have been taken without the approval of top-ranked Syrian security officials, and could not have been further organized without the collusion of their counterparts in the Lebanese security services." Judge Mehlis had the four Lebanese generals arrested in 2005.

When the judge moved to question Syrian officials—including the intelligence chief, Assef Shawkat, who is Syrian president Bashar al-Assad's brother-in law—the Syrians stonewalled and protested the inquest's direction. In January 2006, the U.N. Security Council replaced Judge Mehlis with Serge Brammertz, a forty-three-year-old Belgian lawyer who had served as deputy prosecutor at the International Criminal Court in The Hague.

Brammertz was replaced in 2008 by Daniel Bellemare, Canada's assistant deputy attorney general. In April 2009, Bellemare requested that the four imprisoned Lebanese generals be released because of the "complete absence of reliable proof against them." And so they were.

Meanwhile, Lebanese investigators working on behalf of the U.N. team had re-examined cell phone records from 2005. They uncovered a network of about twenty mobile phones that had all been activated a few weeks before the attack and then silenced just afterward. This so-called second ring of phones had been calling the same phone numbers that had been called by the eight phones that coordinated the attack.

By 2009, investigators had traced the second ring of phones to a command post of Hezbollah's military wing under the notorious Imad Mughniyeh, who had been responsible, according to U.S. intelligence assessments, for other spectacular bombing attacks, including the 1983 U.S. embassy bombing in Beirut. But before this cell-phone evidence could be further examined, the Lebanese chief investigator working on this complex network was killed in Beirut in 2009. (Mughniyeh, who might otherwise have been called as a witness, had himself been assassinated in 2008.)

In April 2010, U.N. investigators summoned twelve Hezbollah members and supporters for questioning. This spurred rumors that the Special Tribunal for Lebanon, which the U.N. set up in March 2008, was on the verge of finally issuing indictments. The political reaction in Lebanon showed the potential costs of pursuing a political crime. Hezbollah's powerful chief, Hassan Nasrallah, said ominously in July 2010 that Hezbollah would not stand by idly if its members were accused of involvement in the assassination. He also denounced what he called attempts to "politicize" the tribunal—as if political consideration could be omitted from political crime.

Nasrallah also moved to discredit the U.N. by saying that its investigators come from "intelligence services closely linked to the Israeli Mossad." He demanded the establishment of a Lebanese committee to investigate "false witnesses." In September 2010 he went further, claiming that Hezbollah had "evidence" that Israel was behind the assassination. Syria, for its part, is claiming to be the victim of planted evidence.

When the Special Tribunal for Lebanon then indicated four members of Hezbollah, the Lebanese government chose to ignore the indictments and terminate its support for the tribunal. The tribunal, which relocated to the suburb of Leidschendam just outside The Hague, then announced that it would try the four members of Hezbollah in absentia. It issued warrants for their arrest, but the Lebanese government refused to act on them. Instead, it declared the tribunal to be illegitimate, leaving the crime officially unsolved.

Three theories have been advanced to fill the judicial vacuum. First, there is the view that the assassination was the work of Syrian intelligence units based in Lebanon. In December 2005, former Syrian vice president Abdul Halim Khaddam, after resigning from the government, said that he heard Syrian

President Assad personally threaten Hariri before the assassination, and that Assad had the means to carry out the plot. Second, according to the U.N. tribunal, the assassination was carried out by Hezbollah, which bought the stolen Japanese van, armed it with the TNT and C4 explosives used in the attack, and killed Hariri. Finally, there is the theory proposed by Hezbollah that Israel's Mossad was behind the attack. In support of this view, it is claimed that the jamming devices for blocking remote-control bombs in Hariri's convoy were manufactured by Israel and that these devices were disabled before the attack. The U.N. investigation, however, found no evidence that any of the three anti-jamming devices had been disabled.

My assessment is that this political assassination was most likely organized by the military wing of Hezbollah, which then ghosted a trail to Syria to cover its tracks. The inability of the government to act on the evidence provided by the U.N. tribunal, or even serve the indictments on those charged, demonstrates again how difficult it is to resolve a crime when vital political interests are at stake.

CHAPTER 25

WHO ASSASSINATED ANNA POLITKOVSKAYA?

The brutal murder of Anna Politkovskaya in Moscow on Vladimir Putin's birthday in 2006 sent shock waves through the media community not only in Russia but around the world. The award-winning Russian journalist was gunned down at close range at about 4:00 p.m on October 7 in the stairwell of her apartment block. Three bullets hit her body, and a fourth bullet was fired into her head, execution-style. Next to her body, there were a Makarov PM pistol, a silencer, and the four shell casings from the bullets. As the Makarov PM ordinarily ejects its shells about ten to fifteen feet behind the shooter, the killer had collected the casings and neatly placed them next to his victim, which police interpreted as the signature of a contract killer. The killer, whose features were obscured from CCTV cameras by a baseball cap, knew the code to access Politkovskaya's building. It was also determined from the cameras that he had entered the building just before Politkovskaya had returned from shopping.

The plot grew more sinister after police investigators examined the videotapes from other surveillance cameras. Politkovskaya's last stop before returning home was the nearby Ramstor shopping center. Here the investigators established that she had been under surveillance by a man in jeans and a woman in black. The CCTV cameras revealed that they had methodically followed her as she shopped. As they examined CCTV video from other locations she had visited early that week, they found that she had also been tailed by these and other trackers. Such surveillance technique suggested that she was being watched by a security service.

Identifying Politkovskaya's trackers turned out to be relatively easy for the police.

According to the chief investigator in the case, the trackers had been linked to other plotters by their cell-phone records, saying, "they called back and forth by phone before the murder, on the day of the murder, and after it." The problem confronting the police was where these tracks led. Some of those identified were current or former agents of the Federal Security Service, or FSB, the successor agency to the KGB. Indeed, it was such a sensitive issue that it took nearly ten months before the police got Russia's prosecutor general, Yuri Chaika, to issue warrants to arrest the suspects. In a press conference on August 27, 2007, after announcing that ten suspects in Politkovskaya's murder had been arrested, Chaika ominously warned, "Unfortunately, this group included retired and acting Ministry of the Interior and FSB officers." The official version was that Politkovskaya had been killed for money by a Chechen criminal gang in Moscow that had paid a lieutenant colonel in the FSB to provide surveillance on her.

The shooter was subsequently identified by authorities as Rustam Makhmudov, a Chechen allegedly employed as a contract killer. He was apparently warned about his imminent arrest and provided with a forged passport, which allowed him to flee Russia. The best that the police could do was to arrest two of his brothers, Ibragim and Dzhabrail Makhmudov, as accomplices. They also arrested FSB Lieutenant Colonel Pavel Ryaguzov, who was charged with abuse of office and extortion in connection with the assassination.

On February 19, 2009, after a three-month trial, a jury

unanimously acquitted the accused. Since Russia does not proscribe double jeopardy, prosecutors filed a motion to re-try the case, which was approved in August 2009. Two years later, they charged Dmitry Pavlyuchenkov, a former police lieu-tenant colonel, with organizing the plot. He then implicated Sergei Khadzhikurbanov, a former Ministry of the Interior of-ficial, who denied the charge. The trial of Pavlyuchenkov in December 2012 was held behind closed doors after the judge ruled that all testimony needed to be kept secret. According to *Novaya Gazeta*, the Moscow-based newspaper for which Politkovskaya reported, Pavlyuchenkov claimed in his pre-trial testimony that Politkovskaya's murder was ordered by two London-based enemies of Putin, billionaire Boris Ber-ezovsky and Akhmed Zakayev, an organizer of the Chechen re-volt (which coincides with Putin's theory that the murder was staged as a provocation). Consequently, on December 13, 2012, Pavlyuchenkov was found guilty as an accomplice and sen-tenced to eleven years imprisonment. None of the testimony in this trial will be made public. (One reason such political crimes remain difficult to resolve in Russia is that potentially embar-rassing testimony can be kept secret.) Even if there is a further trial of the perpetrators, which is by no means certain, it will not resolve the real mystery: Who really gave the orders and paid to have Politkovskaya assassinated on Putin's birthday?

The theory of the prosecution is that the contract to assas-sinate Politkovskaya ultimately came from the leaders of the Russian-backed regime in Chechnya. She had been exposing their illegal activities, and they hired the killers. A second the-ory is that Putin's enemies abroad paid the killers to execute this world-famous journalist on Putin's birthday to undermine Putin. Finally, there is the theory that Putin himself ordered the hit to intimidate journalists.

The problem in a political crime in which elements of the government, security services, and organized crime rings collaborate is that while it is possible to arrest the thugs who carried out the contract, the link to those who issued the contract may disappear. What is clear to me is that the murder involved killers for hire, officers in the FSB, and political leaders in Chechnya. My assessment of the case based on interviews in Moscow is that there had to be police involvement that went beyond that of Lieutenant Colonel Pavliuchenkov. The surveillance of Politkovskaya, which was carried out by Pavliuchenkov's unit, involved, according to the released investigative report, "two shifts: the first one from 8 a.m. to 2 p.m., the second one—from 2 p.m. to 9 p.m. Each shift included no less than two transportation units, and at least six operatives." Such a massive operation, even if it is part of a contract killing, suggests a great deal of money and power behind the murder. It is plausible that the contract was given by those leaders in Chechnya who were the targets of Politkovskaya's investigative reporting. But Moscow's contract-killings are not always explained by plausible motives. One Russian official I interviewed quoted the famous closing line of the movie *Chinatown*, "Forget it Jake. This is Chinatown," to make the point that American investigative logic does not apply to Russian mysteries.

CHAPTER 26
BLOWING UP BHUTTO

On December 27, 2007, Benazir Bhutto was killed by a suicide bomber in the Pakistani city of Rawalpindi. Twenty-four other people were also killed in the explosion. Bhutto had just returned from a nine-year exile as part of a deal arranged by the United States. The plan, if it succeeded, would bring about an American-sponsored regime change: Bhutto would run in a nationwide election, win, and replace the faltering military dictatorship of General Pervez Musharraf.

That afternoon Bhutto spoke at a massive political rally at Liaquat Park, a park named after Pakistan's founding Prime Minister Liaquat Ali Khan, who, in 1951, was assassinated. Bhutto departed at 5:00 p.m. in a white armored Land Cruiser. As the convoy made a right turn onto the main highway, Bhutto was waving to her supporters through the roof hatch in her car. Then a gunman standing a few feet behind her car fired three shots and also detonated a bomb. The video footage shows that only 1.6 seconds elapsed between the time of the first shot and the detonation of the explosives. Bhutto received a large head wound, and she died in the hospital less than an hour later. Her doctors, finding no bullet wounds, postulated that she died from a head injury caused by the explosion. Since authorities did not permit an autopsy to be conducted, even though it is required by law, the cause of her death was not conclusively determined. Access to the crime-scene investigation was also inexplicably limited by authorities.

Only one bullet casing was recovered, which was traced by

the DNA on it to skull fragments of the suspected gunman. The skull fragment, which was found on the roof of a nearby building, was determined to have come from a boy no more than sixteen years old. Since the crime scene itself was hosed down within an hour of the shooting, other potential clues, including any other DNA evidence, were washed away. (The lone bullet casing was found lodged in a sewer drain.) Similarly, Bhutto's Land Rover had been scrubbed clean hours after the blast. The extraordinary cleansing of the crime scene before all the evidence could be recovered had been ordered by police authorities. According to the UN commission that investigated the assassination, "Hosing down the crime scene so soon after the blast goes beyond mere incompetence," and raises the issue of "whether this amounts to criminal irresponsibility." As a result, it was all but impossible to determine whether the bomber had any accomplices.

Despite the lack of forensic evidence, at a press conference arranged by General Musharraf the very next day, it was announced that Bhutto's assassination had been organized by Baitullah Mehsud, the leader of the Taliban insurgency in Pakistan, assisted by al-Qaeda. The government spokesman said that the Pakistan intelligence service had intercepted a message in which Mehsud congratulated a subordinate on the Bhutto assassination. Fugitive warrants were then issued for Mehsud (who was killed in 2009 by a CIA drone attack) and his subordinates. Meanwhile, the UN investigators obtained a transcript of the intercepted message, but it contained no mention of either Mehsud or the Bhutto assassination. Instead, it contained a conversation in which someone called "Emir Sahib" asked another unknown person merely "who were they?" After he was told three names, he said "The three did it?" When U.N. investigators attempted to pursue the matter, the ISI, Pakistan's main intelligence arm, claimed that it had been able to identify "Emir Sahib" as Mehsud through a "voice signature," and that from the context of the conversation, its analysts assumed that the "it" likely referred to the Bhutto assassination. The ISI also refused to divulge the date of the interception, the means by which it was obtained, or how it was verified. So the U.N. commission was unable to authenticate the official theory of the assassination.

Soon after the December 28 press conference, the authorities in Pakistan, according to the U.N. commission's report, "essentially ceased investigating the possibility of other perpetrators, particularly those who may have been involved in planning or directing the assassination by funding or otherwise enabling the assassination," and, by doing so, "ended its efforts to identify the suicide bomber." The closing-down of an investigation that threatens the stability of a fragile state is not unusual after political assassinations, but it leaves unanswered the question of who killed Bhutto.

At least three theories are consistent with the facts of the case. First, there is the official theory, proposed by then–President Musharraf that the suicide attack had been arranged by Baitullah Mehsud, the leader of the Pakistani Taliban. The problem here is that the announced evidence in support of it turns out to be either bogus or vague. Second, it has been suggested by Bhutto supporters that the attack was allowed to take place by Pakistan's powerful intelligence service, the ISI, to prevent Bhutto from winning the election. The proponents of this theory point to videos showing men in dark glasses along the motorcade route and at the scene of the assassination as evidence of the ISI's close surveillance of Bhutto. (These videos can be viewed on YouTube.) Finally, there is the theory that Bhutto's security detail was intentionally reduced by a cabal of ambitious politicians inside Bhutto's own political party to put her in harm's way. The proponents of this theory cite the fact that despite credible assassination threats against her, there were gaping holes in her protection.

It would be a mistake, however, to confuse the activities in support of the cover-up, such as literally washing away the evidence at the crime scene, with the assassination itself. We know, as can be seen from the videos, that a young suicide bomber first fired shots at Bhutto and then detonated his suicide vest. The forensic evidence indicates that he was most likely a fifteen- or sixteen-year-old boy from the tribal areas. As Owen Bennett-Jones pointed out in the *London Review of Books* in December 2012, part of the mechanism used in the suicide bomb that was recovered matched those used in eleven other suicide bomb attacks that year in Pakistan. The teenager used in such attacks is in effect a remote-controlled weapon. His actual identity is no more important to solving the mystery than the serial number of a missile fired from a drone. The issue here is: who operated the remote control? My assessment is that that the suicide bomber was trained and dispatched on this mission by a jihadist organization associated with the Pakistani Taliban. The purpose of the attack was to undermine the U.S. initiative to bring about a regime change in Pakistan.

CHAPTER 27

THE CASE OF THE RADIOACTIVE CORPSE

On December 1, 2006, one of the eeriest autopsies in the annals of crime was conducted at the Royal London Hospital.
Three British pathologists, covered from head to toe in white
protective suits, stood around a radioactive corpse that had
been sealed in plastic for nearly a week. The victim was Alexander Litvinenko, a forty-four-year-old ex-KGB officer who had
defected from Russia to England six years earlier. He had been
brought to the Barnet General Hospital by his wife, Marina,
on November 3, complaining of abdominal pain. During his
stay at the hospital his condition continually worsened. The
initial diagnosis was that he had been poisoned by thallium,
a non-radioactive toxin used in Russian rat poison. Since the
KGB had reportedly used thallium as a poison in the Cold War
era, and Litvinenko was one of the most severe critics of Russian president Vladimir Putin, the theory gained traction in
the press that Litvinenko might have been the victim of the
Russian security service, the FSB, which had been created in
April 1995 out of the remnants of the KGB. As Litvinenko had
been writing exposés of putative FSB operations in London,
it seemed at least plausible that the FSB had taken revenge
on him. The possibility that Russia was poisoning opponents
abroad resonated in the world press, since, less than a month

earlier, Anna Politkovskaya, a crusading journalist, had been murdered in Moscow.

Meanwhile, Litvinenko was moved to University College Hospital and given massive doses of the cyanide-based antidote for thallium, which did not work. As his condition grew critical, one of his associates, Alex Goldfarb, prepared for Litvinenko's end by writing out his "deathbed" statement, which, according to Goldfarb, was drawn from statements that Litvinenko had dictated to him accusing Putin of orchestrating his murder. When Litvinenko died on November 23, 2006, Goldfarb released the sensational deathbed accusation at a hastily called press conference at the hospital. It made headlines around the world.

Just two hours before Litvinenko died, another startling surprise developed in the story: new tests at the hospital discovered that he had not been poisoned with thallium or a rat poison based on it. Instead, they showed that he had in his body one of the world's most tightly controlled radioactive isotopes, polonium-210. Polonium was discovered in 1898 by Marie and Pierre Curie and named in honor of Poland, where Marie was born. The reason that this rare isotope was controlled is that it is a critical component in early-stage nuclear bombs. Both America and the Soviet Union used it as part of the trigger in their early bomb designs. So did most, if not all, countries with clandestine nuclear programs, including Israel, India, Pakistan, and South Africa. North Korea had also used it for its nuclear test just six weeks before Litvinenko's contamination in London. Although most of the major nuclear powers shifted to more sophisticated tritium-based triggers after they tested their weapons, for nuclear-ambitious countries, obtaining polonium-210 was crucial step toward obtaining a bomb. And, as a declassified Los Alamos document notes, the detection of polonium-210 remains "a key indication of a nuclear weapons program in its early stages." When polonium-210 was detected in Iraq in 1991, Iran in 2004, and North Korea in October 2006, it immediately raised suspicions of rogue bomb-building programs. Therefore, its presence would normally be of great interest to the International Atomic Energy Agency (IAEA), the U.N.'s nuclear-proliferation watchdog, as well as the intelligence services of the United States, Great Britain, and Israel.

When polonium-210 was discovered in Litvinenko's body in late November 2006, however, no such proliferation alarm bells went off. Instead, the police assumed that this component of early-stage nuclear bombs had been smuggled into London solely to commit a murder. It would be as if a suitcase nuclear bomb had been found next to an irradiated corpse in London, and everyone assumed the bomb had been smuggled into the country solely to murder that person. Michael Specter, in *The New Yorker*, for example, called it the "first known case of nuclear terrorism perpetrated against an individual." But why would anyone use a nuclear weapon to kill an individual, when a knife, bullet, or conventional poison would do the trick more quickly, efficiently, and certainly?

The mysterious circumstances surrounding the death of Litvinenko from radiation poisoning spawned a different kind of international crisis. British authorities told the press, "We are one-hundred percent sure who administered the poison, where and how," but they refused to disclose their evidence. Nonetheless, the consensus that the Russian secret service was behind the poisoning was so powerful that a *Washington Post* editorial could assert that the poison "dose was almost certainly carried by one or both of the former Russian security operatives—one of them also a KGB alumnus—whom Litvinenko met at a London hotel November 1." The KGB alumnus was a forty-two-year-old Russian security expert, Anatoli Lugovoi. Like Litvinenko, Lugovoi had been exposed to polonium-210, and after Litvinenko's death he was hospitalized. Based mainly

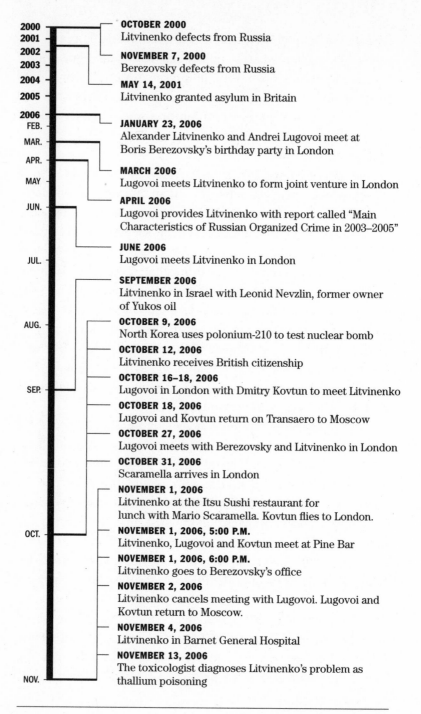

2000
2001
2002
2003
2004
2005

2006
FEB.
MAR.
APR.
MAY
JUN.
JUL.
AUG.
SEP.
OCT.
NOV.

OCTOBER 2000
Litvinenko defects from Russia

NOVEMBER 7, 2000
Berezovsky defects from Russia

MAY 14, 2001
Litvinenko granted asylum in Britain

JANUARY 23, 2006
Alexander Litvinenko and Andrei Lugovoi meet at
Boris Berezovsky's birthday party in London

MARCH 2006
Lugovoi meets Litvinenko to form joint venture in London

APRIL 2006
Lugovoi provides Litvinenko with report called "Main
Characteristics of Russian Organized Crime in 2003–2005"

JUNE 2006
Lugovoi meets Litvinenko in London

SEPTEMBER 2006
Litvinenko in Israel with Leonid Nevzlin, former owner
of Yukos oil

OCTOBER 9, 2006
North Korea uses polonium-210 to test nuclear bomb

OCTOBER 12, 2006
Litvinenko receives British citizenship

OCTOBER 16–18, 2006
Lugovoi in London with Dmitry Kovtun to meet Litvinenko

OCTOBER 18, 2006
Lugovoi and Kovtun return on Transaero to Moscow

OCTOBER 27, 2006
Lugovoi meets with Berezovsky and Litvinenko in London

OCTOBER 31, 2006
Scaramella arrives in London

NOVEMBER 1, 2006
Litvinenko at the Itsu Sushi restaurant for
lunch with Mario Scaramella. Kovtun flies to London.

NOVEMBER 1, 2006, 5:00 P.M.
Litvinenko, Lugovoi and Kovtun meet at Pine Bar

NOVEMBER 1, 2006, 6:00 P.M.
Litvinenko goes to Berezovsky's office

NOVEMBER 2, 2006
Litvinenko cancels meeting with Lugovoi. Lugovoi and
Kovtun return to Moscow.

NOVEMBER 4, 2006
Litvinenko in Barnet General Hospital

NOVEMBER 13, 2006
The toxicologist diagnoses Litvinenko's problem as
thallium poisoning

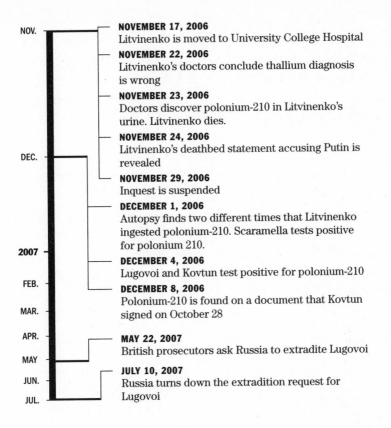

NOV.

NOVEMBER 17, 2006
Litvinenko is moved to University College Hospital

NOVEMBER 22, 2006
Litvinenko's doctors conclude thallium diagnosis
is wrong

NOVEMBER 23, 2006
Doctors discover polonium-210 in Litvinenko's
urine. Litvinenko dies.

NOVEMBER 24, 2006
Litvinenko's deathbed statement accusing Putin is
revealed

DEC.

NOVEMBER 29, 2006
Inquest is suspended

DECEMBER 1, 2006
Autopsy finds two different times that Litvinenko
ingested polonium-210. Scaramella tests positive
for polonium 210.

2007

DECEMBER 4, 2006
Lugovoi and Kovtun test positive for polonium-210

FEB.

DECEMBER 8, 2006
Polonium-210 is found on a document that Kovtun
signed on October 28

MAR.

APR.

MAY 22, 2007
British prosecutors ask Russia to extradite Lugovoi

MAY

JUN.

JULY 10, 2007
Russia turns down the extradition request for
Lugovoi

JUL.

on the fact that Lugovoi had been in contact with Litvinenko
shortly before his death, and contaminated by polonium-210,
Great Britain demanded that Russia extradite him, so he could
be tried for the murder of Litvinenko. When Russia refused,
Great Britain expelled four Russian diplomats from London, in
reprisals reminiscent of the Cold War.

To find out what had brought Lugovoi in contact with Litvinenko, I went to Moscow to see him in May 2008. There was
no doubt that he had been with Litvinenko in London. On November 1, 2006, witnesses saw Lugovoi with Litvinenko in the
Pine Bar of the Millennium Hotel, where Lugovoi was staying
with his family. A waiter recalled bringing Litvinenko tea. This
was less than a day before Litvinenko became ill. Subsequently,

the Pine Bar as well as Lugovoi's room tested positive for polonium-210, leading to an early theory that Litvinenko had been poisoned in the Pine Bar. But then it turned out that Litvinenko had had a sushi lunch at the Itsu restaurant some four hours earlier, and that restaurant, as well as Litvinenko's lunch partner, Mario Scaramella, tested positive for polonium-210. This suggested that Litvinenko had been contaminated prior to his tea at the Pine Bar. Lugovoi had also had a number of earlier meetings with Litvinenko, including one on October 16, 2006, at a lap-dancing club called Hey Jo. The owner, David West, and others recalled seeing both men seated in a VIP booth. The booth then tested positive for polonium-210, as did the seat Lugovoi had occupied on the British Airways flight back to Moscow on October 19. If so, both men were exposed to polonium-210 over a month before Litvinenko died. But how?

When I met Lugovoi in his office in Moscow, he had just been elected to the Duma, the Russian parliament, which gave him immunity, and with that protection he talked freely about his relationship with Litvinenko. He told me that they both had been intelligence officers in the KGB and FSB in the 1990s, but that then he had become a supporter of Putin, while Litvinenko had done everything he could to discredit Putin, and then defected to London. I asked how they came together a decade later. Lugovoi answered in a single word: "Berezovsky."

He was referring to Boris Abramovich Berezovsky, a billionaire living in London, who had been the single most powerful oligarch in Russia in the 1990s. He not only controlled whole sectors of the Russian economy and the country's largest television channel, but he was part of the government apparatus, serving as the deputy secretary of its National Security Council. Both he and Litvinenko acted as Berezovsky's protectors in the FSB. Litvinenko was deputy head of its organized-crime unit, while Lugovoi was in the Ninth Directorate, which was responsible for guarding top Kremlin officials, including

Berezovsky. He said that Berezovsky was so impressed with his work that he hired him as head of security at the television channel, ORT, which Berezovsky co-owned. With an enigmatic smile, Lugovoi said that both Litvinenko and he had performed extraordinary services for Berezovsky. With a gun in one hand and his FSB credentials in the other, Litvinenko had prevented Moscow police from arresting Berezovsky on a murder charge. He then ended his own career in the FSB by exposing an FSB faction's alleged plan to assassinate Berezovsky. As a consequence, Litvinenko was imprisoned. For his part, Lugovoi helped Berezovsky's partner break out of a Moscow prison—an act for which he also served prison time. Meanwhile, Berezovsky moved to London and became Putin's arch-foe. In November 2000, he helped Litvinenko escape to England, where he financially supported him and sponsored his investigations for the next six years.

I asked how Berezovsky had repaid him. Lugovoi answered with a wry smile: "By bringing me to Litvinenko."

The reunion came in January 2006 in London. Berezovsky had rented Blenheim Palace—the birthplace of Winston Churchill—to give himself a lavish sixtieth birthday party. There were some 300 guests in formal attire and, in the center of the room, a giant ice sculpture representing St. Basil's Cathedral on Red Square, covered with Caspian caviar. Berezovsky's seating plan placed Lugovoi at a small table with three men: on his right was Litvinenko, who was now engaged in conducting investigations into Russian atrocities in Chechnya. Across from him was Akhmed Zakayev, the exiled leader of the Chechen resistance who headed the Committee on Russian War Crimes in Chechnya. On his left was Alexander Goldfarb, who ran Berezovsky's foundation, which helped support both Litvinenko's and Zakayev's activities.

As it turned out, the people at his table that night would be among the last to see Litvinenko alive ten months later. Lugovoi saw him in the Pine Bar at 5:00 p.m. on November 1. Zakayev then picked up Litvinenko at the Pine Bar and drove him to Berezovsky's office. Goldfarb later wrote Litvinenko's dramatic deathbed statement. But that evening, as Lugovoi recalls it, there was nothing but good cheer and celebratory toasts.

Soon afterward, Lugovoi explained, Litvinenko called him with a "business proposal." They would form a joint venture, backed by Berezovsky, to gather information in Moscow. The idea, according to Lugovoi, was to use his connections in Moscow to get "business data" that Litvinenko could sell to London clients, including, as it turned out, the former owners of Yukos, the largest oil enterprise in Russia. Yukos was no ordinary oil company: with tens of billions of dollars stashed away in accounts in Cyprus, Gibraltar, and other offshore havens, it had become by the early 2000s a virtual counter-state to the government. In the battle that ensued between Yukos and Putin, Yukos was charged with tax fraud and, through enormous fines, its assets in Russia were effectively expropriated.

Since this "joint venture" would involve Lugovoi in a collaboration with some of President Putin's most determined enemies abroad, including Litvinenko, Berezovsky, and the former owners of Yukos—all of whom Russia was then attempting to extradite from Great Britain and Israel—I asked Lugovoi if he had been concerned that this engagement could cause him problems with the authorities in Moscow. He answered, "I had no such worries." Did this mean that he had informed Russian authorities about his participation in this venture, I asked. He shrugged, and said, "I am now a member of the Duma. What does that tell you?"

As this project developed, much of the "business data" requested from Lugovoi concerned individuals connected in one way or another with Yukos. The two principal owners of its holding company were Mikhail Khodorkovsky, who was imprisoned in Siberia, and Leonid Nevzlin, who had fled to Israel.

In Tel Aviv, Nevzlin had set up a private intelligence company, ISC Global, with divisions in London and Tel Aviv, to gather information that would help him fight Russian efforts to get control of the offshore accounts. It was in its London office, renamed RISC Management, Ltd., that Lugovoi said he next met with Litvinenko. According to Lugovoi, RISC asked him to obtain in Moscow relatively innocuous reports, such as one entitled, "Main characteristics of Russian Organized Crime in 2003–2005." He acquired the report from former FSB officers, and delivered it to Litvinenko, who paid him. Litvinenko then gave him a list of other data to acquire for RISC, including government files on Russian tax officials. Litvinenko threatened that if he did not get this material, Lugovoi might have a "problem" renewing his British visa, and his visa was indeed held up. When he then agreed to get this sensitive data, not only was his visa renewed, but $8,000 was wired to his bank account. This joint venture now had all the earmarks of a classic espionage operation. Lugovoi was compromised, threatened, and paid to deliver intelligence. This incident made him suspicious that Litvinenko, aside from working for Berezovsky, was involved with British intelligence. "How else could he get my visa withdrawn—and reinstated?" he asked rhetorically. (Four years after my meeting with him, Lugovoi's suspicions were confirmed when on December 13, 2012, in a preliminary hearing for an inquest in London, it was disclosed that Litvinenko was indeed on the payroll of the British intelligence services at the time of his death in 2006.)

The game took a further turn in September 2006, when Litvinenko made a trip to Tel Aviv to personally deliver to former Yukos holding-company owner Nevzlin what he called the "the Yukos file." According to Lugovoi, it contained much of the information that he had provided. Nevzlin admits receiving the dossier from Litvinenko, although he insists it was unsolicited. In any case, after Litvinenko returned from Israel, Lugovoi says he found him increasingly on edge. About a month later, on October 27, Lugovoi was summoned to London by Berezovsky. A few hours after he arrived, he recalled that Litvinenko turned up at his hotel. Litvinenko said he needed to retrieve the cell phone that Lugovoi had been given to use for RISC business. After Lugovoi gave it to him, Litvinenko removed the SIM card, which contained a digital trail of his contacts. Litvinenko then told him that the next meeting with RISC would be on November 2.

Lugovoi said that the last time he saw Litvinenko was at 5:00 p.m. on November 1 at the Pine Bar. Litvinenko had come to discuss their planned meeting the next day at RISC, and, as Lugovoi was on his way to a soccer match, he stayed only briefly. The next day, Litvinenko called to say he was sick and canceled the meeting. So Lugovoi returned to Moscow.

When I asked Lugovoi who was providing the expenses for his trips to London, he said Litvinenko gave the money to him in cash but he assumed it came from Berezovsky. Not only had the exiled billionaire been financing Litvinenko ever since he had defected to London, but he owned the house in which Litvinenko lived and the office that he used. He had also come to one of the meetings at RISC, and he frequently called Litvinenko on the cell phone reserved for RISC activities. So, even though Litvinenko did not say so, Lugovoi had little doubt that Berezovsky was behind their venture.

Had he kept the FSB informed about his meetings with Litvinenko, Berezovsky, and RISC officials? I asked. "I did what was necessary," Lugovoi replied, smiling knowingly.

He insisted that he had no knowledge about how Litvinenko, or he himself, got contaminated with polonium-210. Subsequently, he provided the same answer on a polygraph examination, and, according to the examiner, showed no signs of deception.

I next went to see Dmitry Kovtun, who had accompanied

Lugovoi to London for the last two meetings with Litvinenko. Like Lugovoi, Kovtun had been contaminated with polonium-210. Since his seat on the Transaero plane on which he had arrived in London on the morning of October 16 showed no trace of polonium-210, but his flight out of London tested positive for it, he had most likely been contaminated in London. But how?

I met him at the Porto Atrium, an expansive restaurant on the Leninsky Prospect known for its extensive wine cellar. A compact man in his mid-forties with greying hair, Kovtun explained how he got, as he put it, "into this mess." He had just returned from Germany, where he had served in a Soviet Army intelligence unit and married, then separated from, a German woman. He was looking for international business contacts, and Lugovoi had proposed he go to London with him. When they arrived, they were met by Litvinenko, who spent most of his next two days with them. Kovtun's next encounter with Litvinenko came two weeks later, when Lugovoi invited him to come to London for a major soccer match, for which Berezovsky was providing tickets. When he arrived on November 1, he joined Lugovoi and Litvinenko for a pregame drink at the Pine Bar.

When Litvinenko walked him out, he recalled that Litvinenko made an extraordinary proposal. After rambling on about suspicious Russian billionaires who had established residence in Spain, he suggested a new business venture for which he and Lugovoi were going to Spain. All Litvinenko told Kovtun was that the service he would provide was to "solve their problems." Kovtun said he asked, "What kind of problems?" and Litvinenko replied "We'll provide their problems and then fix them." Kovtun assumed that Litvinenko planned to somehow extract money from Russians residing in Spain. (It was subsequently revealed at the December 2012 preliminary hearing in London that Lugovoi and Litvinenko planned to go together to Spain.) This was Kovtun's last contact with Litvinenko.

Since both Lugovoi and Kovtun claimed that they were merely innocent bystanders who themselves had been contaminated by the same polonium-210 that killed Litvinenko, I asked the office of the Russian prosecutor general what evidence the British government had provided to support its extradition request for Lugovoi. Supposedly, the British and Russians had undertaken a joint investigation of Litvinenko's death. I was told that the case had been consigned to a new unit called the National Investigative Committee, which was headed by Alexander Bastrykin, a former law professor and a deputy attorney general from St. Petersburg. His office was located in a nondescript but well-guarded building across the street from Moscow's elite Higher Technical University in the district of Lefortovo.

Before I could meet officials in a conference room there to review the British file, I had to agree to indemnify the Russian government for any costs that resulted from disclosing the British evidence, submit my proposed questions in advance, and agree not to identify by name any of the officials working for the committee and to refer to them collectively as the "Russian investigators." I agreed to these terms, and the Russian investigators then provided me with access to the British files.

What immediately caught my attention was that they did not include the basic documents in any murder case, such as the postmortem autopsy report, which would help establish how—and why—Litvinenko died. In lieu of it, Detective Inspector Robert Lock of the Metropolitan Police Service at the New Scotland Yard wrote that he was "familiar with the autopsy results" and that Litvinenko had died of "Acute Radiation Syndrome."

Like Sherlock Holmes's clue of the dog that didn't bark, this omission was illuminating in itself. After all, Great Britain and Russia had embarked on a joint investigation of the Litvinenko case, which, as far the Russians were concerned, involved the polonium-210 contamination of Russian citizens who had contact with Litvinenko. They needed to determine when, how, and under what circumstances Litvinenko had been exposed to the radioactive nuclear component. The "when" question required access to the toxicology analysis, which usually is part of the autopsy report. There had already been a leak to a British newspaper that toxicologists had found two separate "spikes" of polonium-210 in Litvinenko's body, which would indicate that he had been exposed at two different times to polonium-210. Such a multiple exposure could mean that Litvinenko was in contact with the polonium-210 days, or even weeks, before he fatally ingested it. To answer the "how" question, they wanted to see the postmortem slides of Litvinenko's lungs, digestive tract, and body, which also are part of the autopsy report. These photos could show if Litvinenko had inhaled or swallowed the polonium-210, or gotten it into his bloodstream through an open cut.

The Russian investigators also wanted to know why Litvinenko was not given the correct antidote in the hospital and why his ailment had not been correctly diagnosed for more than three weeks. They said that their repeated requests to speak to the doctors and see their notes were "denied," and that none of the material they received in the "joint investigation" even "touched upon the issue of the change in Litvinenko's diagnosis from thallium poisoning to polonium poisoning." They added, "We have no trustworthy data on the cause of death of Litvinenko since the British authorities have refused to provide the necessary documents."

The only document provided in the British file indicating that a crime had been committed is an affidavit by Rosemary Fernandez, a Crown prosecutor, stating that the extradition request is "in accordance with the criminal law of England and Wales, as well as with the European Convention on Extradition 1957."

The British police report that accompanied the extradition papers did not cite any conventional evidence, such as eyewitness accounts, surveillance videos of the Pine Bar, fingerprints on a poison container (or even the existence of a container), or Lugovoi's possible motive. Instead, the case against Lugovoi was entirely based on a "trail" of polonium-210 radiation that had been detected many weeks after Litvinenko, Lugovoi, Kovtun, and others had been in contact with the polonium-210.

From the list of the sites supplied to the Russian investigators, it is clear that a number of them coincide with Lugovoi's movements in October and November 2006, but the direction is less certain. When Lugovoi flew from Moscow to London on October 16 on Transaero Airlines, no radiation traces were found on his plane. It was only after he had met with Litvinenko on October 16 that traces were found on the British Airways planes on which he later flew, suggesting to the Russian investigators that the trail began in London and then went to Moscow. They also found that in London the trail was inexplicably erratic, with traces that were found, as they noted, "in a place where a person stayed for a few minutes, but were absent in the place where he was staying for several hours, although these events follow one after another."

When the Russian investigators asked the British for a comprehensive list of all the sites tested, the British refused, saying it was not "in the interest of their investigation." This refusal led the Russian investigators to suspect that the British might be truncating the trail to "fit their case."

Despite its erratic nature, the radioactive trail clearly involved the Millennium Hotel. Traces were found both in rooms in which Lugovoi and his family stayed between October 31 and November 2, and in the hotel's Pine Bar, where Litvinenko met Lugovoi and Kovtun in the early evening of November 1. If Litvinenko's tea was indeed poisoned at that Pine Bar meeting, as the British contended, Lugovoi at least could be placed at the crime scene. But other than the radiation, the report cited no witnesses, video surveillance tapes, or other evidence that showed that the poisoning had occurred at the Pine Bar. It could just as well have occurred early in the day at any of several other sites that also tested positive for radiation.

Litvinenko, who was probably the best witness to that day's events, initially said he believed that he had been poisoned at his lunch with his Italian associate Mario Scaramella at the Itsu restaurant. (Even one week after he had been in the hospital, he gave a bedside BBC radio interview in which he still pointed to that meeting, saying Scaramella "gave me some papers.... after several hours I felt sick with symptoms of poisoning." At no time did he even mention his later meeting with Lugovoi at the Pine Bar.)

Not only did Itsu have traces of polonium-210, but Scaramella was contaminated. Since Scaramella had just arrived from Italy and had not met with either Lugovoi or Kovtun, Litvinenko was the only one among those people known to be exposed to polonium-210 who could have contaminated him. If so, Litvinenko had been tainted by the polonium-210 before he met Lugovoi at the Pine Bar. Other evidence from the British radiation trail indicated that Litvinenko had been contaminated well before his meeting with Scaramella. For example, several nights earlier, Litvinenko had gone to the Hey Jo club in Mayfair, and the place where he was seated in the VIP lap-dancing cubicle tested positive for polonium-210.

The most impressive piece of evidence in the British report involves the relatively high level of polonium-210 in Lugovoi's room at the Millennium Hotel. Although the police report does not divulge the actual level itself (or any other radiation levels), Detective Inspector Lock states that an expert witness called "Scientist A" found that these hotel traces "were at such a high level as to establish a link with the original polonium source material." Since no container for the polonium-210 was ever found, "Scientist A" presumably based his opinion on a comparison of the radiation level in Lugovoi's room and other sites, such as Litvinenko's home or airplane seats. Such evidence would only be meaningful if the different sites had been pristine when the measurements were taken. However, all the sites, including the Millennium hotel rooms, had been compromised by weeks of usage and cleaning before they were tested. Therefore the differences in the radiation levels could have resulted from extraneous factors, such as vacuuming, washing, or heating conditions.

The Russian investigators also found that these levels had little evidentiary value because the British had provided "no reliable information regarding who else visited the hotel room in the interval between when Lugovoi departed and when the traces of polonium-210 were discovered." As a result of this nearly monthlong gap, they could not "rule out the possibility that the discovered traces could have originated through cross-contamination by outside parties."

Hospital tests confirmed that Lugovoi, Kovtun, Scaramella, and Litvinenko's widow, Marina, all had some contact with polonium-210. But it was not clear who contaminated whom. The British police never found the container for the polonium-210. The Russian investigators concluded that all the radiation traces provided in the British report, including the "high level" cited by "Scientist A," could have emanated from a single event, such as a leak at the October 16 meeting at a security company in Berezovsky's building (which was also contaminated). But they could not find "a single piece of evidence which would confirm the charge brought against A. K. Lugovoi."

The radiation trail led to what appeared to be a dead end. All that could be established from it was that probably no later than October 16, 2006, by unknown means, individuals in London, including Litvinenko, Lugovoi, and Kovtun, had been tainted by a rare radioactive isotope. The small quantity of polonium-210 found in London could have been made in any country that has an uninspected nuclear reactor—a list in 2006 that included Russia, Great Britain, China, France, India, Israel, Pakistan, and North Korea (which manufactured a substantial quantity for its October 2006 nuclear tests). It could also have been stolen from stockpiles in the former Soviet Union or in America, where, according to the International Atomic Energy Agency's Illicit Trafficking Data Base, there had been fourteen incidents of missing industrial polonium-210 since 2004.

Consequently we not only don't know when it arrived in London; we don't know where it came from. Nor do we know why it was smuggled into Great Britain. It could have been smuggled to sell on the international black market. It also has some utility in the universe of modern espionage, since it can be used to power a miniaturized transmitter that can be planted in such classic targets as an embassy ceiling, a diplomatic vehicle, or an article of clothing. Because a single gram can produce 140 watts of energy, it can be left in place for long periods of time. It can also be used as an exotic assassination weapon, since it is lethal once it is inhaled or otherwise gets into the bloodstream. But if polonium-210 were to be deployed as an assassination weapon, the assassin would need to handle it with great caution, since it is extremely unstable and becomes airborne with ease. Before Litvinenko's death, six people are known to have died of exposure to polonium-210—two in a radiation lab in France, three in a nuclear facility in Israel, and one in a nuclear research lab in Russia. All of these deaths were accidents resulting from airborne leakage.

There is also some mystery about the activities of the men whose persons and premises were tainted by the smuggled radioactive isotope. At the time that his offices tested positive for polonium-210, Berezovsky had an extraordinary agenda, which he himself described as overthrowing the regime of his archenemy, Putin. And he had gathered in London a number of former intelligence officers from Russia and Ukraine to undertake projects that furthered this agenda. Litvinenko was also involved in a convoluted plot with Scaramella, who was also contaminated with polonium-210 in London. A self-styled nuclear-waste investigator in Naples, Scaramella had enlisted Litvinenko in a plot to incriminate putative members of a "Red Mafia" in Ukraine that smuggled arms, including nuclear components. One of their targets was an ex-KGB agent living in Naples, to whom who they arranged for a box of contraband Russian rocket grenades to be delivered. The plan was to tip off the Naples police to the shipment and claim it was to be used for an assassination, but it backfired because Scaramella's and Litvinenko's phone conversations were being listened to by the Italian intelligence service. Scaramella had also provided police with a tip that led them to a suitcase containing enriched-uranium rods that supposedly belonged to other "Red Mafia" agents trafficking in nuclear components. As a result of these entrapment schemes, Italian authorities criminally charged Scaramella with planting false evidence, and, after he returned from London, he was imprisoned in Naples on charges of calumny and arms smuggling.

As for the crime itself, most of the evidence in the case has either vanished or been suppressed. Polonium-210 has only a brief half-life of 138.4 days. By 2012, more than twelve half-lives have passed, meaning that almost all of whatever traces were gathered no longer exist in identifiable quantities. So there is no longer a radioactive trail, if indeed there ever was one. The autopsy results are still classified as a national security secret, and the coroner's report has never been completed.

This void has given rise to a profusion of theories. The most prevalent one, which has received wide circulation from Berezovsky and his associates, is that Putin gave the orders to murder Litvinenko, and that Lugovoi carried them out. Certainly, Putin had a motive, as Litvinenko had been publishing books, articles, and internet reports charging that the FSB blew up six residential buildings in Russia, killing hundreds of innocent people, on Putin's orders. A second theory is that Putin's enemies in London arranged the death of Litvinenko so to cast suspicion on Putin. Even before Litvinenko was dead, websites controlled by Berezovsky and his allies had declared Putin the villain. A third theory holds that the ex-KGB mafia that Litvinenko and Scaramella were trying to frame for smuggling nuclear materials arranged his poisoning. His attempt to incriminate ex-KGB men in Ukraine, Russia, and Italy by planting items with a radioactive signature could also have led to his own exposure. A fourth theory suggested to me by Alexander Goldfarb, who, it will be recalled, was with Litvinenko when he died, is that Litvinenko was killed because of his investigation into organized crime in Spain. According to Goldfarb, Litvinenko, who had made several trips to Madrid in 2006, had uncovered connections between Spanish mafia and criminal elements in Moscow and the Kremlin. He said that Litvinenko planned to provide further information about this liaison to José Grinda González, a special corruption and organized crime prosecutor in Spain, and theorized he was poisoned on November 1 to silence him. Kovtun also told me that Litvinenko was attempting to ferret out compromising data about Russian activities in Spain in November. If he had found such material, and was about to reveal it, it could indeed provide a motive for murder. (Although the choice of a slow-acting poison such as polonium-210 would not have prevented Litvinenko from revealing these secrets during his weeks in the hospital.) Finally, there is the theory that Litvinenko's associates, if not Litvinenko himself, were engaged in smuggling radioactive material and an accidental leak contaminated him. Among other things, his murky operations, including seeking contacts in the Pankisi Gorge, a lawless area in Georgia that had become notorious for nuclear smuggling, could have exposed him to accidental radiation.

My own assessment, after considering the evidence made available to me in London, Washington, D.C., and Moscow, is that Litvinenko was likely contaminated by accidental leakage of polonium-210. If so, his death would be consistent with all the known previous cases of polonium poisoning in France, Israel, and Russia. Such a leak would be even more likely if a vial was handled outside a lab because polonium-210, which can turn into a gas because of the heat produced as it decays, has a propensity to leak from containers. To be sure, polonium-210 is not readily available, other than to people in rarified professions, such as nuclear scientists, smugglers, and intelligence operatives. As for the latter category, Litvinenko was involved with a number of intelligence services, including British intelligence, Russia's FSB, America's CIA (which rejected his offer to defect in 2000), and Italy's SISMI (which was monitoring his phone conversations). One way that an intelligence service might use polonium-210 is in a battery for a miniature transmitter used to track a person of interest. Another way would be to use it in an intelligence game as a sample in an exchange to entrap someone suspected of buying nuclear components.

The British government has gone to considerable lengths to conceal Litvinenko's relationship with its intelligence services (even delaying the coroner's report for, as of this writing, six years). Other intelligence services have no doubt also made sure that their dealings with Litvinenko will not surface. But we know Litvinenko and a number of his associates, whether wittingly or not, were in contact with a container of polonium-210. My conclusion is that it leaked.

We will never know how or why Litvinenko came into contact with this substance, because all the evidence that might answer our questions, such as the autopsy report, is locked away in the realm of national-security secrecy. A British inquest may reveal further details of the crime, but in the cases of such sensitive political crimes, evidence that vanishes seldom reappears in a creditable form. As a result, the radioactive death of Litvinenko likely will remain an unsolved crime.

CHAPTER 28
THE GODFATHER CONTRACT

On March 20, 1979, Carmine "Mino" Pecorelli, a fifty-year-old journalist who was paid not to publish unsavory news in his scandal sheet, was assassinated in his office on the Via Orazio in Rome. When the gunman entered, Pecorelli was editing the next week's issue of his *Osservatorio Politico*. The assassin killed him with four well-placed bullets, and, Mafia-style, left the shell casings next to the body. The casings established that the bullets were of the Gevelot brand, which is not commonly used. The Gevelot brand was used, however, by an organized group of killers called the Magliana gang. The police assumed that this was a professional contract killing, and learned from their informers in the Rome underworld that the contract to kill Pecorelli had come from the Sicilian Mafia. At the time, there was no shortage of people with a motive. Any of the well-connected politicians and power brokers that Pecorelli was either blackmailing or threatening to expose could have put a contract out on him. In view of this surfeit of motives, and the lack of witnesses to the murder itself, the police did not pursue the case.

After fourteen years, however, a sensational lead emerged that would strike at the heart of the Italian political establishment. It came from a Mafia "pentito," or former Mafia member who was now cooperating with the police in return for leniency. This turncoat was Tomasso Buscetta, and on April 6, 1993, Italian investigating magistrates announced that

Pecorelli's murder contract had been arranged by the Mafia on behalf of one of Italy's most important political leaders, Giulio Andreotti. Buscetta said that Andreotti wanted to eliminate Pecorelli because Pecorelli was planning to publish documents that would implicate Andreotti in the death of former Prime Minister Aldo Moro, who was kidnapped by the Red Brigade in 1978, held in captivity for sixty-four days, and then executed. The request came to the Mafia via two Sicilian politicians, according to Buscetta.

If there was a political Godfather of postwar Italy, it was Andreotti. He had served as Prime Minister three times between 1972 and 1992. He also had been minister of the interior in 1954 and 1978, defense minister from 1959 to 1966 and again in 1974, and foreign minister from 1983 to 1989. He had made the Christian Democratic party into America's key ally in Italy. Even though many of his colleagues had been indicted in the infamous Tangentopoli, or "bribe city," in the early 1990s, Andreotti was not himself implicated and was elected a senator for life.

Now he was accused of complicity in murder. His accuser, Buscetta, had had a bloody criminal career in the Mafia. He was a major heroin trafficker in South America and implicated in two murders in the United States. After being extradited to the United States from Brazil in 1984, he agreed to provide information to U.S. authorities about Mafia activities in return for his freedom, and was subsequently given a new identity and put into the U.S. Witness Protection Program. According to Buscetta, Andreotti had been the Mafia's "man in Rome" for decades, using his immense power to "adjust," or reduce, Mafia prison sentences. In return, the Mafia, according to Buscetta, did his dirty work, which included murder. Buscetta himself did not claim to have ever met or even seen Andreotti. His allegations proceeded from stories relayed to him by other Mafia members, all of whom were either dead or silent.

Two separate magistrates, one in Rome, the other in Palermo, were unable to even establish that Andreotti, or any of his associates, had ever adjusted any Mafia sentences, so the magistrates developing the case relied on the accounts of two other imprisoned pentiti. Both of these men had been convicted of murder, and by testifying against Andreotti, they both literally got away with murder.

The first witness was Baldassare Di Maggio, who had admitted murdering fifteen people before he was arrested in 1993. He alleged that in September 1987 he had witnessed Andreotti receive a "kiss of honor" from the top Mafia leader in Sicily, Toto Riina, in the Palermo apartment of Sicilian politician Ignazio Salvo. There were two immediate problems with his story. For one, the entrance to Salvo's apartment was guarded by police because Salvo was under house arrest in September 1987, so it seemed highly unlikely that Riina, who was then the most wanted fugitive in Sicily, would choose a venue under police surveillance for a Mafia gathering. Second, Andreotti was foreign minister in 1987 and had a twenty-four-hour security detail that kept detailed records, which do not show that Andreotti was in Palermo at the time of the meeting. To attend, he would have had to elude his security detail. As the inquiry proceeded, Di Maggio's credibility was further damaged when investigators discovered that he had committed a murder after he had been admitted to the Italian witness protection program and then falsely claimed that he had been given permission to commit the homicide by Italian authorities. The investigating judges concluded that Di Maggio's "kiss of honor" story was a total fiction. The other witness in 1993 was Marino Mannoia, who claimed that in 1980 he had personally witnessed Andreotti arrive in a bulletproof Alfa Romeo sedan at a villa in Sicily in the company of several Mafia leaders. Since none of these leaders was alive, there were no witnesses who could confirm or disprove the putative meeting. In addition, Mannoia was unable to recall the exact place or date of this alleged meeting, so his story could not be checked against the records of Andreotti's security detail. Aside from these two witnesses, the magistrates heard a number of secondhand stories recounted in prison. While such hearsay testimony is ordinarily not admissible in court because it denies the accused the ability to confront the accuser, the magistrates made an exception here on the grounds that "one of the inflexible rules of the Mafia is that men of honor must tell the truth when speaking of facts relating to other men of honor." This rule turned out to be flawed, because one of the hearsay stories told by Buscetta about a Mafia heroin trafficker proved to be untrue.

For his part, Andreotti denied all the charges and pointed out that the Mafia had reason to discredit him. He had been personally responsible for initiatives against the Mafia, such as the international bilateral agreements that allowed the United States to extradite mafiosi (including Buscetta); the Decree-laws that prevented the release of Mafia suspects before trial; and the dissolution of twenty-nine Mafia-penetrated municipal councils in Sicily. His party had also passed laws allowing the internal exile of Mafia suspects without trial, which led the Mafia to engage in a full-scale attack on civil authorities in the early 1990s and blowing up anti-Mafia investigators.

In 1996, Andreotti was formally charged, on the basis of the pentiti evidence, with complicity in Pecorelli's murder, and, after a long trial, fully acquitted. In Italy, the prosecution can appeal jury verdicts, and in an appeal the verdict was overturned, and Andreotti was convicted of complicity of murder in 2002. But then that verdict was quickly overturned by the superior appeals court, and Andreotti was again declared innocent. As a result of these trials, the murder of Pecorelli remains an unsolved crime.

Almost all the theories about the murder proceed from possible motives. Since Pecorelli had been in the political-blackmail business for a decade, it is not difficult to identify parties that might have a reason to put out a contract on his life. The theory that Andreotti was the culprit has persisted even after his acquittal. The 2008 movie *Il Divo* makes the case that Andreotti's allies in Sicily had made deals with the Mafia to win elections, and that they used the Mafia to eliminate Pecorelli when he threatened to link Andreotti to the death of Moro. Other theories focus on groups involved in major scandals in the late 1970s, such as Licio Gelli's Propaganda Due lodge (of which Pecorelli was reportedly a member), the Gladio paramilitary networks, and the beneficiaries of the secret accounts in Panama of the Banco Ambrosiano. Indeed, almost any shadowy group with a secret to hide could be considered to have a motive in silencing Pecorelli.

My own assessment is based on documents that I received in Rome from lawyers involved in the case against Andreotti. From them, I conclude that the charges against him were politically motivated and with little, if any, basis in fact. The most likely killer of Pecorelli is one of the individuals from whom he was attempting to extort a price for his silence. Such a party, rather than paying him for his silence, could have decisively gained his silence by having him killed.

The lesson is that while it is possible to elicit stories from sociopaths, especially if they are provided with incentives, the resulting testimony cannot be relied on in the service of truth. Magistrates concocted the case against Andreotti almost entirely out of Mafia turncoat stories that could not be corroborated. Almost all of it was hearsay, allowed because of the myth that ex-Mafia men cannot lie to one another. Yet, this myth is refuted by numerous cases in which Mafia members have lied to each other. By casting suspicion on the man responsible for the extradition agreement with America, they diverted attention from others in the Mafia who were their criminal allies.

CHAPTER 29
THE VANISHINGS

In the 2004 film *The Forgotten*, a seemingly delusional mother played by Julianne Moore discovers that the government is part of an elaborate conspiracy to abduct children. Even in the fictional realm of Hollywood, this notion of alien abduction might have qualified as the height of political paranoia, but that same year, Japanese parents whose children had left home and disappeared in the late 1970s and early 1980s learned that the children had been systematically abducted by an alien state, North Korea. This revelation came in September 2002 when Kim Jong-Il, North Korea's supreme leader, admitted to Japanese Prime Minister Junichiro Koizumi that his intelligence service had carried out abductions of Japanese youth. What remained a mystery even after the admission of this political crime was how many people were kidnapped in this state-sponsored program, and why.

Initially, police in Japan understandably viewed these vanishings as isolated incidents. After all, the 1970s in Japan, as in the United States, was a time of drugs, rock music, and youth rebellion, and missing youth were not necessarily victims of forcible abductions. When parents persisted in believing that their children had been kidnapped, they themselves were often considered out of touch with reality.

One such incident occurred in the rural prefecture of Niigata on the Sea of Japan. On November 15, 1977, Megumi Yokota, a thirteen-year-old student, left badminton practice at

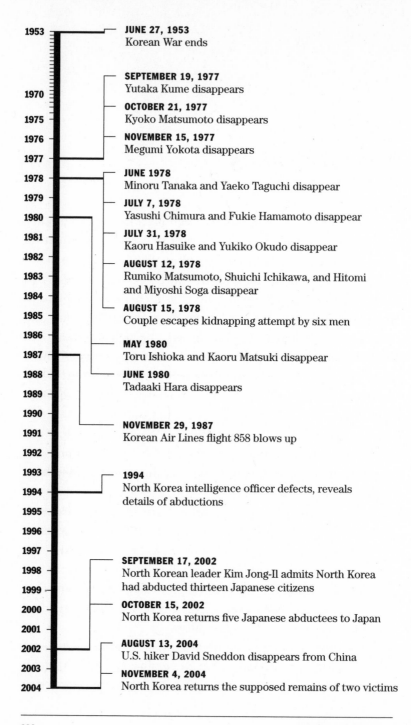

1953

JUNE 27, 1953
Korean War ends

SEPTEMBER 19, 1977
Yutaka Kume disappears

1970

OCTOBER 21, 1977
Kyoko Matsumoto disappears

1975

1976
NOVEMBER 15, 1977
Megumi Yokota disappears

1977

1978
JUNE 1978
Minoru Tanaka and Yaeko Taguchi disappear

1979
JULY 7, 1978
Yasushi Chimura and Fukie Hamamoto disappear

1980

1981
JULY 31, 1978
Kaoru Hasuike and Yukiko Okudo disappear

1982

1983
AUGUST 12, 1978
Rumiko Matsumoto, Shuichi Ichikawa, and Hitomi
and Miyoshi Soga disappear

1984

1985
AUGUST 15, 1978
Couple escapes kidnapping attempt by six men

1986

1987
MAY 1980
Toru Ishioka and Kaoru Matsuki disappear

1988
JUNE 1980
Tadaaki Hara disappears

1989

1990

1991
NOVEMBER 29, 1987
Korean Air Lines flight 858 blows up

1992

1993
1994
North Korea intelligence officer defects, reveals
details of abductions

1994

1995

1996

1997

1998
SEPTEMBER 17, 2002
North Korean leader Kim Jong-Il admits North Korea
had abducted thirteen Japanese citizens

1999

2000
OCTOBER 15, 2002
North Korea returns five Japanese abductees to Japan

2001

2002
AUGUST 13, 2004
U.S. hiker David Sneddon disappears from China

2003
NOVEMBER 4, 2004
North Korea returns the supposed remains of two victims

2004

school, and never arrived home. The local police conducted a massive search for her, and they called in a team of underwater divers to scour areas along the shore in which she might have drowned. They found no trace of her. Nor did any witnesses come forward when her photo was published in local newspapers.

Many of the Japanese who disappeared after Megumi were young couples. In these cases, the police could not discount the possibility that they had run away to Tokyo or another large city to get married. In all of that year, more than a dozen people were reported missing in northern Japan. Then, on August 15, 1978, an incident occurred on a beach outside Takaoka City that suggested that these vanishings might be part of a conspiracy. A twenty-eight-year-old man and his twenty-year old-fiancée, returning from a swim on a solitary beach, were attacked by six men. The man was handcuffed, gagged, and forced into a body bag; the woman had her arms and legs tied and was gagged with a towel. Then, a barking dog distracted the kidnappers long enough for the woman to escape and obtain help. Her fiancée was found still in the bag. Even though the six kidnappers escaped, police discovered equipment at the scene that appeared to be designed to kidnap people without injuring them, including a gag that allowed breathing, ear covers to prevent hearing, handcuffs, binding material, and green nylon body bags. The girl also told police that the men seemed to be speaking a foreign language.

At this point, Japanese security officials suspected that the six abductors were agents for a foreign intelligence service that for unknown reasons had orders to kidnap Japanese youth. Since they fled the beach, they also probably had orders not to allow themselves to be seen or captured.

The next piece of the puzzle emerged nine years later on November 29, 1987, when Korean Air Lines flight 858 blew up in midair, killing all 115 people aboard. The attack had been the work of the North Korean intelligence service. It dispatched two North Korean agents, a man and a woman, disguised as Japanese tourists, who carried a bomb aboard concealed in a Japanese-made Panasonic radio. They stored it, together with liquid explosives concealed in a liquor bottle (which would intensify the explosion), in the overhead storage compartment. They then deplaned at a stopover in Abu Dhabi and went to Bahrain, where police became suspicious of their forged Japanese passports. They both attempted suicide by smoking cyanide-laced cigarettes. The man died, but the woman survived and confessed. During her interrogation, she said she had been employed by the "investigation department" of North Korea's intelligence service and had been taught Japanese for the mission by a thirty-year-old Japanese women at its headquarters in Pyongyang. The description that she provided matched that of Yaeko Taguchi, who had disappeared from Tokyo in June 1978 after dropping her young children off at a day-care center. If this story is true, at least one of the abductees was working in Pyongyang for North Korean intelligence.

The next piece of the puzzle fell into place in 1994 with the defecting of a North Korean intelligence officer to South Korea. He told South Korean debriefers about a Japanese girl, used as an instructor by the North Korean intelligence service in Pyongyang, whose age and physical description matched that of Megumi Yokota. In addition, he provided details, such as the fact that she had been abducted after badminton practice, that left no doubt as to her identity, or that these abductions were part of a North Korean operation.

Japan was outraged when this information about Yokota was reported in the press. Even though North Korea categorically denied any involvement for another eight years, the Japanese government blocked any further consideration of World War II reparations until this issue was resolved. It was only in 2002, with a famine-starved North Korea expecting $10 billion in reparation payments, that its dictator acknowledged that his intelligence service had abducted Japanese citizens. Even so, many questions were left unanswered. For instance, North Korea claimed that it had abducted only thirteen people, yet in Japan alone there were more than one hundred unexplained disappearances and police investigations attributed at least seventeen of them to state-sponsored abductions. Moreover, North Korea said that eight of the thirteen abductees had died, including the two who been previously identified in Pyongyang, Megumi Yokota and Yaeko Taguchi. As proof, it supplied death certificates from a North Korean hospital and the cremated ashes of Megumi Yokota. But when Japanese forensic experts examined the death certificates, they found so many irregularities that they could not preclude the possibility that some of them were forgeries. Even more disturbing, DNA taken from supplied ashes did not match that of Megumi Yokota. The North Korean explanation was further undermined by reported sightings of abductees, including Megumi Yokota, after their supposed deaths.

Once it was unambiguously established that state-sponsored abductions were not a paranoid fantasy, Western intelligence services began to examine missing-person cases outside Japan, and they found that in more than a dozen countries North Korean agents had either abducted or attempted to abduct individuals, including a movie star and director in Hong Kong, a violinist in Croatia, and five businesswomen from Singapore. It was not clear when, or even if, this abduction program has been ended. Intelligence analysts suspect that the vanishing of David Sneddon, a twenty-four-year-old American hiker from Utah, on August 13, 2004, in the city of Shangri-la in western China may have been an abduction by North Korea. If so, the 2002 admission by Kim Jong-Il had not ended state-sponsored abductions.

Since North Korea is a closed society in which even the

movements of foreign diplomats are tightly controlled, the purpose behind this program of international kidnappings remains elusive. One theory is that North Korean agents initially snatched young people abroad to "re-educate" them for intelligence tasks or to use them to force their relatives to cooperate, and then, as the program expanded, found other uses for them, such as language instruction. A second theory, provided by a CIA analyst, suggests that the 2002 return of five language instructors was at best a "limited hang-out" meant to divert attention from North Korea's employment of unknown abductees for more sinister operations, including assassinations, sabotage, smuggling, and other covert actions.

My own assessment is that North Korea engaged in an extensive program of abductions, of which the Japanese abductions may be just the tip of the iceberg. We do not know how many other missing persons were in fact abducted. During this period, it has been established that North Korea was using its intelligence apparatus for a wide range of criminal enterprises, including counterfeiting money, drug trafficking, prostitution, and money laundering. I assume that the purpose behind these and other abductions was to supply the country's criminal networks with false identities. As with many political crimes, the full extent and purpose of these state-sponsored abductions remains a mystery.

What is clear, however, is that because a theory appears to be paranoid does mean that it is wrong. In this case, the parents who believed that their missing children had been kidnapped by an alien government turned out to be right in a spectacular way: The alien government, North Korea, returned some of the victims.

PART FIVE
SOLVED OR UNSOLVED?

CHAPTER 30
THE OKLAHOMA CITY BOMBING

At 9:02 a.m. Central Standard Time on April 19, 1995, a huge truck bomb destroyed a large part of the Alfred P. Murrah Federal Building in Oklahoma City, damaging more than 300 other buildings and killing 168 people, including nineteen children at a day-care center. The building, which housed fourteen government agencies, including the DEA, the Alcohol, Tobacco, and Firearms Agency (ATF), and U.S. Army recruitment offices, was a symbol of the power of the U.S. government. The truck bomb was a massive device, containing over 5,000 pounds of ammonium nitrate, 165 gallons of nitromethane, and over 100 pounds of Tovex explosives, with a sophisticated dual-fuse ignition device, packed into a truck rented from Ryder under a false name. More than a dozen witnesses recalled seeing the truck driven through Oklahoma City that morning, and at 8:57 a.m it was recorded by CCTV cameras approaching the Murrah building. It was then parked under the day-care center in the building, locked, and vacated minutes before it detonated. The bombing was the deadliest terror attack America had experienced before the 9/11 assault and, understandably, caused a public outcry for justice.

The first conspirator arrested was Timothy McVeigh, a twenty-seven-year-old Army veteran, who had been awarded the Bronze Star during the first Gulf War. As the evidence clearly showed, McVeigh had driven the truck bomb to Oklahoma City and detonated it. The second conspirator arrested was Terry Nichols, a forty-year-old farmer who had befriended McVeigh in the Army and who had helped him prepare and arm the truck bomb.

Both McVeigh and Nichols were found guilty of a conspiracy to use a weapon of mass destruction. McVeigh was sentenced to death and executed on June 11, 2001. Nichols was sentenced to life imprisonment with no possibility of parole. The only other person charged was Michael Fortier, who pleaded guilty to not warning authorities of the attack. Since he was not involved in the attack itself and cooperated with authorities, he was sentenced to only twelve years and then released into the witness-protection program.

There is no doubt that McVeigh, Nichols, and Fortier were guilty. Their convictions, however, do not settle the question of who else, if anyone, was involved in this act of organized terrorism. A decade after the execution of McVeigh, investigative journalists Andrew Gumbel and Roger Charles, sorting through more than 18,000 FBI witness interviews for their book *Oklahoma City*, found holes in the investigation that left open the possibility of a wider conspiracy. A major gap proceeds from the fact that no fewer than twenty-four witnesses said that they saw McVeigh, just before and after the crime, while he was either driving the truck or in the truck rental office, with an unidentified man who could not have been either Nichols or Fortier. This man's fingerprints may have been among the more than 1,000 unidentified latent fingerprints found in the investigation, but that was not established, because, through an inexplicable investigation failure, the FBI did not attempt to match these unknown prints to the computerized FBI database or even to perform a comparison among them to see how many belonged to the same people. Since neither McVeigh nor Nichols had the military training necessary to build the complex bomb that was used, the existence of another conspirator might have provided some explanation of how the bomb was designed, built, and rigged.

One reason this gap was not plugged, as the ATF and FBI documents unearthed by Gumbel and Charles show, is that there had been enormous pressure from the federal prosecutors to cut off the investigation. The prosecutors' case against McVeigh and Nichols—who were tried separately—would not necessarily be strengthened by an increased numbers of conspirators. So, once Fortier had agreed to testify against McVeigh and Nichols, the prosecutors had no need to call many of the eyewitnesses to testify. Yet, even though convictions were obtained, the legal process failed to answer several key questions: How many conspirators were involved, and who, if anyone, was behind McVeigh and Nichols?

On this score, there are three theories worth considering. First, there is the theory of the prosecution: that McVeigh and Nichols, acting by themselves, planned, financed, built, and detonated the truck bomb. In this view, all twenty-four eyewitnesses are mistaken and it is a closed case. Second, there is the theory advanced by Gumbel and Charles in their well-researched book that McVeigh and Nichols were in league with right-wing activists. Their investigation found that McVeigh and Nichols were in contact with dozens of members of militias, armed religious sects, White Supremacist groups, and neo-Nazi cabals that robbed banks and sold drugs to buy guns. They also dealt with individuals at a gun show who were involved in bomb-making. They therefore conclude that the mystery man in the truck came from a right-wing group that was involved in the plot.

Finally, there is an Islamic-terrorist theory. Since Nichols made many trips to Cebu City in the Philippines in 1994, where his Filipino wife was attending Southwestern University, it has been suggested that he may have had contact with Islamic extremist groups based there, including Abu Sayyaf, an affiliate

of al-Qaeda. For example, Stephen Jones, one of the trial attorneys for McVeigh, claimed to have evidence that Nichols
attended a meeting with the Islamic terrorist Ramzi Yousef,
who in November 1994 was on the same campus of Southwestern University as Nichols' wife. It was Yousef who had organized the first attack of the World Trade Center in New York
in 1993, using the same modus operandi as was used in Oklahoma City—a truck bomb in the parking lot. In November 1994,
when Nichols came to Cebu City, Yousef was in the final stages
of the so-called "Bojinka plot." This scheme to plant twelve
bombs on twelve American planes that would simultaneously
detonate on January 21, 1995, was aborted in the Philippines in
early January by police who arrested Yousef's co-conspirator
Abdul Hakim Murad. In what may have been a coincidence,
Nichols meanwhile flew back to America on one of the targeted
flights of Northwest Airlines. About four months later, after the
bomb went off in Oklahoma City, Murad made statements from
prison, verbally and in writing, claiming responsibility for it.
Aside from this prison bluster, and the fact that they were both
in the same city in November 1994, the only actual evidence
cited in this theory is Yousef's phone records from the months
before he detonated the first World Trade Center bomb in 1993,
which showed calls placed to a close neighbor of Nichols' in-
laws in New York.

My own assessment of the evidence is that there was another conspirator involved in the plot. Although eyewitness
testimony is notoriously unreliable, I find it difficult to accept
the prosecution theory that *all* the eyewitnesses' identifications of a fourth man are wrong. Even though the FBI investigation collected a vast amount of data, including thirteen million
hotel and motel records, none of it precludes the possibility
that McVeigh and Nichols had help. The al-Qaeda theory, as
intriguing as it is, lacks a smoking gun. In addition, if Nichols
had such information, I find it difficult to believe that he would

not have used it to bargain with prosecutors to avoid a life sentence. The most plausible theory, in my view, is that McVeigh received assistance from the right-wing activists with whom he was known to be in contact.

Even in what was then the most deadly terrorist attack in American history, there can be no doubt that as the McVeigh trial approached, there was enormous pressure put on the FBI not to pursue leads that could be used by the defense team to advance doubts with the jury. The fact that the investigation was cut off before a fourth conspirator could be located demonstrates that the need for prosecutors to bring high-profile cases to trial can result, as it did in this case, in an unsolved mystery.

CHAPTER 31

THE O. J. SIMPSON NULLIFICATION

Evidence is, by its very nature, controvertible. Nowhere is this proposition better illustrated than in the murder trial of O. J. Simpson. Late in the evening of June 12, 1994, Simpson's ex-wife, Nicole Simpson Brown, and her friend Ronald Goldman were brutally stabbed to death outside Nicole's condominium on Bundy Drive in Los Angeles.

Since Orenthal James Simpson, better known as O. J., one of America's all-time great football heroes, had threatened her with violence on previous occasions, and had left Los Angeles immediately after the bloodbath, he became a suspect in the double homicide, and he agreed to voluntarily surrender to the Los Angeles police on June 17.

After he had retired from professional football, O. J. Simpson had remained in the public eye as a movie actor, television-show host, and product endorser, which made his surrender a media event. More than one thousand reporters had gathered at police headquarters to witness his agreed-upon surrender. When Simpson failed to arrive, they became fixated on the pursuit of his Ford Bronco in which a passenger had warned on his cell phone that Simpson was suicidal and holding a loaded gun to his head. As a convoy of police cars slowly trailed the Bronco on the throughways, one network after another canceled its schedule to carry the strange chase from helicopters live on television. By the time Simpson returned home, surrendered to waiting police, and was handcuffed, *USA Today* reported that it was already "the most publicized crime in history."

Although no murder weapon or any eyewitness to the double homicide was found, the police quickly amassed a wealth of incriminating evidence, including a bloody footprint, hairs, and fibers, and, on July 7, they proceeded to indict O. J. Simpson.

He pleaded "absolutely not guilty," retaining what the media termed a "dream team" of nine top lawyers, including two world-renowned experts in DNA evidence, to defend him. The televised trial, which began on January 25, 1995, turned on the prosecution's DNA evidence. To compare samples from those taken at the crime scene with those specimens furnished by Simpson, the prosecution used a technique called "restriction fragment length polymorphism." It requires the breaking of each DNA sample into pieces via restriction enzymes, then separating them according to their lengths, and comparing these results with the DNA furnished by Simpson. According to the prosecution's expert witness, police criminologist Dennis Fung, this DNA evidence, including samples taken from the bloody footprints leading away from the bodies, perfectly matched that of O. J. Simpson. If this was true, he could be placed at Nicole Brown Simpson's townhouse at the time of the murders. But in eight days of cross-examination, defense lawyer Barry Scheck elicited testimony that showed flaws in the process. For example, the police scientist who collected blood samples from Simpson to compare with those from the crime scene carried them around in his lab-coat pocket for nearly a day before handing them over as evidence, raising the possibility of cross-contamination between the samples. Scheck argued that this and other mishandling of the blood samples made it impossible to determine whose DNA was found at the crime scene.

The prosecution had also relied heavily on seemingly cogent glove evidence. It presented a left leather glove, found

EDWARD JAY EPSTEIN

at the crime scene, that contained blood that matched that of murder victim Goldman, and a similar right glove that was found in the police search of Simpson's compound. However, when the prosecutor asked Simpson to try on the left glove in front of the jury, it was much too small to fit on his hand. This mismatch led defense lawyer Johnnie Cochran to argue to the jury, "If it [the glove] doesn't fit, you must acquit."

The dream team of lawyers so effectively impeached the evidence supplied by the police investigation that on October 3, 1995, after only three hours of deliberation, the jury returned a unanimous verdict of not guilty. The one-hundred-and-thirty-five-day trial was over, and O. J. walked out of the court room a free man.

How could Simpson not be guilty of the double murder? Such a verdict was so much at odds with the narrative that had begun in the media, from the day of the televised car chase fifteen months earlier, that an explanation had to be provided to the public for this apparent contradiction. The theory offered by prosecutors, police, and pundits was "jury nullification," a doctrine that allows a jury to ignore the evidence and acquit the accused if they believe the law itself is unfair. It can be traced back to runaway slave cases in the early 1800s, when juries in anti-slavery states refused to convict runaway slaves because they believed slavery laws were unfair. As Simpson was being tried for murder, and his legal rights were well represented, intentionally ignoring the evidence—if indeed that is what occurred—would also be a miscarriage of justice on the part of the jurors. In any case, the relatives of Goldman and Nicole Brown Simpson sued O. J. Simpson for wrongful death in civil court, which uses a lower standard of proof than a criminal trial. In February 1997, the jury awarded the plaintiffs $33.5 million—a judgment that literally bankrupted Simpson.

He was still technically not guilty of the murders, so a confession was needed to remedy the jury verdict and restore the narrative. In 2006, Judith Regan, the editor of ReganBooks, a subsidiary of Rupert Murdoch's News Corporation, persuaded Simpson to sign his name to a work of fiction that would be called *If I Did It: Here's How It Happened*. She offered him a $1.1 million advance, as well as a percent of the profits, at a time when he was desperate for money. The plan was to make the book into a TV special for the Fox television network, also a subsidiary of News Corporation. As Regan explained it, the purpose was to bring "closure" to the case. A ghostwriter, Pablo Fenjves, was hired to write the fictional account of how an O. J.–like character comitted the murders. Before it could be published, word of it leaked to the *National Enquirer*, causing such a firestorm of charges that O.J Simpson, Regan, and Fox television, were exploiting the crime for profit, that Murdoch fired Judith Regan, canceled the television show, and withdrew the book from publication.

But the effort to publish a confession from Simpson continued. A Florida bankruptcy court awarded the rights to the ghostwritten book to the Goldman family, which changed its title, without O. J.'s approval, to *If I Did It: Confessions of the Killer*. They then effectively dropped the key word "if" by printing it in such minute letters that it actually fitted in the dot over the "I" in the title. So the title appeared to be: *I Did It: Confessions of the Killer*. In addition to this legerdemain, the book included a chapter by Dominick Dunne implying falsely that Simpson had actually confessed to the crime. The ghostwritten fiction, passed off to the public as a truthful confession by O. J. Simpson, became a huge best-seller in 2007. In the court of public opinion, a confession, albeit a fraudulent one, had finally been extracted from Simpson. On the books of the L.A. police department, the 1994 murders remain, however, unsolved crimes.

The only viable alternative theory is that another party, possibly one with whom Simpson was acquainted, committed the murders, and O. J. later stumbled on the crime scene and cut himself there. While such a theory could account for the DNA evidence, it does not account for the awareness of guilt that Simpson displayed after the crime, first by fleeing to Chicago, and then, during the car chase, holding a gun to his own head. These actions, in conjunction with the evidence at the trial, convince me that he was the perpetrator. In my view, the jury, which was subjected to unprecedented media exposure, opted to nullify the legal process.

CHAPTER 32

BRINGING DOWN DSK

May 14, 2011, was a fateful day for Dominique Strauss-Kahn, at the time the head of the International Monetary Fund and the odds-on favorite to replace Nicolas Sarkozy as the president of France. By late afternoon, instead of flying to Europe for a meeting with German Chancellor Angela Merkel, he would be imprisoned in New York on a charge of sexual assault. He would then be indicted by a grand jury on seven criminal counts, including attempted rape, sexual assault, and unlawful imprisonment; spend four days in the Rikers Island jail; would be placed under house arrest for over a month; and, two weeks before all the charges were dismissed on August 23, 2011, would be sued for sexual abuse by the alleged victim.

Strauss-Kahn, better known in France by his initials, "DSK," had been arrested for allegedly attempting to rape a hotel maid at the Sofitel Hotel in New York. At first, prosecutors assumed that this was a simple case of a lustful master of the universe disregarding the laws of New York State. But they soon learned that things were not as they initially seemed, and they dropped all charges against Strauss-Kahn.

After the prosecutors dismissed the charges against Strauss-Kahn, it was revealed that DSK had become a prime target of French intelligence at least two months before the Sofitel incident. French authorities were intercepting communications of his associates, and, as is evident from the hotel's security cameras, anticipating his arrival at the hotel. This raises the mystery: Did Strauss-Kahn's political downfall proceed from his own lust, or from the machinations of those out to derail his election? Or was he a victim of both? To reconstruct the elements of this continuing mystery, I have used videos from the hotel's CCTV cameras, electronic key-swipe records, and cell-phone records. Here is what unfolded.

The day began normally enough. According to room-service records, a waiter knocked on the door of DSK's four-room suite shortly after 9:30 a.m. and brought in the breakfast DSK had ordered. It was left for DSK in the dining room on the far side of the living room. But when DSK went through his messages, he discovered that he had a potentially serious problem with one of his BlackBerry cell phones, which he called his IMF BlackBerry. This was the phone he used to send and receive texts and emails, for both personal and IMF business. According to DSK, who I interviewed in Paris in April 2012, he had received a text message that morning from a friend in Paris. She warned him that at least one private email he had recently sent from his BlackBerry to his wife, Anne Sinclair, had been read by his political foes. It is unclear how these foes might have been able to receive this email, but if it had come from DSK's IMF BlackBerry, he had reason to suspect that he might be under electronic surveillance in New York.

Since DSK had taken measures to protect his phone a month earlier, the warning that his BlackBerry might have been hacked was all the more alarming. At 10:07 a.m. he called his wife in Paris on his IMF BlackBerry, and in a conversation that lasted about six minutes, he told her that he had a big problem. He asked her to contact a friend, Stéphane Fouks, who could arrange to have both his BlackBerry and iPad examined by one or more experts in such matters. He wanted Fouks and his team to meet him at Charles de Gaulle Airport, where he would make a short stopover en route to Berlin.

DSK had no time to do anything else about it that morning.

He had scheduled an early lunch with his twenty-six-year-old daughter, Camille, who wanted to introduce him to her new boyfriend. After that, he had to get to the JFK airport in time to catch his 4:40 p.m. Air France flight to Europe.

DSK finished packing his suitcase at around noon, according to his own account, and then took a shower in the bathroom, which is connected to the suite's bedroom by an interior corridor. Just minutes later, there were several entries to his suite. The first entry was at 12:05 p.m., according to the hotel's electronic key-swipe records (which are accurate only to the nearest minute). The key belonged to Syed Haque, a room-service waiter. According to Haque's police statement, he had come to the suite to remove DSK's breakfast dishes. If so, he turned left on entering the suite and proceeded through the living room to the dining room, where he would collect the breakfast dishes on his cart.

It is not clear how long Haque spent in the suite, or when he left, because the electronic key system records only entries, not exits.

The second entry came only about a minute later, at 12:06 p.m. This time, the key belonged to a hotel maid, Nafissatou Diallo, who was a thirty-two-year-old immigrant from Guinea. Ordinarily, cleaning personnel do not enter a room to clean when a guest is still in it. The presidential suite, however, is a large four-room apartment, so Diallo may not have known that DSK was in the suite when she entered. If her purpose was to clean the suite, she would need the cleaning equipment on her cart. But, according to her own testimony, her cart was locked in room 2820. (According to hotel records, the guest in 2820 had checked out at 11:36 a.m.) Diallo then left DSK's suite, and the door locked behind her. The third entry was also made by Diallo. It was also recorded at 12:06 p.m., so she had spent very little time in the hall. We do not know why she returned, but when she did, she still lacked her cleaning equipment. At this time, depending on whether or not the room-service waiter had yet exited, there was either one or two staff in the presidential suite.

Shortly after her second entry, she encountered DSK. What followed, and where it happened, is a matter of dispute, but there is no doubt about the sexual nature of the encounter. DNA evidence found just a few feet outside the bathroom door showed a combination of her saliva mixed with his semen. DSK does not deny that a sexual encounter occurred. The prosecutors determined that this encounter, whether forced or not, was "hurried," because DSK's phone records show that by 12:13 p.m. he was speaking to his daughter on his IMF Black-Berry—a call that lasted for thirty-six seconds. Since it was not a call that Diallo witnessed, according to her own account, she must have already left the room. If so, the sexual encounter had lasted no more than seven minutes.

In the maid's account, she encountered DSK in the entrance area when he emerged naked from the bedroom. He then dragged her first to the bedroom and then to the end of the interior corridor across from the bathroom, and there, after molesting her, he forced her to perform oral sex on him.

In DSK's version, the maid was already standing just outside the bathroom door when he opened it. If so, she had crossed through the bedroom before she encountered him. The sex act then took place and, according to him, was consensual.

What is known from phone records is that DSK completed his call before 12:14 p.m. He then dressed, put on a light black topcoat, and left the suite with his bag and briefcase (which contained his iPad and several spare cell phones). As he recalled, when I later discussed it with him, he left no gratuity for his one-night stay in the $3,000-per-night presidential suite. He left the room at about 12:26 p.m.

At 12:27:08, he was recorded by the ground-floor CCTV cameras arriving in the lobby. On the twenty-eighth floor at

12:26 p.m (just moments after DSK got into in the elevator), Diallo used her electronic key to reenter the presidential suite. It was her third entry to the presidential suite in just twenty minutes, and she remained there very briefly before encountering another maid in the hall at 12:30 p.m. or shortly after.

Like many hotels built in the twenty-first century, much of what happens at the Sofitel hotel is recorded by CCTV cameras. Outside, they are located at both the main entrance on 44th Street and the employees' entrance on 45th Street. On the ground floor, they are located, among other places, in the concierge area, the main lobby, the lounge, the reception area, the elevator entranceway, the security-office corridor, and the loading dock. They are also located in the sub-basement. There are no cameras in the upper-floor corridors, elevators, or rooms. The photos from these cameras are digitally stored, and they can be viewed on a state-of-the-art monitor in the security office, located in the corridor between the employee entrance and the lobby.

These cameras show DSK's departure at 12:28:20 p.m. on May 14. DSK emerged from the elevator at 12:27:12 p.m. Fifty seconds later, at 12:28:03, the head engineer, Brian Yearwood, emerged from another guest elevator. DSK reached the reception desk at 12:28 p.m. At 12:28:30 p.m., Yearwood moved toward a vantage point in the lobby from which the reception area was visible. By 12:28:50, DSK had checked out and walked through the lobby exit to 44th Street.

Yearwood, a former corrections officer at the Mid-Orange Correction Center in Warwick, New York, was also visible in CCTV footage from the previous night, when DSK arrived in a taxi from JFK airport. The time-stamped video showed DSK's taxi arrive at the 44th Street entrance of the Sofitel at 7:08 p.m. on May 13. Just before that, Yearwood came out of the hotel with a cell phone pressed to his ear. He walked out into the street and handed the phone to a doorman. They both looked down 44th Street. Yearwood then returned to the sidewalk and continued speaking and gesturing to the doorman, who then walked down 44th Street (out of the range of the camera) and then ran back with DSK's cab. The doorman then unloaded DSK's bag and briefcase as DSK paid. DSK then carried his own baggage to the hotel, pulling a small wheeled bag behind him, while Yearwood was standing in the entranceway, and then Yearwood appears to have followed DSK to the reception area, which is on the 45th Street side of the building. As DSK signed in at 7:11 p.m. and provided his passport for the reception clerk, Yearwood can be seen framed in the lounge doorway looking toward him. Then, at 7:12:16 p.m., DSK, accompanied by the reception clerk, walks to the elevator lobby. Three seconds later, Yearwood comes out of the doorway, walks past the reception desk. These near-encounters with DSK may have been pure coincidence, or Yearwood may have been assigned by the hotel the task of making sure that DSK's arrival—and his departure the next day—went smoothly. Such a task could be a perfectly proper precaution, since DSK, a possible future president of France, was one of the hotel's most important clients. But if Yearwood was assigned that role, how did he, or the person on the telephone, know when DSK's cab was arriving?

Yearwood also became part of the unfolding drama on the 28th floor shortly after DSK's departure on May 14. At 12:39 p.m., he can be seen on the CCTV video receiving a phone call while talking to a woman in a pink cardigan in front of the hotel. The call was from Renata Markozani, the head of housekeeping. At that time, according to key records, she was in the presidential suite, and according to police reports, she was with Nafissatou Diallo, with whom DSK had had the encounter about a half-hour earlier. Diallo had by now told the head of housekeeping that she had been attacked in the suite. At 12:43 p.m., Yearwood got into a guest elevator. He was joined on the 28th floor by Derek May, a security guard (and the hotel's union representative). May, a large, muscular man wearing an earpiece, and Yearwood appear to have been working closely together that afternoon, since they are frequently shown together on the CCTV videos.

At 12:45 p.m. Yearwood used his electronic key to enter the presidential suite, where Markozani was with Diallo. About fifteen minutes earlier, Diallo had encountered another maid near the 28th-floor linen closet, and she asked a hypothetical question about what a hotel guest could do to a maid. After that, Diallo said she had been sexually attacked by a guest, which led this maid to call the head of housekeeping. It is not known what was said at this meeting, but it could not have lasted long. At 12:51:56 p.m., Diallo and Markozani, along with May, got out of the elevator on the ground floor, as recorded by a CCTV camera. May stayed with them as far as the main lobby, and the head housekeeper and Diallo continued to the corridor used by employees, located at the 45th Street entrance. The hotel's security office is there. It has a set of Dutch doors, the upper half of which were opened.

Behind the doors sat Adrian Branch, the Sofitel's head of security. Diallo stood next to a solitary bench just across the corridor from this half-opened door. She remained standing or sitting there for the next hour and fifteen minutes. Yearwood did not immediately accompany Diallo downstairs. He remained behind on the 28th floor and, according to the electronic key records, reentered the presidential suite at 12:51 p.m.

Whatever his reason for this second visit, it was brief. By 12:53 p.m., the cameras recorded him leaving the elevator on the ground floor. He walked briskly through the lobby to the security area, where he spoke briefly to Diallo; thirty seconds later, he returned to the reception area, where he rejoined May in a curtained office to the right of the reception desk. As there was no CCTV camera in this office, we do not know what they did there for the next five minutes. Possibly, they were checking the records to verify Diallo's story. If they had consulted the hotel's computerized guest records, they would have seen that the client in the presidential suite was DSK, and that he had checked out at 12:28 p.m. (which Yearwood may have himself seen him do). If they checked electronic key records, they would have ascertained that only two employees had entered the suite prior to his checkout—the room-service waiter Haque at 12:05, and Diallo three times, twice at 12:06 and once at 12:26 p.m. They would also have seen that both before and after her visit to the presidential suite, Diallo had gone to another room across the hall, room 2820.

By 1:00 p.m., both men had returned to the security area. They would spend a good part of the next hour there, either talking on their cell phones or inside the security booth (which was not covered by the CCTV cameras). At 1:03 p.m., a call was made to the cell phone of John M. Sheehan (Sheehan's cell-phone calls are a court document). Sheehan was the director of safety and security at the Sofitel's parent company, Accor, which is a part of the French-based Accor Group. He also had a similar position and office at the Sofitel (the Accor Group's only hotel in New York). He was off that day at his home in Washingtonville, New York. Nevertheless, he had been in frequent touch with the head engineer earlier that day, exchanging no fewer than thirteen text messages with him between 10:21 and 10:35 a.m., according to the log of his cell phone.

After receiving the 1:03 p.m. call, Sheehan headed to the Sofitel, which is about an hour- and-a-half drive from his house. While en route, according to his cell phone records, he called the number 646-731-4400 in the United States. When I called the number, a man with a heavy French accent answered and asked whom I wanted to speak with at Accor. The man I asked to talk to—and to whom I was not put through—was René-Georges Querry, Sheehan's ultimate superior at Accor and a well-connected former chief of the French anti-gang brigades, who was now head of security for the Accor Group. Before joining Accor in 2003, he had worked closely in the police with Ange Mancini, who then became coordinator for intelligence for President Sarkozy. At the time that Sheehan was making his call to the 646 number, Querry was arriving at a soccer match in Paris, where he would be seated in the box of President Sarkozy. Querry denies receiving any information about the unfolding drama at the Sofitel at this time or until after DSK was taken into custody about four hours later.

Another person at the Accor Group whom Sheehan (or the operator at Accor) might have alerted was Xavier Graff, the duty officer at the Accor Group in Paris. Graff was responsible that weekend for handling emergencies at Accor Group hotels, including the Sofitel in New York. His name only emerged five weeks later when he sent a bizarre email to his friend Colonel Thierry Bourret, the head of an environment and public health agency, claiming credit for "bringing down" DSK. After the email was leaked to *Le Figaro*, which reported that he had said that he had "*faire tomber* DSK" (made DSK fall), Graff described it as a joke. (It resulted, however, in his suspension as director of emergencies by the Accor Group.) Jokes can often have a basis in fact. In this case, the joke was made by the person who was directly responsible for passing on information to his superiors, including the head of security at Accor, René-Georges Querry—information that, if Querry acted on it by informing the American authorities, could have helped destroy DSK's career. But like Querry, Graff denied receiving any calls or messages from New York until later that evening, telling a French newspaper that the failure to inform him was an incredible blunder.

Whatever communications might have passed between New York and Paris, the victim in the drama received no medical attention. The CCTV video shows Diallo repeatedly pointing to different parts of her body and making a series of hand gestures. It appears to be a reenactment of her story. At one point, she uses the head housekeeper Markozani to play the part of her attacker. At 1:07 p.m., the room-service waiter, Haque, who is the only known person who could have witnessed her entry into the presidential suite, and who was in the room only a minute before she entered, was brought into the apparent reenactment. He can be seen in a discussion with the head engineer and Diallo. The CCTV videos contain no sound component, so we do not know what was said, but, if this was part of the reenactment, at least two potential witnesses—the room-service waiter, who had preceded Diallo in the room, and the head housekeeper, who had heard her outcry on the 28th floor—had an opportunity to hear Diallo's version of the incident and refresh their memory before the police were called in.

It is not clear who finally made the decision to call the police. At 1:28 p.m., the Accor safety director, Sheehan, who was still on the way to the hotel, called the head engineer, who had entered the security office. After that, the Sofitel's head of security, Branch, made the 911 call.

The 911 operator recorded the time as 1:31 p.m., which was just over one hour after Diallo had first reported that she had been assaulted by the client in the presidential suite.

The call can be heard in its entirety on a 911 tape. After giving the address of the hotel, Branch reported only that a "room attendant" had been assaulted in a "sexual manner" by a hotel guest. When the 911 operator asked him if an ambulance should be sent, he replied that it was unnecessary because the victim had "no sustained injuries." Even though the records were available at the hotel, the security officer provided a time-line that falsely minimized the amount of time that had elapsed before the 911 call was made. He stated that the incident had taken place "thirty or forty minutes ago," when in fact it had occurred eighty minutes earlier, and that the guest had checked out of the hotel "twenty minutes ago," when in fact, DSK had checked out sixty-four minutes earlier. In any case, at about 1:32 p.m. the 911 operator said she would dispatch a "squad car." So the police were now on their way.

By this time, Yearwood, who was on and off his cell phone, had received another text message from Sheehan. He briefly went outside then returned just as the 911 call was concluding.

At 1:34:40, he walked past May, who then followed him through a door leading to the loading area. Here Yearwood and May were observed by another CCTV camera. The men speak for a moment. Then they high-five each other, clap their hands, and briefly dance. The security guard then actually lifts the head engineer off the floor. This performance, which spans about thirteen seconds, looks very much like the sort of victory dance seen in a football game after a touchdown is scored.

While the celebratory dance was taking place at the Sofitel, DSK was lunching seven blocks away at McCormick & Schmick's, a restaurant on 52nd Street between Sixth and Seventh avenues. When he left the hotel at 12:28 p.m., he had caught a taxi, which then became delayed by heavy traffic and a street fair on Sixth Avenue. By the time he got to the restaurant, as its CCTV camera showed, it was 12:54 p.m. His daughter Camille and her boyfriend were already there. Because it was to be a short lunch, DSK deferred to his daughter's request that he not use his cell phone. At 2:15 p.m., DSK hailed a taxi to go to the airport. Almost immediately, when he sought to make a call, he discovered that his IMF BlackBerry was missing. It was the phone he had arranged just that morning to have examined for bugs after he arrived in Paris, and it was the phone that contained the earlier text message warning him about the interception of his messages.

At 2:16 p.m. he called Camille, who had also just left the restaurant, on one of his spare BlackBerrys. He asked her to go back to the restaurant and search for his missing phone. CCTV footage at the restaurant shows her crawling under the table.

At 2:28 p.m., she sent him a text message saying that she could not find the phone. Meanwhile, as DSK continued on to the airport, he was still attempting to locate the missing phone. At 3:01 p.m., he was calling it from his spare phone. He received no answer.

What DSK did not know was that his phone had remained at the Sofitel after he had left the hotel. As late as 12:51 p.m., which was twenty-three minutes after DSK left the hotel, the GPS on the phone showed that it was still at the Sofitel, according to the records of BlackBerry parent company Research In Motion. The company could determine this time because a BlackBerry, like many other smartphones, continues to send a signal as to its location even when it is turned off. BlackBerry could also electronically determine that the GPS signals on DSK's phone had abruptly stopped at 12:51, indicating either that the battery had run out or that the GPS had been intentionally disabled. (A forensic expert later concluded from the strength of the previous signals that the latter most likely occurred.) So, either the phone was still in the presidential suite or someone at the hotel had taken it from the Sofitel after 12:51 p.m. (when it was no longer traceable).

At 3:29 p.m., evidently still unaware of what was happening at the Sofitel, DSK called the hotel from the taxi, saying, according to the police transcript, "I am Dominique Strauss-Kahn, I was a guest. I left my phone behind." He then said he was in room "2806."

At that time, Diallo had just left the hotel en route to St. Luke's–Roosevelt Hospital to be examined, but the police were still at the hotel. DSK was asked to give a phone number, so that he could be called back after someone searched for his phone. He furnished it.

At 3:33 p.m., police and security staff, using a security electronic key, then reentered the presidential suite. The police did not find the phone.

When DSK was called back thirteen minutes later, he spoke to a hotel employee who was in the presence of police detective John Mongiello. The hotel employee falsely told him that his phone had been found (it has never been found) and asked where it could be delivered. DSK told him that he was at JFK airport and said, "I have a problem because my flight leaves at 4:26 p.m." He was reassured that someone could bring it to the airport in time.

"OK, I am at the Air France terminal, gate four, flight twenty-three," DSK responded. At 4:45 p.m., the police called DSK off the plane and took him into custody. He was then driven back to New York City.

The police arrived on the scene at the Sofitel at 2:05 p.m. Two uniformed policemen can be seen on the CCTV video. They walked through the main lobby to the security area, where they were greeted by the hotel's manager, Florian Shotz, who himself arrived only ten minutes earlier on his motor scooter. The police then escorted Diallo to a private room. It is not clear when they began to question her or officially took control of the case. According to the prosecutor's bill of particulars, members of the hotel security staff had remained in contact with Diallo for at least another twenty-five minutes, since it states that at 2:30 p.m. "a photograph of the defendant was shown to the witness [i.e. Diallo] by hotel security without police involvement." If so, even after leaving the bench (and video surveillance) and going into a room with the police, she remained available to the Sofitel staff. (I asked both Deputy Commissioner Paul Browne and Deputy Inspector Kim Royster why, according to the bill of particulars, the police were not officially involved at this point, but they declined to comment.) Nor was the presidential suite entered by the police, according to the records, until 2:52 p.m., which was five minutes after Sheehan, the Accor safety director, arrived at the hotel. It was not until 3:28 p.m. that the police took Diallo to the hospital, and that she was finally

MAY 12

MAY 13

MAY 14

1:00 A.M.

2:00 A.M.

3:00 A.M.

4:00 A.M.

5:00 A.M.

6:00 A.M.

7:00 A.M.

8:00 A.M.

9:00 A.M.

10:00 A.M.

11:00 A.M.

12:00 P.M.

1:00 P.M.

2:00 P.M.

3:00 P.M.

4:00 P.M.

5:00 P.M.

6:00 P.M.

7:00 P.M.

8:00 P.M.

9:00 P.M.

10:00 P.M.

11:00 P.M.

MAY 15

MAY 12–13, 2011
DSK attends sex party at the W Hotel in Washington, D.C.

MAY 13, 2011, 7:09 P.M.
DSK arrives at Sofitel by taxi

MAY 14, 2011, 1:53 A.M.
DSK enters 2806 with blond woman

3:56 A.M.
Blond woman leaves hotel

10:00 A.M.
DSK gets text warning emails are compromised

10:07 A.M.
DSK calls his wife Anne Sinclair to have BlackBerry and iPad checked for bugs

12:05 P.M.
Syad Haque, room service waiter, enters 2806

12:06 P.M.
Diallo, the maid, enters 2806 twice

12:13 P.M.
DSK calls daughter

12:26 P.M.
DSK gets in elevator, two bags, briefcase with phones, overnight bag. Diallo re-enters 2806

12:28 P.M.
DSK checks out of the hotel, hails taxi

12:30 P.M.
Diallo reports DSK incident

12:51 P.M.
DSK BlackBerry goes dead

12:52 P.M.
Diallo, Markozani in security area

12:54 P.M.
DSK arrives at lunch with his daughter at McCormick & Schmick on W. 52 St.

1:31 P.M.
Sheehan sends text to Yearwood

1:32 P.M.
Hotel Security chief, Adrian Branch, makes 911 call to police to report "sex assault"

2:16 P.M.
DSK discovers his cell is missing in taxi to JFK

3:29 P.M.
DSK calls Sofitel about the phone

4:40 P.M.
DSK is called off plane

MAY 15, 2011, 8:00 P.M.
DSK bail deal is canceled

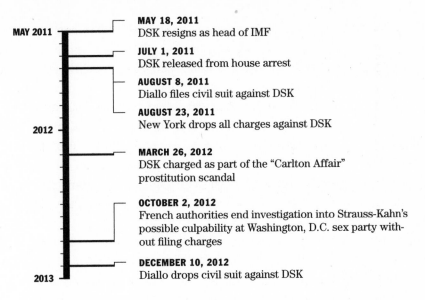

MAY 2011

MAY 18, 2011
DSK resigns as head of IMF

JULY 1, 2011
DSK released from house arrest

AUGUST 8, 2011
Diallo files civil suit against DSK

AUGUST 23, 2011
New York drops all charges against DSK

2012

MARCH 26, 2012
DSK charged as part of the "Carlton Affair"
prostitution scandal

OCTOBER 2, 2012
French authorities end investigation into Strauss-Kahn's
possible culpability at Washington, D.C. sex party without filing charges

DECEMBER 10, 2012
Diallo drops civil suit against DSK

2013

medically examined and then formally interviewed by police detectives.

The account she provided was of a brutal and sustained sexual attack. She described how her attacker locked the suite door, dragged her into the bedroom, and then dragged her down the inner corridor to a spot close to the bathroom door—a distance of about forty feet—and, after attempting to assault her both anally and vaginally, also forced her twice to perform fellatio.

After that, she said she fled the suite and hid in the far end of hallway until he left. She later identified DSK in the lineup as her attacker.

Based on her description, the police crime-scene unit sealed off two crime scenes—the presidential suite and the far end of hallway—and located five areas of the carpet in the interior hallway leading to the bathroom of the presidential suite that potentially had stains of semen or saliva. The next day, May 15, police detectives brought sections of the carpet from the hallway, as well as the wallpaper, to the police forensic biology lab. A preliminary examination showed that one of the five stains in the carpet, located about six feet from where Diallo had said she was assaulted, contained a mixture of semen and amylase (an enzyme from saliva) that was consistent with the DNA of DSK and Diallo. This was direct evidence that they had engaged in fellatio, as Diallo had claimed. (Three of the other stains also tested positive for semen, as did the wallpaper, and a fourth stain showed a mixture of semen and saliva, but these stains were determined to be from six other individuals, and their sexual activity was assumed to be unrelated to the incident under investigation.)

The next issue was whether force had been used. To this end, DSK was examined at St. Luke's–Roosevelt Hospital for any telltale bruises, traces of her DNA under his fingernails, or any other evidence of a struggle. None was found. Then, on Sunday, May 15, DSK was formally arrested.

The Manhattan district attorney office, under DA Cyrus Vance, Jr., was possibly the best staffed prosecution team in the United States. Its trial division alone had more than fifty assistant district attorneys, as well as dozens of investigative analysts and paralegals. Its sex-crimes unit, which had been assigned the case, had been the subject of a laudatory HBO documentary. Immediately after DSK's arrest, Lisa Friel, who had headed the sex-crimes unit, began examining the case, as did John "Artie" McConnell, the prosecutor assigned to the case; Ann Prunty, his "second" chair; and Joan Illuzzi-Orbon, the assistant DA who headed the newly created hate crimes unit. The first issue facing this formidable team of prosecutors was bail.

Bail is not unusual in the case of a first-time offender with no previous criminal background who is employed. DSK was the managing director of the IMF. His lawyers, William W. Taylor, III, and Benjamin Brafman, immediately moved to arrange bail. According to DSK's lawyers' understanding of their conversation with the prosecutors, a deal was arranged at 4:00

p.m. on May 15 whereby the prosecution would recommend $250,000 cash bail and DSK would relinquish his passport. But at 8:00 p.m. that Sunday, Lisa Friel told Brafman on the phone that "things had changed and there was no more agreement." Instead, the DA would recommend that bail not be granted. (Friel herself left the case shortly afterward and resigned from the district attorney's office.)

What had reportedly happened in the four-hour interim was that Vance had received information from Paris bearing on the case. Although it had been initially reported that this phone call concerned a Frenchwoman, Tristane Banon, who had charged that DSK had attacked her, that accusation had not even been officially filed on May 15 (and it was subsequently dismissed).

Instead, an investigation in the French newspaper *Libération* by Fabrice Rousselot found that the call came from the phone of a senior official in the French government. The official, according to Rousselot's investigation, said that DSK was implicated in a prostitution case that involved, among other things, transporting prostitutes to Washington, D.C. If it turned out to be true that DSK might be involved in a Washington prostitute ring, releasing him on bail could embarrass the DA's office, especially if he fled.

There may have been more than one phone call from Paris. At the bail hearing the next day, according to the court transcript, McConnell requested that Judge Melissa Jackson hold DSK without bail, explaining in an apparent reference to the communications with Paris that "we are obtaining additional information on a daily basis regarding his behavior and background." He continued, "Some of this information includes reports he has in fact engaged in a conduct similar to the conduct alleged in the complaint." He added that these reports were as yet unverified, but he did not specify who was supplying his office with these reports "on a daily basis" less than two days after DSK's arrest. But if the reports concerned DSK's sexual activities at the W Hotel in Washington earlier that week, where he had attended a sex party on May 13, this raises the question of how the French government, or whoever was supplying the reports, had obtained such up-to-date intelligence on DSK's private activities in Washington.

For their part, the prosecutors now strongly deny that this information from France was the decisive factor in their opposing bail. Their principal concern, according to a source in the prosecutor's office, was that DSK, if released on bail, might use his connections to flee to France. Whatever shaped the decision, Judge Jackson acquiesced and denied DSK bail.

The prosecutor's opposing bail had two immediate consequences. First, DSK was imprisoned on Rikers Island for four days (after which another judge granted bail). Second, it started a relatively brief clock for the prosecutors. New York state law required the prosecution to gather evidence and present it to the grand jury within 144 hours. This rush resulted in a presentation before all the facts could be assembled. For example, within that period, the prosecutors had not yet obtained electronic key-swipe records. When they did the following month, those records cast a very different light on the case.

The reasons that the prosecutors may have been willing to risk this rush to judgment is, as the district attorney publicly stated, that it was assumed that there was a solid case against DSK. After all, preliminary DNA evidence established that DSK had a sexual encounter with Diallo. The semen stains, moreover, placed it in the presidential suite in the area that she described to the police. Neither DSK nor his lawyers had denied that it had occurred. Instead, they said that it was not forced. So the only legal issue was whether or not it was consensual. That would be up to a jury to decide. And as is common in sex-crime prosecutions, the verdict would depend heavily on the credibility of the prosecution's only real witness. If the jurors believed Diallo beyond a reasonable doubt that force was used,

DSK would be convicted. And, as far as her creditability went, the prosecutors believed that they were on solid ground. The initial police investigation had turned up no "red flags" in Diallo's background. She had, for example, never been arrested or accused of a crime. Although she had entered the United States under an alias (as do many refugees), she had been granted political asylum by the U.S. Immigration Court. Diallo had worked for the Sofitel for three years without any reported problems and was described by her supervisor as a "model employee." And while she was the only witness to the attack itself, two other hotel employees—the room-service waiter and the head housekeeper—had given police statements that supported her story (although, as it later turned out, these witnesses had the opportunity to hear Diallo tell her story in the security area before the police were called in).

When the prosecutors went to court on May 15 and argued against bail, they assumed they had a credible witness.

Diallo also impressed them subsequently with the vivid account she gave of experiencing a previous rape by soldiers in Guinea. She had been so convincing that she brought tears to the eyes of one of the prosecutors. After hearing the testimony of Diallo, the grand jury indicted DSK on May 18. It charged him with two counts of criminal sexual acts, one count of attempted rape, two counts of sexual abuse, one count of unlawful imprisonment, and one count of forcible touching.

DSK pleaded not guilty to all the charges. He was then granted bail on conditions tantamount to house arrest. The case was adjourned to July 18, 2011. In the interim, the prosecutors continued to subpoena records, including cell-phone transmissions, credit-card records, and CCTV videos. However, as they gathered this evidence, the case became, as one person in the prosecutor's office said, "curiouser and curiouser." On June 7, Diallo's lawyer, Ken Thompson, who was a former prosecutor himself, delivered an unexpected bombshell. He told the prosecutors that his client had been untruthful in her interviews with the prosecutors in describing her background and circumstances. Specifically, he said that she had fabricated the story she had told them about being raped by soldiers in Guinea. While she had not told this story under oath, and it had no bearing on the DSK case, the revelation stunned the prosecutors. Among other things, it meant that she could provide a convincing description of a sexual encounter that she had invented. But why would she have been untruthful about such an embarrassing event? It was initially suggested that she had told this false account to support a similar account she had used in her immigration application. But when prosecutors then examined her immigration records, they found that she had told no such story. When re-interviewed on June 8, Diallo admitted that the prior rape story was untrue. Then the prosecutors found that she had told a far more damaging untruth, since it was about the DSK case itself. Diallo testified to the grand jury that immediately after she had been assaulted, she had fled the room and gone to the far end of the 28th-floor hallway. This was the story that she had also told to police and prosecutors. When she was asked why she had not used her keycard to go into another room from which she could call for help, she said they all had "Do Not Disturb" signs on their doors. But when the prosecutors obtained the electronic key records from the Sofitel hotel for the rooms on the 28th floor, which was not until late June, they showed that Diallo had entered another room, 2820. If so, she had been untruthful under oath about her whereabouts before her outcry. The prosecutors could not immediately re-interview her because, for more than a week in June, she refused to speak further to them, claiming she was ill. Finally, on June 28, Diallo admitted that she had been untruthful about not going into 2820. She now said that she went directly into 2820 after running out of the presidential suite, and that she then spent considerable time cleaning and vacuuming the room. This version would explain where she had been between 12:13 and 12:30 p.m. (when she met the other maid). The problem here is that the key records show that she did not use her key to enter room 2820 until 12:26 p.m., thirteen minutes after the encounter. When confronted with this discrepancy one month later, she changed her story yet again. On July 27, in what the prosecutors describe as "Version 3," she says she waited in the hallway for most of that time. Then, when she saw DSK leave the presidential suite, which was at 12:26 p.m., she entered 2820 to pick up her cleaning equipment, which she had left there earlier. And she then went back to the now-empty presidential suite.

The prosecutors now had to contend with the fact that not only had she been untruthful under oath to the grand jury about this case, but that she had concealed her visit to room 2820 from the police, which had effectively obstructed the investigation. The prosecutors noted that if she had mentioned her visits to 2820, that room would have been declared part of the crime scene and searched for fingerprints and DNA by the police. But she did not do so, and the room was immediately rented out.

In addition, it also developed that soon after DSK had been arrested, Diallo discussed with her fiancé DSK's ample financial resources. Since her fiancé was in prison on drug charges at the time, the conversation was recorded. While a victim is entitled to recover financial damages, this conversation might be used by DSK's lawyers in cross examination to suggest that she had had a financial motive. She was also vulnerable because she had made possible fraudulent statements elsewhere for financial gain. For example, she admitted that she repeatedly excluded her earnings from the Sofitel from her low-cost housing applications so as to be eligible for lower rent. After extensive interviews, the prosecutors noted "In sum, the complainant has been persistently, and at times inexplicably untruthful in describing matters of both great and small significance. In our repeated interviews with her, the complete truth about the charged incident and her background has, for that reason, remained elusive." Diallo was not a witness whose credibility they could recommend to a jury.

Nor did the other evidence prove that force had been used. The DNA samples taken from Diallo's clothing and the carpet of the interior hallway in the presidential suite showed that there had been a sexual encounter between Diallo and DSK, but they in themselves did not show that it was forced. Neither did the medical examinations. Diallo claimed that DSK had dragged her around the suite, but when both parties were examined at the hospital and scrapings were taken from under their fingernails, doctors could find no clear signs that force was used by DSK to overpower Diallo. Five weeks later, Diallo's lawyers reported that an MRI showed a "SLAP type 2 tear" in her left shoulder, but when the prosecutors' expert orthopedic surgeon examined the MRI, he concluded that the injury had not been sustained during her encounter with DSK, but well afterward, and in his opinion had been self-induced by "repeated overhead use of the upper extremity." So the prosecutor could find no medical evidence, other than an injury that its own expert said was caused by Diallo herself after the incident, that proved the encounter was not consensual.

By the end of July, Diallo had changed her story on this chronology at least three times, leaving it uncertain which, if any, of the versions was true. The prosecutors came to the conclusion that they could not bring the case to trial. In August, the task of preparing a recommendation for dismissal of all the charges was given to Assistant District Attorney Joan Illuzzi-Orbon, a well-regarded prosecutor who by June had become "second chair" to McConnell.

On August 22, the prosecutors submitted a twenty-five-page recommendation for dismissal of all the charges. It was signed by Illuzzi-Orbon and McConnell, who wrote in the submitted motion, "the nature and number of the complainant's falsehoods leave us unable to credit her version of events beyond a reasonable doubt." They said that Diallo "has given irreconcilable accounts of what happened," and had told untruths not only to the prosecutors but under oath to the grand jury about her whereabouts after the encounter. It was a startling turn of events for prosecutors to discredit their own star witness. The judge had little choice but to approve the motion. DSK had been indicted on the basis of testimony of a witness who had been untruthful under oath. DSK then left the court, an innocent man in the eyes of the law. (Diallo's later civil suit against DSK was settled in December 2012 for an undisclosed sum.)

But there may have been another crime committed in the effort to end DSK's political career. The French spy agency *Direction Centrale du Renseignement Intérieur*, or, as it is called, the DCRI, reportedly made DSK a target of its surveillance. According to the 2012 book *The President's Spy* by Didier Hassoux, Christophe Labbé, and Olivia Recasens, the director of the DCRI, Bernard Squarcini, had set up "a special group" in collaboration with the Élysée Palace (the French equivalent of the White House) to focus on DSK in March 2011—two months before he was arrested in New York. The authors, all investigative journalists with the French weekly *Le Point*, based their findings heavily on interviews they had with present and former members of the DCRI. They describe in detail the capabilities of the DCRI to intercept emails and to monitor tablets and computers. If this was true, Sarkozy's staff was likely privy to the intelligence that was being collected by the DCRI at the time DSK arrived at the Sofitel in New York. Such surveillance might also explain why, ninety seconds before his taxi pulled up to the Sofitel hotel at 7:08 p.m. on May 13, its arrival was apparently anticipated by the hotel staff.

There is also the mystery of DSK's missing IMF BlackBerry.

Twenty-three minutes after DSK departed the hotel, his phone was still there. But the police did not find it there when they searched the presidential suite. Nor was it found in the corridor, elevator, check-out desk, or lobby. The room was locked at 12:51 p.m. and not reopened until the police arrived later that afternoon. It is reasonable to conclude that some unknown party took the phone between 12:14 and 12:51 p.m.

Assuming the police search was thorough, and they were specifically looking for the phone, its disappearance presents a locked-room mystery. One possibility is that DSK left it behind in the rush to meet his daughter. That would account for the continued signals from the Sofitel. But if that was the case, the phone would have been found in the room after he departed at 12:26 p.m. We know that the door was locked, because Diallo swiped her key to reopen the suite at 12:26 p.m. Aside from Diallo, the only employees to use their electronic keys to enter the room were the head housekeeper, who entered the suite at 12:38 p.m. along with Diallo, according to her statement, and the head engineer, who entered the suite at 12:45 p.m. and a second time at 12:51 p.m. But none of these employees reported seeing the phone. Nor did the police who then entered the suite.

The other possibility is that the phone was taken before DSK had left the presidential suite. Since it is a large four-room suite—pantry, dining room, living room, and bedroom—it cannot be ruled out that someone else was in the suite, possibly even before Diallo had entered at 12:06 p.m. That person could have taken the phone from DSK's briefcase or elsewhere while he was getting dressed, and had it taken somewhere else in the Sofitel. In that case, the phone would continue to send out GPS signals from the hotel—as it did—until it was disabled at 12:51 p.m. The phone has never been found. We don't know who took it from the room, when it was taken, or why it stopped sending GPS signals at 12:51 p.m.

Another mystery proceeds from the key records. When analyzed together, the records produce three intriguing possible interventions.

First, there is a possible intruder in DSK's suite. DSK arrived at the Sofitel on the evening of May 13. At 7:13 p.m., after checking in, he used his newly issued electronic key to enter the presidential suite on the 28th floor. The suite had been prepared for him earlier in the afternoon, and the maid on duty, O.Y. Fong, had turned down the bed at 5:47 p.m. Then, at 6:13 p.m., just as DSK's plane was landing at the airport, a person entered the suite using the electronic key belonging to a Sofitel employee named A.C. Chowdhury. The hotel's personnel records, however, show that Chowdhury was not working that evening. If so, an unknown person used an employee's ID to gain entry. At 6:54 p.m., there was another unidentified entry by a person using the generic "HK1" key, kept in the housekeeping department. This key does not identify the individual.

Second, there is the issue of the double entry. A maid cannot clean a hotel room without the cleaning equipment on his or her cart. For that reason, a maid normally takes a cart to the room he or she is about to clean and leaves it parked outside the door of the room while cleaning it. On May 14, however, Diallo did not have her cart when she went to the presidential suite after noon. It will be recalled that she had left it in the room on the other side of the elevator bank, room 2820, where it remained until 12:26 p.m. Yet the key records show that Diallo entered the presidential suite not once but twice within one minute at 12:06 p.m. She entered the first time, according to her account, because a room-service waiter told her that the room was empty. Since the electronic key records do not record seconds, we do not know how much time she spent on her first visit or how much time she spent in the hall afterward.

The room-service waiter, Syed Haque, who had entered the room only one minute or less before Diallo's first entry, may possibly have still been in the suite. He told prosecutors that he had entered the suite to remove the breakfast dishes. These dishes were in the dining room at the far end of the suite. Wherever Haque was at 12:06 p.m., Diallo did not remain long after that first entry. It is also possible that she met someone else outside the suite between her first and second visits.

If she still intended to clean the room, she needed her cart of cleaning equipment. But she did not get that equipment. Instead, she returned to the presidential suite without it again. Whatever reason she had for returning to the room, she did so without the means to clean it.

Third, there is the issue of the room across the hall, 2820. If the prosecutors had been given the key records on May 14, room 2820 might have been less of a mystery. It was not until late June that the prosecutors learned that Diallo had gone into room 2820, and, by that time, the room had been rented out many times, and it was too late to find evidence. Prosecutors found her concealment of her presence "inexplicable." In doing so, she prevented the police from searching room 2820. It was not only Diallo who did not provide the authorities with this information about room 2820. The hotel would not identify the registered guest other than to say he was a "French businessman." There was no key entry between 11:37 a.m. and 12:26 p.m., so, if Diallo was telling the truth to the prosecutors in June that she ran directly to room 2820 after leaving the presidential suite, an unknown person in room 2820 may have opened the door for her at 12:13 p.m. But given Diallo's conflicting accounts, all that we really know for certain is what the electronic key records disclose: Diallo entered room 2820 three times before the registered guest left and once afterward at 12:26 p.m. We don't know if anyone else was in the room when she was there, why she left her equipment there before the guest had checked out, or, if her June version is true, how the door was opened at 12:13 a.m. without leaving a swipe record.

Finally, there is the issue of the time lapse. There was a gap of well over one hour between the time when Diallo had her encounter with DSK and the time that it was reported to the police. She had run out of the presidential suite when, or before, DSK called his daughter at 12:13 p.m. The 911 call by the Sofitel security chief was received at 1:32 p.m., according to the 911 report. This is a seventy-nine minute delay. Part of the gap was due to Diallo not immediately reporting the incident to anyone. First, at 12:26 p.m., as the key-card records show, she briefly went back into the presidential suite but did not stay to clean it. Then, approximately four minutes later, she asked a hypothetical question to another maid, and only when that maid asked whether the hypothetical situation had just happened to Diallo did Diallo state that she had been attacked by the guest in the presidential suite. This allegation was made at 12:30 p.m. But even after her outcry, there was a one-hour delay before the hotel staff reported it to police or attempted to get Diallo any medical attention. As a result, Diallo did not arrive at St. Luke's–Roosevelt Hospital until 3:57 p.m., nearly four hours after the alleged attack.

We know from CCTV videos, phone records, and police reports that members of the hotel staff, including the hotel's head engineer, a security guard, and the head of housekeeping, were heading up to the 28th floor within ten minutes of her outcry. By 12:37 p.m., according to key records, the head housekeeper and Diallo had reentered the presidential suite. They were joined at 12:45 p.m. by Yearwood and the security guard, and they remained there for approximately five minutes. If Diallo told them the same story she later told police, they knew only that she had been violently attacked by a naked man who came out of the bedroom of the presidential suite at about noon. Since Diallo had not previously seen DSK—she had not been on duty when DSK arrived the previous evening—she could not have known that he, and not an intruder, was the attacker. The hotel staff, according to prosecutors' documents, did not show her a photograph of DSK until 2:30 p.m., so, when they first heard her story, they could not rule out the possibility that an intruder had gotten into the suite after DSK had left it and attacked her. If that was true, it was possible that a criminal was still lurking in the hotel and could be a danger to others. That was reason enough to call the police immediately. In addition, they had to consider the well-being of their fellow employee. Diallo said she was dragged across a room and molested. Even if there were no visible injuries, she might require immediate medical attention or trauma counseling. The suite had a phone. Yet, instead of calling for police and medical help, they took Diallo downstairs, through the main lobby, and to a bench in the employees' entranceway across from the security office. Here, without any privacy or comfort, she waited for fifty minutes before the call was finally made.

During this wait, there was no interruption of communications. The CCTV videos show that both the head engineer and the security guard frequently used their cell phones. Yet no one from the hotel's human resources department, which deals with employee welfare, was brought down to talk to Diallo. If the hotel staff was waiting for some development, what was it?

One possibility is that Diallo was initially unwilling to file a complaint. Such a theory was suggested by Lanny Davis, the Washington lawyer retained by the Sofitel's owner, the Accor Group, in an interview on NBC's *Today Show* in December 2011. Presumably, as the crisis manager for the Sofitel, he had access to its employees. In attempting to explain the weird dance between the security guard and head engineer following the call to the police, Davis said it was possible that the two men were celebrating Diallo's finally agreeing at 1:30 p.m. "to allow the hotel to call 911." The implication is that for an hour she had not agreed to such a call. While such a scenario is possible, the prosecutors specifically cited the promptness of her outcry for help as a factor that made them believe her story. If she had been unwilling to make a complaint for over an hour, it raised the question of what or who changed her mind at 1:30 p.m.

Another possibility is that the hotel staff was awaiting authorization from a higher level before calling 911. After all, DSK was a possible future president of France, and making the 911 call would likely involve the French-owned hotel in a major scandal. The CCTV videos depict the head engineer and security guard almost constantly on their cell phones in the three minutes prior to the 911 call. The cell-phone records also show that Accor's chief of security in New York called Yearwood at 1:28 p.m. and also sent a text to the hotel manager, who then sped to the hotel on a motor scooter (arriving only seven minutes before the police). A flurry of cell-phone communications preceded the 911 call, and the employees at the hotel could have been influenced by these calls.

Ordinarily, a scandal is not good news for a first-class hotel. It is particularly onerous if it involves the arrival of uniformed police in the lobby, authorities subpoenaing CCTV videos, and the sealing off of VIP rooms with yellow tape as crime scenes. For the security staff, it can also mean many hours of work preparing incident reports and being questioned by police, prosecutors, defense lawyers, and management. Given such consequences, it is not clear why two hotel employees would engage in the sort of victory dance that would be appropriate after a touchdown in a football game. Yet the security guard and the head engineer at the Sofitel did such a dance following the call to the police. They did not do this dance in the view of others; instead, they went into a loading-dock area, where no one in the security area could see them.

Neither man has offered an explanation for the dance. According to an Accor Group spokesman, they both said their minds were blank on the subject and they could not recall the dance. So we do not know what made both men suddenly go to a private area and dance at 1:34 p.m. We do know that these two men had been working together throughout that day, as can be seen on the CCTV videos, and that they had many earlier opportunities to high-five each other but didn't. No significant sports event ended at 1:34 p.m. What did happen at that time was that the 911 dispatcher said she was sending a squad car to the hotel.

The unresolved mystery of what brought about the downfall of the man who seemed likely to become the next president of France has given rise to three main theories. First, there is the theory that DSK himself was the sole author of his disgrace in New York. According to this view, DSK forcibly attempted to rape Diallo and did everything else attributed to him in the dismissed indictment. Whatever delayed her outcry to the police and led her to give false testimony to the grand jury were innocent mistakes. The other anomalies, such as the unidentified semen and saliva stains in the presidential suite, were irrelevant coincidences, as was DSK's missing phone, the multiple entries in his suite, and the near encounters he had with the head engineer when he arrived and departed from the hotel. Second, there is the theory that DSK was set-up by parties acting on behalf of Sarkozy to derail his presidential bid. According to this view, Diallo was sent into the room because of his known attraction towards woman, and when he took the bait, the trap was sprung. He was thus the victim, albeit a willing one, of a well-orchestrated conspiracy. The third theory was that there was an after-the-fact conspiracy, set in motion only after his sexual encounter with the maid, to shape the incident so that it would lead to his arrest and imprisonment. In this view, DSK had been under surveillance by French intelligence since March to find information that could be used to discredit him. To this end, freelancers, including individuals possibly working at the hotel, were used to track his activities and to take his phone once he realized it was compromised and arranged to have examined. Then, when the maid voiced a complaint against DSK after he checked out, the operatives helped her articulate an incriminating story and convinced her to go to the police. Once that had been accomplished, the after-the-fact conspirators provided information about DSK that led prosecutors to argue against bail, which irreparably destroyed his candidacy.

After reviewing the evidence and speaking to DSK and some of the prosecutors, my assessment is that the court acted correctly in dismissing all the charges against DSK. While DSK might have acted crudely and reprehensively, I do not believe that there is any credible evidence that he committed a crime at the Sofitel Hotel. On the other hand, there was another crime committed that day: an after-the-fact conspiracy to shape and alter the event so as to destroy DSK's career. As the prosecutors themselves established, DSK's humiliating imprisonment proceeded from an indictment based on false testimony given under oath to the grand jury by its principal witness, Diallo. That witness concealed important information from the police about her activities. But why? It is clear to me from viewing the CCTV videos that she met with a number of people in the hotel, including potential witnesses, both in the presidential suite and the security area, during the one hour and fifty minutes that elapsed between her leaving DSK's suite and the arrival of the police. We also know both from her statements and CCTV videos that she engaged in several reenactments of the incidents. While we don't know what was said, she had an opportunity to modify, if not change, elements of her story to fit in with other considerations during this critical period. The otherwise-inexplicable omissions and untrue parts of her testimony about her movements may have been the result of these considerations. We now know that she initially was reluctant to go to the police. It was only after an hour that she agreed to making the report that would bring DSK down. The prosecutors could have pursued the issue of when and why she changed her story, since falsely testifying to a grand jury could constitute a felony, but they chose not to go into that potential minefield. Consequently, what influenced her remains part of the mystery.

From my discussions with former CIA and NSA officials, I also have no doubt that French intelligence had the capability to intercept DSK's communications and monitor his movements in both Washington, D.C., and New York. Further, it is now clear from the work done by French journalists that DSK had been a target of French surveillance at the time. I therefore believe it to be likely that French intelligence learned through its contacts at the hotel before the police were called that DSK had a potential problem. If so, French intelligence could take full advantage of the situation by making sure that it proved an acute embarrassment to DSK and badly damaged his ambitions. And, in my view, French operatives did intervene on both May 14 and May 15.

The riposte to this is that Sarkozy did not need to use the New York incident to derail DSK because he could use a prostitution scandal in France to achieve the same objective. The problem here, however, is the chronology. As early as March 2011, French authorities were tracking DSK's participation in a series of sex parties with French prostitutes operating out of the Carlton Hotel in Lille. The organizers included three associates of DSK: Jean-Christophe Lagarde, the police commissioner for the Lille region; David Roquet, an executive of the French construction group Eiffage; and Fabrice Paszkowski, the owner of a medical supply company. The fact that DSK, a possible presidential candidate, had attended ten or more of these sex parties with prostitutes, made it a high-profile case when DSK attended the last such party at the W Hotel in Washington, D.C., on May 12. There is no doubt that French operatives were aware of these liaisons, since bugs had been placed on the phones that DSK and his associates were using. In light of the relations between French intelligence and the Élysées Palace, it seems inconceivable that Sarkozy's staff did not know about DSK's attendance at these parties. But attendance in itself did not constitute a crime in France, where it is legal to use the services of prostitutes and to attend sex parties. Moreover, if Sarkozy's forces revealed the salacious details of these parties in the midst of the run-up to the election, the revelation could backfire by exposing the fact that French intelligence was spying on the head of the IMF. So, up until May 14, 2011, Sarkozy's forces had potentially compromising spying that they could not safely use. Indeed, they did not get the evidence they sought until September 2011, five months after the Sofitel incident, when the three organizers of the Lille sex parties suggested DSK may have been complicit in procuring women for the parties, a possible criminal offense. As DSK had been rising in the polls that May, and Sarkozy forces could not be certain in which direction the sex-party case would go, the accusation of DSK at the Sofitel of a crime that would be pursued by American authorities presented a way of derailing him before he gained the nomination. And it succeeded. In my view, the true crime in the DSK case was the manipulation of the American justice system.

CHAPTER 33

THE MACDONALD MASSACRE

When military police arrived at the Fort Bragg, North Carolina, home of Captain Jeffrey MacDonald at 3:50 a.m. on February 17, 1970, they found a bloody massacre. Captain MacDonald, a twenty-seven-year old military doctor, had multiple wounds, including stab wounds in his stomach and chest, and a collapsed lung. His pregnant wife, Colette, twenty-seven, was lying dead in a pool of blood. Their two daughters, Kimberley, six, and Kristen, three, had been beaten and stabbed to death. The word "pig" was scrawled in blood on a wall. There were apparent signs of a struggle, including a table standing on end, magazines strewn around the room, and torn clothing. They also found three possible weapons—a paring knife, an ice pick, and a club. When Macdonald was revived by the military police through mouth-to-mouth resuscitation, he gave a descriptions of three men and a blond woman who he said broke in and attacked him. He said that the woman wore boots and a floppy wide-brimmed hat, and held a candle.

The gory murder scene itself lent itself to two theories. The first one, based on MacDonald's story, was that home invaders had broken in and attacked him while he slept on the couch. Such home invasions happened in that era. Just about six months earlier in Los Angeles, the Charles Manson "family" had broken into two homes and murdered seven people, including the actress Sharon Tate. They had also written the word "pig" in blood. Since Fort Bragg was an open base, anyone, including drug-crazed murderers, could have broken into the MacDonald home that night.

The second theory is that MacDonald, the lone surviving member of the family, murdered his pregnant wife and daughters. He then staged the appearance of a hippie home invasion by upsetting furniture, throwing objects around, writing "pig" in blood, and inflicting multiple deep wounds on himself. According to police statistics of spousal murders, the husband is usually the perpetrator, especially if he was at home at the time of the murder.

Husbands become prime suspects in such cases because they have the opportunity and the means (in the form of household knives, ice picks, and blunt instruments) and a possible motive to kill their wives, even if it is only a domestic spat. Often, as seen in the Dr. Sam Sheppard case, husbands claim that the deed was done by strangers. But if none are immediately found, the husband almost automatically becomes the focus of the investigation. (On this logic, Roman Polanski, the husband of Sharon Tate, would have been a suspect if he had not been in London shooting a movie at the time of the crime.)

In the MacDonald case, even when Captain MacDonald was still in the hospital, military investigators proceeded on this latter theory. In May 1970, MacDonald was brought before an Article 32 hearing, the military equivalent of a grand jury, presided over by Colonel Warren V. Rock. Since military investigators could find no apparent motive, the only evidence they presented was of staging. Their expert witness testified that multiple experiments persuaded him that the coffee table at the crime scene could not have landed on its edge as a result of a fight, and that therefore MacDonald had arranged it in that position to simulate the appearance of a home invasion. At that point, Colonel Rock went to the crime scene and, to settle the matter, kicked the coffee table once. It landed on its edge, and he dismissed the case against MacDonald for lack of evidence.

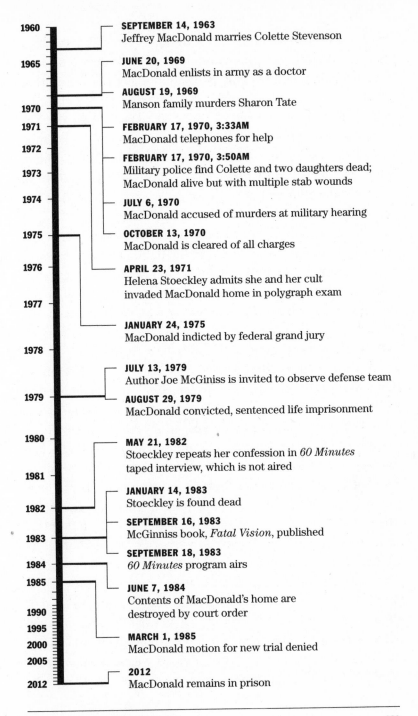

SEPTEMBER 14, 1963
Jeffrey MacDonald marries Colette Stevenson

JUNE 20, 1969
MacDonald enlists in army as a doctor

AUGUST 19, 1969
Manson family murders Sharon Tate

FEBRUARY 17, 1970, 3:33AM
MacDonald telephones for help

FEBRUARY 17, 1970, 3:50AM
Military police find Colette and two daughters dead;
MacDonald alive but with multiple stab wounds

JULY 6, 1970
MacDonald accused of murders at military hearing

OCTOBER 13, 1970
MacDonald is cleared of all charges

APRIL 23, 1971
Helena Stoeckley admits she and her cult
invaded MacDonald home in polygraph exam

JANUARY 24, 1975
MacDonald indicted by federal grand jury

JULY 13, 1979
Author Joe McGiniss is invited to observe defense team

AUGUST 29, 1979
MacDonald convicted, sentenced life imprisonment

MAY 21, 1982
Stoeckley repeats her confession in *60 Minutes*
taped interview, which is not aired

JANUARY 14, 1983
Stoeckley is found dead

SEPTEMBER 16, 1983
McGinniss book, *Fatal Vision*, published

SEPTEMBER 18, 1983
60 Minutes program airs

JUNE 7, 1984
Contents of MacDonald's home are
destroyed by court order

MARCH 1, 1985
MacDonald motion for new trial denied

2012
MacDonald remains in prison

After MacDonald reentered civilian life, he was indicted by a Federal grand jury for the murders in 1975. It then took four years to adjudicate his claims of double jeopardy and other procedural issues, so the trial did not commence until nine years after the crime itself. At the trial, experts from the FBI crime lab presented more sophisticated evidence of staging, including the alignment of puncture wounds in his clothing, which convinced a jury that he was guilty. On August 29, 1979, he was convicted of first-degree murder and sentenced to life imprisonment.

The prosecution's successful narrative of the crime was then so thoroughly established in the public mind by massive media attention, including Joe McGinniss' best-selling book *Fatal Vision*, a TV miniseries, a *60 Minutes* investigation, and Janet Malcolm's book *The Journalist and the Murderer*, that most people, including myself, assumed there was no reasonable doubt of his guilt. It appeared to be a closed case.

But in 2012, Errol Morris, an Academy Award–winning filmmaker and former private investigator, published his book *A Wilderness of Error: The Trials of Jeffrey MacDonald*. It is based on an extraordinary investigation, documented with a wealth of affidavits, diagrams, and interview transcripts, and pursues the other theory—that a home invasion had been neglected by police for over forty years. He found several witnesses who saw a girl matching MacDonald's description of the girl with a candle, including Kenneth Mica, the MP officer who first answered the call to go to the MacDonald house. As he raced home at 3:30 a.m., he recalled seeing a young woman in a wide-brimmed floppy hat. Then six other witnesses identified Helena Stoeckley, a twenty-eight-year-old drug user, self-styled witch, and narcotics informer, as a person wearing such a hat that night. One police officer, for whom she worked as an informer, saw her in such a hat, a blond wig, and white boots arriving home that morning in the company of a group of men.

So did a neighbor. She eventually admitted to no fewer than six people that she was in the MacDonald home on the night of the murder, high on drugs, accompanied by three male Vietnam veterans. She also recalled such details of the home invasion as holding a candle, riding a broken toy rocking horse in the home, and answering the MacDonalds' phone. (A soldier named Jimmy Friar told the FBI that he had called the Mac-Donald number and heard the woman who answered break into hysterical laughter when he asked for Dr. MacDonald and then hang up.) Not only did Stoeckley pass a lie detector test; one of the veterans she named, Greg Mitchell, had written, according to three witnesses, in bright red paint on a white wall in the farmhouse where he was staying, "I killed the MacDonald's wife [sic] and children."

Stoeckley gave her account in an 1982 interview taped for CBS's *60 Minutes*. She told of how she taken a large amount of mescaline that night, wore a blond wig, hat, and boots, and went from room to room with a candle. "I entered the [Mac-Donald] house with another member of the cult. There were three members there already, talking with Dr. MacDonald." Then she said "someone knocked him unconscious" and other cult members were beating his wife. After the phone call, she recalls that the group left in two cars. Morris cites a half-dozen other witnesses who spotted Stoeckley and her confederates earlier and later that night.

Yet the jury never heard Stoeckley's account. Instead, as Morris discovered, Stoeckley was reportedly discouraged from testifying, when she arrived at the courthouse, by the assistant U.S. attorney, James Blackburn. This alleged warning emerged only in 2005, when Jimmy B. Britt, the U.S. marshal charged with bringing Stoeckley to the courthouse for the trial, came forth. In his affidavit, Britt said that on arriving at the courthouse with Stoeckley, he first brought her to see Blackburn. He then witnessed her giving Blackburn a detailed confession, essentially the same story that she had told Britt on their trip to the courthouse. Then, according to Britt, Blackburn told her that if she repeated that story under oath in court, he would indict her for first degree murder. (Blackburn, who was disbarred in 1993 for ethical transgression, denies Britt's account.) When she appeared in court, she totally changed her story, saying now that she could not recall ever being in the MacDonald house. Without her testimony, the defense could not call the corroborating witnesses.

Nor was her confession ever broadcast on CBS's *60 Minutes*. CBS producers decided against airing it. Instead, the *60 Minutes* report focused on McGinness's sensational story of a drug-crazed doctor who slaughtered his family. Stoeckley's confession would undercut the program's narrative line, and, by 1982, the accepted conventional wisdom was that MacDonald would not have been convicted if he were innocent.

We are left with the same two theories that existed four decades ago, but thanks to Morris, more evidence as to what happened. However abhorrent the idea may be of an innocent man spending his life in prison, I believe that the evidence now supports the intruder theory. To be sure, the prosecutors made a powerful case for the husband-did-it theory and for the claim that the crime scene had been staged. That assertion was seemingly substantiated after from the testimony of expert witnesses interpreting the results of complex experiments conducted at the FBI crime lab. One FBI fiber expert testified, for example, that the neat pattern of puncture wounds in MacDonald's clothes indicated that, in his opinion, the shirt was stabbed when he was not wearing it. Morris, however, found that many of the experiment results were distorted by cherry-picking the parts that supported the staging narrative and omitting those consistent with the break-in narrative. Such distortions are not unheard of at the FBI crime lab: In 1997, a Justice Department historic review of the FBI lab's work discovered some 3,000 such suspect incidents of misconduct. In any case, even if taken at their face value, the experiments proved not that MacDonald killed his family but that his account was inconsistent with clues found at the scene. But as MacDonald was woozy when resuscitated, trauma alone—and not murder—could account for his lack of clarity.

My assessment of the evidence is that home invaders, including Helena Stoeckley and her boyfriend Greg Mitchell, murdered the wife and children of Jeffrey MacDonald. We have an eyewitness evidence of a break-in in the statements of Helena Stoeckley. Mitchell corroborated part of her account by writing that he murdered MacDonald's family on the wall of the house in which he was staying.

There was also a motive for the break-in, according to Stoeckley. She said that her friends were seeking drugs at the MacDonald house. Since he was a doctor, this is a plausible motive. Her claim that the violence began when MacDonald attempted to call the police is also plausible, since MacDonald, a trained Green Beret, would no doubt respond to the break-in. It also seems likely that once the violent rampage began, the "cult," as she describes her friends, imitated elements of the then-notorious Manson murders by painting the word "pig" on the wall. As there were unidentified fingerprints found in the house—which were accidently destroyed by a military technician before they could be compared with prints of people outside the household—it is not possible to preclude such a home invasion. I am also persuaded by elements of Stoeckley's story that were later confirmed, such as candle drippings on the floor that did not chemically match any candles found in the MacDonald home, twenty-four-inch Dacron strands found on a hairbrush that did not match anything owned by the MacDonald family but were consistent with strands in the type of blond wig Stoeckley wore, and the finding of a witness who confirmed details of the phone conversation described by

Stoeckley. The police chose the path of least resistance in focusing on MacDonald, as is often the case in a domestic crime, but in doing so they woefully neglected the counter-narrative of a home invasion. Francis Bacon summed up the problem bedeviling this case four centuries ago when he wrote in *Novum Organum* that "The human understanding when it has once adopted an opinion ... draws all things else to support and agree with it. And though there be a greater number and weight of instances to be found on the other side, yet these it either neglects or despises, or else by some distinction sets aside or rejects." It took a truly extraordinary book by the documentarian Errol Morris to break the journalistic paradigm that had congealed around this case. Even though MacDonald remains in prison, it is, in my view, a miscarriage of justice.

CHAPTER 34

THE KNOX ORDEAL

On the night of November 1, 2007, Meredith Kercher, a twenty-one-year-old exchange student from South London, was murdered in a cottage on the Via della Pergola in the ancient university city of Perugia in Umbria, Italy. Her body was found by police the next day, locked in her ground-floor bedroom and covered in a blood-soaked quilt. She had deep stab wounds in her neck. The only clothing on her body was a cotton shirt pulled up to the neck. Bruises indicated that she had been held down, and there was male DNA in her body, indicating possible rape. The exact time of death could not be determined because the coroner had not been allowed to immediately take the body's temperature. The autopsy could only establish a time frame for the death, between 8:55 p.m. and 12:50 a.m. There was also evidence of a burglary, since house keys, money, cell phones, and credit cards were missing and a ten-pound rock had been thrown through the window of the adjoining room. When the crime scene was further processed, fingerprints, palm prints, and semen were found that did not match any of the residents of the cottage. There was also a footprint of a Nike sneaker in blood. Two witnesses had seen a young black man running down Via della Pergola from the direction of the cottage at 10:30 p.m. They said that he nearly collided with them.

The black man seen running away might have been sought as a suspect if the investigators from the police's "flying squad" believed that an outsider had killed Meredith, but, within hours of finding the body, they concluded that all the evidence of burglary, including the broken window, strewn clothing, and missing belongings, had been staged to mislead them. For one thing, some of the glass fragments of the window had landed on top of the clothing on the floor, indicating that the rock had been thrown through the window *after* and not before the crime, and probably from inside the room. For another thing, it seemed unlikely that an intruder had climbed the 11.5-foot wall to enter through the window when he could have broken a lower window for entry. The investigators therefore assumed that it was an inside job done by someone who lived in the cottage.

The insider theory narrowed the police investigation down to just seven suspects: four young Italian students who rented rooms in the basement of the house, where they grew Cannabis plants; and, upstairs, Filomena Romanelli, Laura Mezzetti, and Amanda Knox, who, along with the victim, shared the ground-floor flat. Each of the women had a separate bedroom that could be locked from the outside only with a key. As it then turned out, it was a holiday week in Italy, and all four of the Italian men had gone away that weekend to visit their families (and they had asked Meredith to water their Cannabis plants). Romanelli and Mezzetti, both legal trainees in their late twenties, were also away and had solid alibis. That left only one other suspect, Amanda Knox, a twenty-year-old American student from Seattle, who was at the house when the police arrived, kissing her boyfriend Raffaele Sollecito. She was stunningly beautiful. Knox's alibi was provided by Sollecito, whom she had met the previous week at a classical musical recital. The two told police that they were together at Sollecito's nearby flat all night. According to Knox, they had smoked marijuana, watched a DVD of the French movie *Amélie*, and slept together. She claimed she only returned to her apartment at 11:00 a.m the next morning to change her clothing, and that she then noticed blood in the shower. Even though Sollecito initially fully supported her alibi, during the three days of interrogation, he changed his story, now saying that Knox had left his apartment at 9:00 p.m. to go to a bar, Le Chic, where she worked, and that she did not return until after midnight. So neither of them had an alibi for the time when Kercher was murdered. Under intensive interrogation, in which Knox was threatened with imprisonment, and without being given a lawyer, she also altered her story, suddenly implicating Patrick Lumumba, the Congo-born owner of the Le Chic bar. She told police that Lumumba had murdered her flatmate. On November 6, police arrested Knox, Sollecito and Lumumba for the murder of Meredith Kercher. Even though Knox subsequently retracted her accusation, claiming that she had been traumatized by police threats, the theory of the prosecutors now was that the murder proceeded from an orgy that got out of control. But a problem developed when a Swiss professor, who had been at the Le Chic bar on November 1, swore that he had had an extended conversation with Lumumba during the time the murder was committed. In light of this alibi, and Knox's admission that she had falsely accused him, Lumumba had to be released.

Meanwhile, on November 15, the prints in Kercher's room were identified. They belonged to Rudy Guede, a twenty-year-old unemployed gardener from Ivory Coast. His palm print was clearly visible on the bloodstained pillow under Kercher's hips. His DNA was found on her clothes and inside her vagina. He also wore Nike Outbreak 2 sneakers that were consistent with the bloody footprint on the floor. In addition, he also fit the description of the man seen running down the street at 10:30 p.m. He also had knowledge of the cottage. He had met the Italian men living downstairs in the cottage in mid-October while playing basketball, and in the week of the murder he went to the apartment to watch an auto race and smoke hash with them. On that occasion, he met both Kercher and Knox.

This hard evidence unambiguously established that Guede

was in Kercher's room, had sexual contact with her, and left the room after her blood was spilled. According to witnesses, he also had been involved in other recent break-ins in Perugia and Milan. In September 2007, a witness said that Guede had broken into his home in Perugia (through a window) at 6:00 a.m. on the morning after the murder, brandished a knife, and stole his credit cards. On October 13, he apparently broke into a lawyer's office in Perugia through a second-story window and took a laptop and cell phone (which were later found in his backpack). Less than one week before the murder, he had been briefly detained by police in Milan for breaking into a nursery and stealing an eleven-inch kitchen knife.

Guede, who had fled to Germany, was extradited. But by that time Amanda Knox had become such a focus of the media's attention, and the putative sex games by an angel-faced killer such a cornerstone of the story, that the prosecutors, even after releasing Patrick Lumumba, were not about to abandon their group murder theory.

To maintain his theory, chief prosecutor Giuliano Mignini posited a conspiracy by teaming up the two insiders, Knox and Sollecito, with the outside burglar, Guede. Mignini had previously achieved considerable notoriety in Italy in the 2001 "Monster of Florence" case when he unsuccessfully attempted to attribute the suicide of a Perugian doctor to a secret satanic cult. Now, he proposed a similar satanic scenario in which Guede, Sollecito, and Knox went to the cottage together and then attempted to force Kercher to have sex with them. When she refused, Guede and Sollecito took turns molesting her. Knox, who he described as a "she-devil," then stabbed her to death.

One stumbling block was the total absence of evidence that Guede was with either Knox or Sollecito, or that he ever had ever met Sollecito. While two witnesses had seen Guede run away, no one had seen Knox or Sollecito with him at the cottage. Nor did Guede claim that either Knox or Sollecito were with him. His story was that Kercher herself had invited him to the cottage at about 9:00 p.m. They then had consensual sexual contact, but, lacking a condom, he left the room and went to the bathroom. When he emerged, he saw an unknown man run out of the cottage, and he found Meredith bleeding. So he ran away. In light of the abundance of evidence against Guede, he was convicted of murder in a separate "fast track" trial. The investigation had trouble even placing Sollecito in the cottage. The police failed to find a single print in the room that was Sollecito's or, for that matter, Knox's. Since Guede's prints were found in the room, it was difficult to explain he had washed them away. In addition, the speculation that the bloody footprint came from Sollecito's Nike proved wrong. It was from Guede's Nike sneaker. So up until mid-December 2007, the police and prosecutors could not place either Knox or Sollecito at the murder scene. This gap was bridged by a belated DNA analysis of Kercher's bra clasp (which had accidently remained at the crime scene for forty-six days). DNA on it matched Sollecito's.

DNA analysis also identified both Knox's and Kercher's DNA on a kitchen knife in a cutlery drawer in Sollecito's home. No blood was found on it, and, it later developed, the blade was too long to be the murder weapon (which was never found). Even so, Knox said she never removed the knife from Sollecito's home, nor did Kercher ever visit Sollecito's home. So the presence of her DNA on it suggested that Sollecito took it to the cottage on the night of the murder.

In the trial, which began January 16, 2009, the prosecutor painted a gory picture of a "she-devil" who tortured her roommate with a knife while Sollecito and Guede sexually abused her, and who, when the orgy ended, slashed her throat and staged a burglary to dupe the police. This story was based largely on the DNA evidence of Sollecito's presence at the scene. Both Knox and Sollecito were convicted of both murder and sexual violence. In December 2009, Knox was sentenced to twenty-six years' imprisonment, and Sollecito to twenty-five years' imprisonment.

The case was then appealed, and an independent panel of forensic experts was appointed to review the crucial DNA evidence. It found in its 145-page report that the collection of the DNA evidence linking Sollecito to the crime scene had been egregiously flawed. Not only was the DNA testimony not consistent with the actual lab reports, but a video showed that the key items were picked up with a dirty glove that might have transferred DNA samples from the suspects to them. So cross-contamination was possible. That left no credible evidence, and on October 3, 2011, the court threw out the murder and sexual violence convictions of Sollecito and Knox. Both were immediately released from prison, and, in a happy ending, Knox flew back to America and got a book contract.

There are still three theories about the murder. First, the inside-job theory advocated by the prosecutors, who are appealing the acquittal. Second, the lone-burglar theory that holds that Rudy Guede broke into the cottage and encountered and killed Kercher. Third, the two-burglar theory, based on an alleged jailhouse confession that Guede made to a fellow prisoner (who testified at the appeals hearing).

My assessment is that Amanda Knox and Raffaele Sollecito are both innocent of the murder. The police investigation was wedded from the outset to the wrong narrative. It assumed that the crime scene had been staged to look like a burglary and so focused on the only available insider, Knox. In doing so, the police neglected eyewitness sightings of a possible black burglar running from the direction of the house at the approximate time of the crime. If they had investigated that obvious lead, it would have quickly led them to Rudy Guede, who the other residents in the house could identify. His fingerprints, palm prints, sneaker print, and DNA would have established him beyond a doubt as a person at the bloody scene, and he likely would have been arrested before he had a chance to flee to Germany.

Guede had the opportunity, means, and motive to commit the crime alone. He had been to the cottage earlier that week to watch a sports event, so he could have cased it for a later burglary when its residents went on holiday over the long November 1 weekend. He was experienced in such jobs, since he had broken into three other places that fall. There were a number of ways that he could have entered the cottage. It is possible that, with the help of a box, he climbed through the broken window. He could also have easily scaled the grate in the rear of the cottage and entered through the empty basement apartment (where Kercher had agreed to water the Cannabis plants). Alternatively, he could have gone in through a lower window. Afterward, he might have smashed the window from the inside to create an expedient means of exit, especially if he was in a panic. His DNA was found in Kercher's pocketbook and credit cards and 300 euros were missing, which he likely took. And, with a small pocketknife, he had the means to force Kercher to the floor and stab her. In short, there was no evidence at the murder scene to show that this was not the work of a single home invader.

The appeals court stated that the murder and sexual-violence charges against Knox and were "not corroborated by any objective element of evidence." The lesson here is that denying a suspect a lawyer can result in egregious injustice. If Amanda Knox had been provided with a lawyer, she would not have been allowed to succumb to police pressure and give untrue statements that resulted in her arrest, as well as the arrest of two other innocent people. Meanwhile, forensic evidence would have unambiguously identified the perpetrator as Rudy Guede. There would then be no need for a prosecutor to conjure up an orgy out of thin air.

THE ENDURING MYSTERY
OF THE JFK ASSASSINATION

The jigsaw puzzle surrounding the assassination of President John F. Kennedy has taken me more than four decades to understand. I began my effort in 1965 at a time when it was generally believed that the Warren Commission had left no stone unturned in arriving at its conclusion that the assassin Lee Harvey Oswald had acted alone. Then one of the Commission's lawyers, J. Wesley Liebeler, turned over to me two file cases of records, which included work logs and internal memoranda documenting the Commission's work, as well as FBI reports furnished to the Commission, which demonstrated the Commission's investigation was anything but exhaustive. In its rush to issue its report before the 1964 election, the commission left many areas not fully investigated, including Oswald's possible involvement with foreign intelligence services—particularly those of Cuba and the Soviet Union.

In 1974 the United States Senate Select Committee to Study Governmental Operations with Respect to Intelligence Activities, headed by Senator Frank Church, began releasing information about CIA plots to assassinate Fidel Castro, which led me to investigate U.S. entanglements with the Cuban intelligence service shortly before JFK was assassinated. Further information was released through Freedom of Information requests, including ones that I had filed, and, finally, on June 23,

1998, the CIA released its own inspector general's report on these assassination conspiracies. There were also defectors from Castro's intelligence service, some of whom are interviewed in Wilfried Huismann and Gus Russo's 2006 documentary *Rendezvous With Death*, who furnished another key piece of the puzzle. As a result, after nearly fifty years, we now know that there were two different assassins at work on November 22, 1963. This is the story of their deadly dance—and how it tragically ended.

I. THE TARGETS

Fidel Castro Ruz was born out of wedlock in rural Cuba on August 13, 1926, the son of a wealthy landowner. After attending a Jesuit-run college, he studied law at the University of Havana, where he became deeply involved in revolutionary movements. He organized revolutionary activists both in Cuba and abroad, and in the 1950s he participated himself in armed attacks on government forces in Colombia, the Dominican Republic, and Cuba. He was captured during his attempt to seize the Moncada Barracks outside of Havana in 1953 and served a year in prison. Then, in 1955, he went from Cuba to Mexico. There he, along with his younger brother Raul and Che Guevara, an Argentinian revolutionary, formed a group aimed at overthrowing the American-backed dictator of Cuba, Fulgencio Batista. It was called the "26 of July Movement."

On November 15, 1956, Castro and eighty-one of his followers armed with rifles, pistols, and three machine guns, sailed on a small yacht named *Granma* from Tuxplan, Mexico, to Playa Las Coloradas in eastern Cuba. They landed in a mangrove swamp, and most of his force was killed or captured by Batista's army. But Castro, along with nineteen others, survived, escaping into the thickly forested Sierra Maestra mountains.

EDWARD JAY EPSTEIN

Rebuilding his force, Castro waged a successful two-year guerrilla war, and on New Year's Eve in 1958, Batista fled Cuba.

Castro then proceeded to appoint avowed Marxists to key cabinet posts and made Che Guevara the governor of the Central Bank and then the minister of industries. Next, with help from the Soviet Union's KGB, he organized a foreign-intelligence service, the Dirección General de Inteligencia, or DGI, which his brother Raul staffed personally with his close confederates. Even though the Cold War was raging between the United States and the USSR, Castro agreed to provide the USSR with sugar in return for crude oil. He added insult to injury by ordering American companies in Cuba to refine the Soviet crude. When they refused, he nationalized them, and then most other U.S.-owned assets in Cuba. Not only did America retaliate with an embargo on trade with Cuba, but President Dwight D. Eisenhower secretly authorized the CIA to covertly overthrow Castro in 1960.

Castro was now engaged in a life and death covert war with the United States. At stake was not only the survival of his regime in Cuba—but, as he came to realize, his own life.

When John F. Kennedy was elected in 1960, he was only forty-three, and would shortly become America's second-youngest president—only Theodore Roosevelt had been younger—and the first president born in the twentieth century. He brought with him to the White House a thirty-one-year-old wife, Jacqueline Bouvier Kennedy, a socially prominent photographer known to the world as "Jackie," as well as a three-year-old daughter, Caroline, and an infant son, John. JFK also brought to Washington so many men of distinction, including thought-provoking academics from his alma mater, Harvard, that journalists began describing his administration as "Camelot."

Behind the Camelot aura that permeated the public's

perception lay a vexing problem: Castro had installed a Marxist government in Cuba. No sooner had JFK been inaugurated in January 1961 than he was briefed by his national security adviser on the urgent need to unseat the regime in Havana. In the assessment made by U.S. intelligence, with every day that passed Castro was moving closer to America's Cold War enemy, the Soviet Union, and it was only a matter of months before Castro gave it military and intelligence-gathering outposts ninety miles from Florida. The CIA had already been authorized by JFK's predecessor, Dwight D. Eisenhower, to bring about regime change in Cuba. The plan involved using a 1,400-man force of Cuban exiles trained by the CIA in Guatemala for an invasion of a remote area of Cuba, which would be followed by air strikes by U.S. bombers. A CIA-backed "United Revolutionary Front" in Miami would then establish, in the territory held by Cuban exiles, a "government" that the U.S. immediately would recognize. The idea was that this government could call for U.S. help. JFK approved a modified version of the plan, and on April 17, 1961, a brigade of some 1,300 Cuban exiles landed at the Bay of Pigs on the island's southern coast. But JFK decided against providing U.S. air support, which allowed Castro's army to quickly encircle the brigade. Ninety exiles were killed and the other 1,200 surrendered and were held for ransom, requiring a humiliated Kennedy Administration to negotiate a deal for their release. Even though JFK's brother, Attorney General Robert F. Kennedy, was able to persuade U.S. pharmaceutical companies to give Castro $53 million worth of medicine and baby food in exchange for the prisoners, the invasion was a clear defeat for JFK.

Meanwhile, to deal with Castro on his own terms, JFK set up in the White House the "Special Group (Augmented)," headed by his brother Robert, to use covert tactics to dispose of Castro. Infuriated by this humiliating failure, Kennedy summoned the CIA's director of clandestine operations, Richard

Bissell, to the Cabinet Room and chided him for "sitting on my ass and not doing anything about getting rid of Castro and the Castro regime," as later Bissell testified.

The name of the CIA unit responsible for covert actions against Cuba was changed from JM WAVE to the Special Affairs Section, or, as it was called in CIA memos, SAS. The CIA executive who became its head was Desmond FitzGerald, a trusted ally of Robert Kennedy. His rugged good looks and surname led many people in Washington to mistakenly believe he was a distant relative of John Fitzgerald Kennedy. In February 1962, JFK approved "Operation Mongoose," which covert warfare specialist general Edward Lansdale would run under the supervision of Attorney General Robert Kennedy.

As part of the Kennedy-led reorganization of the CIA, Bissell was replaced by Richard Helms, a career CIA officer, who described Operation Mongoose as a "no-holds-barred" enterprise. It included such "planning tasks" as using biological and chemical warfare against Cuban sugar workers; employing Cuban gangsters to kill Cuban police officials, Soviet bloc technicians, and other people; using infiltrators to sabotage mines; and, in what was called "Operation Bounty," paying cash payments of up to $100,000 for the murder or abduction of government officials.

Castro responded by allowing the Soviet Union to establish missile bases in Cuba. The first shipment of medium-range missiles armed with megaton nuclear warheads arrived on September 8, 1962, followed by a second shipment the next week. Then, on October 15, 1962, high-altitude photographs taken by the CIA's U-2 planes revealed the presence of these missiles in Cuba, which nearly led to a nuclear confrontation between the Soviet Union and the United States. Threatened with nuclear war, the Soviet Union withdrew all forty-two missiles, and the United States agreed not to intervene in Cuban affairs.

Although this deal ended the missile crisis and Operation

Mongoose, JFK was still determined to eliminate Castro. The point man remained FitzGerald at the CIA's SAS. Initially, FitzGerald assumed that the technological ingenuity of the CIA's workshop would produce a means either to discredit or to kill Castro. Since Castro was an avid diver and seashell collector, it worked on a booby-trapped seashell. The idea was to place it where Castro frequently swam underwater in the hope that he would see it and attempt to bring it to the surface. If so, he would be blown up, and it would appear that he had been killed by a derelict mine. It would leave no witnesses, and unlike hitmen, no assassin that could be captured. And if Castro ignored it, nothing would be lost. The workshop, however, decided that the construction of such a lethal seashell was technically too difficult. Another idea out of the workshop was a killer gift for Castro, a wetsuit whose breathing apparatus was impregnated with tuberculosis bacilli. The concept was that the implanted bacilli, the only evidence of the assassination, would be destroyed by the seawater, and the Cubans would not be able to determine how Castro contracted tuberculosis. Again, this device would leave no witnesses. The problem was to find a means of delivering it. At the time, James Donovan, an American lawyer, was negotiating the release of the Cuban exiles captured in the Bay of Pigs disaster. The CIA's idea was that somehow Donovan, who was not privy to its machinations, could be induced by the CIA to give the contaminated suit to Castro as a gift. But before it could be delivered, Donovan, acting on his own, coincidentally gave Castro a pristine wetsuit. The plan then had to be aborted.

August of 1963 had been especially hot for the CIA. Richard Helms said he could feel "white heat" from Attorney General Robert Kennedy after yet another of the CIA's coup d'état attempts against Castro failed to materialize. Helms recalled almost daily phone calls from the attorney general wanting to know if he was taking action to remove Castro from power. As the CIA inspector general's report noted, "We cannot overemphasize the extent to which responsible Agency officers felt themselves subject to the Kennedy administration's severe pressures to do something about Castro and his regime." At the time, the CIA had one candidate who both showed a willingness to carry out an assassination and had direct access to Castro. The CIA had broken off contact with him a year earlier, in August 1962, because he had turned down a CIA request that he submit to "fluttering," the CIA's term for a polygraph or lie-detector examination, which was then a standard CIA procedure for protecting against a double agent. At the time, he seemed too great a risk. In September 1963, under relentless pressure from Robert Kennedy, Helms authorized his reactivation. Codenamed AMLASH, his real name was Rolando Cubela.

II. THE ASSASSINS

Rolando Cubela Secades was born in Havana in 1933. After completing medical school in 1956, he joined Castro's mountain guerrillas in fighting Batista's army and became an early comrade-in-arms of Castro. He proved his mettle on October 27, 1956, by assassinating Antonio Blanco Rico, the head of Batista's secret police, and in March 1957, he took part in a bloody assault on the presidential palace in which five of Batista's guards were killed. Castro made him head of the Student Directorate, which took control of the presidential palace after Batista fled on New Year's Eve, 1958. Cubela, given the rank of major in Castro's new Cuban army, was put in command of Castro's youth organizations. In 1961, as head of the Cuban chapter of the International Federation of Students, he was able to carry out sensitive missions abroad for Castro. His close proximity to Castro led him into an intelligence game with the CIA in the early 1960s. As early as March 1961, he sent word to the CIA through another agent claiming that he wanted to defect, but the CIA took no action. Then, on July 30, 1962, while attending an international conference on youth in Helsinki, he met with a CIA officer and offered his services. The offer of a close friend of Castro's to secretly serve America was not one that the CIA could refuse. As the CIA inspector general's *Report on Plots to Assassinate Castro* later recounted in detail, Cubela, under the code name AMLASH, said he would "execute" Carlos Rodriguez, one of Castro's key operatives, and also blow up the Soviet Embassy for the CIA. So at a time when the CIA was searching for an inside man in Havana, Cubela was volunteering to work for it as an assassin and bomber. The CIA declined to take him up on his offer.

A year later, in September 1963, Cubela received word that the CIA again wanted to see him in Brazil. So began his extraordinary mission.

Lee Harvey Oswald was born on October 18, 1939, at the Old French Hospital in New Orleans. His father, Robert E. Lee Oswald, an insurance-premium collector named after the Civil War general, had died of a heart attack two months before. Since he had problems at school, on October 24, 1956, having just turned seventeen, he joined the U.S. Marines. In October 1960, after receiving a hardship discharge from the Marines, he defected to the Soviet Union. He spent nearly eighteen months in Moscow and Minsk, and he married a Russian woman, Marina Nikolayevna Prusakova. He then returned to the United States in June 1962 with Marina and moved to Dallas. Ten months later, he attempted his first assassination. His target was General Edwin A. Walker, who had been forced to resign from the Army because of his open support for right-wing extremist causes. Walker had also called for an American invasion of Castro's Cuba. Walker lived in the upscale Turtle Creek section of Dallas. On March 10, 1963, Oswald used his Imperial

Reflex camera to photograph the alley behind Walker's house. According to Marina's later testimony, he put the photographs and other information into a journal that he kept in his study. He then ordered a Mannlicher-Carcano rifle with a telescopic sight from Klein's Sporting Goods Store in Chicago, using the alias "A. Hidell." On April 10, 1963, Oswald left a note for his wife instructing her to go to the Soviet embassy if he was killed or captured by the police. He then, according to Marina's testimony, went to General Walker's house, fired at him, and returned home at 11:30 p.m. The shot missed only by inches, but, with police investigating the assassination attempt in Dallas, Oswald fled to New Orleans.

III. APPOINTMENTS

Porto Alegre, Brazil. September 5–8, 1963.

Nestor Sanchez, a Spanish-speaking CIA case officer, flew to Porto Alegre, Brazil, in the first week of September 1963. He had been dispatched there by SAS chief Desmond FitzGerald to offer Cubela a highly sensitive assignment. The Brazil meeting had been prearranged through a third party in Havana. Cubela would be in Porto Alegre from September 5 to 8, representing Castro at the Pan American Games. At the meeting, Cubela discussed possible ways for the CIA to approach Cuban military officers. He then suggested almost precisely what the CIA had been under pressure to accomplish: the elimination of Castro himself, a prerequisite to regime change. As a candidate for the mission, Cubela seemed almost too perfect: a trusted colleague of Castro, with direct access to him, who had carried out a prior assassination. Sanchez now asked the key question: Would Cubela be willing to carry out an elimination mission for the CIA? Cubela responded that he would consider such a mission if he knew it had been properly authorized by President Kennedy.

The next day, Sanchez returned to Washington to speak to his superiors. Cubela returned to Havana.

Havana, Cuba. September 7, 1963.

When the CIA made its approach to Cubela, it was unaware that Cubela had an undisclosed motive for meeting Sanchez. He was what is called in the intelligence game a "dangle," or double agent. In this wilderness of mirrors, Cubela was dispatched by Castro's intelligence service, the DGI, to make contact with the CIA, feign disloyalty to Castro, and report back on what he gleaned from his meetings. It was not until 1992, nearly thirty years later, that the CIA learned from a defector the truth about Cubela. The defector, Miguel Mir, had served in Castro's security office in Havana prior to his defection to the United States, and he reviewed Cubela's intelligence file, which showed Cubela was working as a double agent under the control of Cuban intelligence when he met with the CIA in Brazil. His mission was to report back to Havana on the CIA's offer to him. If so, Castro would have learned by or before September 7, 1963, that the CIA had attempted to recruit an assassin.

That very day, September 7, Castro went to the only piece of Brazilian territory in Havana, the Brazilian embassy. It was holding a reception attended by the international press. When he arrived, Castro sought out Daniel Harker, the U.S. correspondent for the Associated Press, and gave him an extraordinary scoop in an on-the-record interview. He warned U.S. leaders against "aiding terrorist plans to eliminate Cuban leaders," adding that, if they did so, "they themselves will not be safe." It implied an ominous threat. Harker's story was sent out by the AP and made headlines in newspapers around the world.

EDWARD JAY EPSTEIN

Washington, D.C. September 8–12, 1963.

Castro's message unsettled the CIA. Ray Rocca, the chief of research on the CIA's counterintelligence staff, immediately brought it to the attention of his boss, James Jesus Angleton. Angleton, as he later told me, did not believe that it was a coincidence that less than twenty-four hours after the CIA had approached a possible candidate to eliminate Castro in Brazil, Castro had taunted the U.S. at the Brazilian embassy about such plots. Angleton took it as evidence that Castro knew of the plot that the CIA had hatched in Brazil. According to Angleton, by continuing the attempt to recruit Cubela, the CIA could give Castro evidence of the involvement of the highest echelon of American government in the assassination plot. He sent a memo to FitzGerald saying that he considered the operation "insecure."

The threat of reprisals against American leaders had to be considered and evaluated by the Kennedy Administration. The CIA's covert activities against Cuba, under the direct supervision of a special group in the National Security Council that was augmented by Attorney General Robert Kennedy and General Maxwell Taylor, designated a special committee composed of FitzGerald and a representative of both the Attorney General and the Secretary of State to weigh the risks involved in proceeding with covert actions against Cuba.

The committee met at 2:30 p.m. at the Department of State on September 12 for a "brainstorming" session, as it was described in the memorandum of the meeting, which concluded that although "there was a strong likelihood that Castro would retaliate in some way," it would probably be at "a low level." The specific possibility of "attacks against U.S. officials" was assumed to be "unlikely." Shortly after this review, FitzGerald, disregarding Angleton's warning, ordered Sanchez to continue with the efforts to recruit Cubela.

New Orleans. September 9, 1963.

On September 9, 1963, Castro's message reverberated in New Orleans. The AP story by Harker was splashed across three columns in the *New Orleans Times-Picayune*, the local newspaper read by Lee Harvey Oswald. Castro's warning presumably would have been of great interest to Oswald. According to Marina, Castro was his hero. Oswald had also opened a branch office of the Fair Play for Cuba Committee, an organization dedicated to opposing U.S. policy toward Cuba. He had gone on local talk radio and handed out leaflets on the street to show his support for Castro, and these pro-Castro activities had brought him to the attention of the local police, which arrested him briefly, and even called the FBI. At one point that summer, Oswald considered hijacking an airliner and forcing it at gunpoint to fly to Havana, as his wife later divulged. Not only did Castro now raise in the press the specter of American assassination plots directed against him, but he suggested that Cuba might need to retaliate. Oswald, who, according to Marina, spent hours practicing with his rifle in the backyard, now swung into action.

He made arrangements for Marina and his daughter to return to Dallas, and for a tourist card to go to Mexico City, which was the nearest city with a Cuban embassy.

Paris, France. September 14, 1963.

On September 14, 1963, Cubela arrived in Paris. He was there ostensibly to study French at the Alliance Française. At least, that is what he told the CIA. But, as he was acting under the control of the Cuban DGI, his likely purpose was to continue his "dangle" operation in a city in which the Cubans had an embassy and could conduct counter-surveillance. The CIA accommodated Cubela by arranging a safe house for his meetings with the CIA.

Dallas, Texas. September 25, 1963.

On the night of September 25, in Dallas, Oswald and two dark-skinned men came to the home of Sylvia Odio, a young Cuban refugee. Her father had been involved in a plot to kill Castro the year before—a plot in which Cubela had also been involved. Unlike Cubela, however, her father had been captured in Cuba and was still imprisoned there. The visitors related to her "details about where they saw her father and what activities he was in," as she later told the Warren Commission investigators. Oswald, who was introduced as "Leon Oswald," was described to her in Spanish by one of the men as an ex-Marine and expert shot. Odio abruptly ended the conversation when they started discussing the Cuban underground because, as she later told me, she became "highly suspicious" of them. The next day, she received a call from them saying that they were on their way to Mexico.

Later that same day, Oswald crossed the border into Mexico at Nuevo Laredo, Texas, on a Continental Trailways bus.

Mexico City, Mexico. September 27, 1963.

On September 27, at 10:00 a.m. Oswald arrived by bus in Mexico City. He registered at the Hotel Comercio under the alias O. H. Lee. To get to Cuba, he believed that he also would need a visa from the Soviet Union—then Cuba's closest ally—so he first visited the Soviet embassy, which was only a block away from the Cuban embassy compound. He then walked to the Cuban Embassy, where he was interviewed by Silvia Tirado de Duran, who had been hired there months earlier to be part of the consular section. Oswald told her that he was "a friend of the Cuban revolution" and presented the documentary evidence of his pro-Castro activities in New Orleans.

Silvia Duran strongly supported Castro, although she was a Mexican citizen, and wrote on his visa application: "The applicant states that he is a member of the American Communist Party and Secretary in New Orleans of the Fair Play for Cuba Committee. He displayed documents in proof of his membership in the two aforementioned organizations." Meanwhile, Oswald, after again going to the Soviet embassy, returned in the afternoon to the Cuban embassy and asked to see a higher-ranking Cuban official, Eusebio Azque. According to witnesses, they engaged in a heated exchange about what Oswald could do to help Cuba. Oswald returned the next day, even though it was Saturday and the embassy was officially closed, and a number of other times in the next three days. He also met Silvia Duran and possibly other embassy employees outside the embassy—and beyond the range of the CIA's surveillance of it. Pedro Gutierrez, a credit investigator for a Mexican department store, later stated that he saw Oswald leaving the Cuban embassy that same Tuesday in the company of a tall Cuban, and that both got into a car. Early the next morning, Oswald checked out of the hotel and boarded the 8:30 a.m. Transporte del Norte bus headed for Texas.

Paris, France. October 3–13, 1963.

Nestor Sanchez arrived in Paris on October 3, 1963. Accompanied by two other CIA officers, he immediately went to the safe house to complete the recruitment of AMLASH. The mission now had been fully approved by CIA headquarters at Langley.

Cubela, however, had a surprise for the CIA. Before he would go ahead with the plan to eliminate Castro (which he had himself proposed in Brazil), he wanted some sort of personal assurance or "signal" from Attorney General Kennedy that the Kennedy Administration would actively support him in this endeavor. On October 11, Sanchez cabled his superiors at CIA headquarters that "Cubela was insistent upon meeting with a senior U.S. official, preferably Robert F. Kennedy, for assurances of U.S. moral support for any activity Cubela undertook in Cuba." He further suggested that the "highest and profound consideration be given" to Cubela's request. The assessment of those in contact with Cubela "is that he is determined to attempt op[eration] against Castro with or without U.S. support." Sanchez received a cable in reply that ordered him to return to the United States via London "before entering final round discussions with AMLASH."

Dallas, Texas. October 17, 1963.

After Mexico, Oswald moved to a rooming house on North Beckley Street in the Oak Cliff section of Dallas under the alias "O. H. Lee." He had moved his wife Marina and young daughter June to the home of a friend, Ruth Paine, in Irving, Texas. He had also stowed his rifle there in the Paine garage. Acting as if he were on a secret mission, he forbade his wife to tell anyone where he was living or working. On October 17, he had gotten a job paying a $1.25 an hour filling orders for textbooks at the Texas School Book Depository. The building, in downtown Dallas, overlooked at least one of the possible routes that a presidential motorcade would likely take en route to the airport.

Washington, D.C. Mid-October 1963.

Overruling objections by his own unit's counterintelligence officer, FitzGerald decided to meet with Cubela himself as a "personal representative" of the president's brother. The risk of possibly compromising the president was apparently outweighed in his opinion by the gains in advancing the Kennedy Administration's goal of a coup d'état in Cuba. The contact plan for the meeting stated: "FitzGerald will represent himself as personal representative of Robert F. Kennedy who traveled to [Paris] for specific purpose of meeting AMLASH and giving him assurances of full support with the change of the present government."

Meanwhile, the CIA counterintelligence staff notified the FBI, the Department of State, and Naval intelligence of Oswald's contact with the Cuban and Soviet embassies. Since the CIA was then restricted from investigating U.S. citizens in the absence of a "special request," it "did nothing further on the case," according to its own files on Oswald, except to request on October 23 a photograph of Oswald from the Navy to check against its files.

Havana, Cuba. Mid-October, 1963.

On October 15, 1963, Oswald's visa was processed in Havana. Castro would later claim that Oswald had acted crazily in his visits to the embassy, talking wildly about taking action to "free Cuba from American imperialism." But that assessment did not prevent the Cuban Foreign Ministry from approving his application. Three days later the Ministry notified the Cuban embassy in Mexico that it could issue Oswald his Cuban visa, provided that he showed proof that he had obtained a Soviet entry visa. If Oswald had still been in contact with Duran or other Cuban Embassy employees, he would have learned that he had been provided with a way of getting to Cuba.

Paris, France. October 29, 1963.

FitzGerald met with Cubela at the safe house—this time a hotel suite—on October 29, 1963, using the alias "James Clark."

Cubela said he wanted confirmation from a senior U.S. official, not a member of the CIA. FitzGerald assured Cubela that once the coup had succeeded and Castro had been removed from power, the Kennedy Administration would be fully prepared to aid and support the new government. Cubela asked for the delivery of a specific weapon—a rifle with telescopic sights capable of killing Castro from a distance.

Although FitzGerald did not use his real name, he was a well-known figure in Washington, and, if Cubela were debriefed on this meeting, FitzGerald would have been readily identifiable to Cuban intelligence from Cubela's description. Castro would then have further proof that the plotters in Paris were no rogue group in the CIA.

New York City. November 14, 1963.

The CIA was informed by one of its agents that Cubela was not at all happy that he was denied by the CIA "certain small pieces of equipment which promised a final solution to the problem." Presumably, this referred to the high-powered rifle with telescopic sight that he had specifically requested from the man representing himself as Kennedy's personal emissary.

Miami. November 18, 1963.

FitzGerald arranged a further "signal" for Cubela. He wrote a section of the speech that President Kennedy was to deliver in Miami on November 18. It described the Castro government as a "small band of conspirators" that, "once removed," would ensure United States assistance to the Cuban nation.

The day after Kennedy delivered this "signal," FitzGerald ordered Sanchez to arrange another meeting with Cubela, one in which the specifics would be discussed. The memorandum for the CIA files notes: "C/SAS (FitzGerald) approved telling Cubela he would be given a cache inside Cuba. Cache could, if he requested it, include ... high power rifles w/ scopes ... C/SAS requested written reports on AMLASH operation be kept to a minimum."

Cubela agreed to postpone his scheduled return to Cuba for a meeting in Paris. He expected that by the time of the meeting the CIA would already have delivered the high-powered rifle with the telescopic sight to Cuba. As he was in fact working for Cuban intelligence, the CIA weapon could be intercepted by Cuban authorities and used as proof of a plot. The date agreed on for the Paris meeting was November 22.

IV. THE DAY OF THE ASSASSINS

On November 22, 1963, shortly before 7:00 a.m. in the suburb of Irving, Texas, Oswald slipped off his wedding ring and left it, along with $170 of his savings, in a dresser drawer at the Paine home. It was for Marina. She had lived there, along with his rifle, since he had gone to Mexico. He then walked over to the home of Buell Wesley Frazier, a fellow worker at the Texas Book Depository, who lived on the same block as Ruth Paine. The night before, Oswald had hitched a ride with him to Irving. As there would be traffic because of the president's announced visit to Dallas that Friday, Oswald and Frazier had to leave early to be back in Dallas in time for work at the Book Depository. Oswald carried with him an oblong package wrapped in coarse brown paper. When Frazier saw it, he assumed it contained the curtain rods that Oswald had told him he needed to get from Irving. Just before 8:00 a.m., they arrived at the Book Depository, and Oswald walked quickly into the building, his package tucked under one arm.

Air Force One landed at Love Field in Dallas at 11:40 that morning and taxied to a terminal building usually used for international arrivals. President Kennedy stepped out onto the top step of the ramp, and he then helped his wife Jackie into their waiting Lincoln limousine. Texas Governor John Connally got into the jump seats in front of the president and his wife. It was a clear November day, and the president decided against using the transparent bubble top for the motorcade through Dallas. By noon, the fifteen-car procession had left Love Field.

At noon in Paris, Nestor Sanchez kept his appointment with Cubela at the CIA's safe house. As he had been instructed by FitzGerald, he referred Cubela to the lines in the speech that President Kennedy had made four days earlier, lines that were intended to signal to Cubela American support of an anti-Communist government in Cuba once Castro was "removed" from power. FitzGerald had also authorized Sanchez to supply Cubela with a weapon that Dr. Edward Gunn at the CIA lab had hastily devised. It was a Paper Mate ballpoint pen with one hidden enhancement: a tiny needle engineered to release a lethal toxin. The poison for it, Blackleaf 40, could be either injected into a beverage Castro might drink or, as it was transdermal, it could be put on an object that Castro might touch. According to the CIA plan, Cubela would surreptitiously administer the poison and casually discard the pen. At the meeting, Sanchez showed Cubela the almost-invisible needle that shot out from an otherwise innocent-looking ball point pen. Cubela ridiculed the pen and expressed dismay that the weapon promised to him, a high-powered rifle fitted with telescopic sights, had not been delivered to his associate in Cuba. In the midst of the discussion, another CIA officer rushed into the room to inform Sanchez that President Kennedy had been shot in Dallas. The assassin had used a rifle with a telescopic sight.

The president, taken to Dallas's Parkland Hospital, was pronounced dead at 1:00 p.m. By this time, police had found a rifle with a telescopic sight on the sixth floor of the Texas Book Depository. Near it were three spent shells. Boxes had been arranged to create a makeshift sniper's nest. From it, an assassin could see the three main streets of Dallas—Elm, Main, and Commerce—converge in the plaza below before they reached the elevated expressways that carried traffic out of town. In checking employees on the six floor, it was found that Oswald was missing.

After walking seven blocks up Elm Street, Oswald caught a bus going in the exact opposite direction. He stayed on it for only two blocks, then, after walking another few blocks, hailed a taxi. He told the driver to take him to Neely Street in Oak Cliff, only a block from his rooming house on North Beckley Street, where he lived under a false name. He then went to his room, put on his grey zippered jacket, and took from the closet his snub-nosed Smith & Wesson revolver. According to his landlady, he left about 1:00 p.m.

Shortly afterward, in Oak Cliff, a Dallas police officer, J. D. Tippit, was found bleeding to death next to his radio car. Witnesses at the scene said he had been shot repeatedly by a man in a grey jacket. The description matched that of Oswald.

In Paris, late that night, Sanchez received, as he recalled, an urgent cable from FitzGerald telling him that "everything was off." He was ordered to return to Washington immediately. Meanwhile, Cubela was heading back to Havana via Prague, where presumably he would be debriefed by his controlling officers in Cuban intelligence.

Just before noon, on November 23, 1963, the CIA station chief in Mexico, Winston Scott, received word that Mexican police were about to arrest Silvia Duran and hold her "incommunicado until she gives all details of Oswald known to her" about Oswald's dealings with the Cuban embassy. Scott telegraphed Washington headquarters. The CIA's concern, as Richard Helms later recalled, was that Duran might say under the brutal techniques used by Mexican interrogators that Cuban intelligence officers had made a deal with Oswald. Whether true or not, that would precipitate a crisis. It could also reveal one of the CIA's darkest secrets: the CIA's AMLASH plot to assassinate Castro. Langley cabled Scott in Mexico,

> Arrest of Silvia Duran is extremely serious matter which could prejudice U.S. freedom of action on entire question of Cuban responsibility. Request you ensure that her arrest is kept absolutely secret, that no information from her is published or leaked, that all such info is cabled to us, and that the fact of her arrest and her statements are not spread to leftist or disloyal circles in the Mexican Government.

To assist the Mexican interrogation, the CIA then provided a list of questions concerning Oswald's September visit to Mexico. It included highly provocative queries, such as: "Was the assassination of President Kennedy planned by Fidel Castro and were the final details worked out inside the Cuban Embassy in Mexico?"; "Who were Oswald's contacts during the period 26 September 1963 to 3 October 1963?"; and "If Castro planned that Oswald assassinate President Kennedy, did the Soviets have any knowledge of these plans?" They made it crystal clear to the Mexican authorities, as they were probably intended to do, how explosive the Oswald situation could be for Mexico. If Duran were to say under Mexican-style hostile interrogation that Oswald had met with Cuban intelligence officers, had discussed his assassination capabilities, and been told that his visa was approved, or provide further evidence that the JFK assassination had been organized in Mexico as a response to CIA assassination plots against Castro, Mexico would find itself in the center of the crisis and under enormous pressure to take action against Cuba. The Soviet Union might even be involved. The implications of the CIA's pointed questions were evidently taken seriously by Mexican authorities. The interrogation was ended, Duran was quietly released from custody, and Cuban officials at the embassy who might have had contact with Oswald were encouraged to return to Havana.

Lee Harvey Oswald did not get to Cuba, or even to Mexico City to pick up his visa. On November 22, at 1:50 p.m., after a suspect in the Tippit shooting had been reported running into a Texas movie theater, Dallas police arrested Oswald, who was holding a snub-nosed revolver in his hand. Dragged out of the movie house in handcuffs, he was shoved into the back of a patrol car.

By that time, the rifle found at the Texas Book Depository had been traced to his post office box, making him a prime suspect in the JFK assassination. On route to his arraignment on November 24, escorted by a phalanx of Dallas police detectives, he was himself shot in the police headquarters basement at 11:21 a.m. by Jack Ruby, a Dallas bar owner. Oswald never regained consciousness. At 1:07 p.m, he was pronounced dead at Parkland Hospital, the same hospital at which President Kennedy had died barely 48 hours earlier.

Cubela returned to Cuba, where he was presumably fully debriefed by the Cuban intelligence officers controlling him. But the game was not yet over. He again contacted the CIA through messages using secret writing technology, "s/w" in CIA parlance. He asked for a cache of weapons and money. He also kept asking the CIA about assassinating Cuban leaders. On December 6, 1964, Sanchez again met with Cubela in Paris. According to the memorandum of the meeting written by Sanchez, Cubela said that "his solution to the Cuban problem was the only one feasible and that he had to continue trying." By now, Helms had firmly banned further assassination missions, so Sanchez replied that "the U.S. Government could not and would not in any way become involved or provide assistance in the task he had planned for himself." Cubela then said that he would proceed without direct CIA help, and Sanchez provided him with a potential ally by arranging for him to meet with Manuel Artime in Spain. Sanchez later explained to the CIA's inspector general, "The thought was that Artime needed a man inside and Cubela wanted a silenced weapon, which CIA was unwilling to furnish to him directly. By Sanchez putting the two together, Artime might get his man inside Cuba and Cubela might get his silenced weapon—from Artime." Artime, who had been a key figure in the Bay of Pigs invasion, now ran one of the CIA-supported anti-Castro networks in Cuba. As it turned out, Cubela's involvement proved disastrous for Artime's network in Cuba.

Angleton, the head of counterintelligence, watched in frustration as the deadly dance with Cubela continued, but he had no control over FitzGerald's SAS. He was principally tasked with advising Helms on Soviet strategy, and FitzGerald's unit was responsible for Cuban operations.

The end of this long intelligence game came on June 23, 1965, when CIA headquarters cabled the SAS, saying that it had

> convincing proof that entire AMLASH group insecure and that further contact with key members of group constitutes menace to CIA operations against Cuba as well as to the security of CIA staff personnel in Western Europe. Under the circumstances headquarters desires that contact with key members of the group or peripherally involved in AMLASH conspiracy be warned of danger implicit in these associations and directed to eliminate contacts ASAP.

Within a month, Cuban security police began rounding up the anti-Castro agents with whom Cubela had been in contact. In March 1966, Cubela was put on trial in Havana, for his 1964–65 "counter-revolutionary activities" with Artime and the CIA, including "having planned the assassination of Fidel Castro." The evidence produced included the rifle with telescopic sight from Artime. Cubela confessed and cooperated. What caught the CIA's attention was that no mention was made of the November 22 plot, although since Cubela was now a cooperating witness, he could have cited the poison pen and his meeting with FitzGerald. To Angleton, this was an indication that Castro, like others involved, wanted to keep the lid sealed on that Pandora's box. Cubela was convicted, but although such a crime ordinarily would result in execution by a firing squad, Castro personally intervened. He wrote the court asking that Cubela be given a prison sentence rather than death because of his past service to the revolution.

In Washington, D.C., Richard Helms, now director of Central Intelligence, needed to close this sorry chapter. He ordered the CIA's inspector general to prepare a report on the CIA's involvement in the assassination attempts against Castro, instructing, when it was completed in 1967: "Retain it in personal, EYES ONLY safekeeping. Destroy the one burn copy retained temporarily by the Inspector General. Destroy all notes and other source materials originated by those participating in the writing of this report." Even the typewriter ribbons were destroyed. So except for this one document locked away in the safe of the director of Central Intelligence, all evidence of the plot was expunged. Helms then certified for the record that only one copy existed, which had been read "either in whole or in part," by him and only three other people at the CIA. They were Inspector General J. S. Earman, and the two authors of the report, Inspectors K. E. Greer and S. D. Breckinridge. Since all of these men were sworn to strict secrecy about what they read, these measures were believed to have sealed the case shut. What could not be foreseen at the time was that a Senate investigation a decade later would break the seal.

In 1979, Cubela, who had worked during his confinement as a prison doctor, was allowed to emigrate to Spain. He received financial assistance from the Cuban government to buy a home in Madrid. For him, the dance was over.

Castro continued to rule Cuba until 2007, when, at the age of eighty and in failing health, he turned the reins of power over to his brother Raul. There were no further efforts made by the CIA to assassinate him after the aborted poison pen plot on November 22, 1963.

How do all of these dates connect? The first theory is that Oswald acted alone. This was the theory of the Warren Commission in 1964. To be sure, the seven members of the Commission did not know when they signed this report that a second jackal, sponsored by the CIA, was in play on November 22. In particular, a jackal requesting that same day a weapon to kill Castro that was similar to the one found in the Texas Book Depository. Yet the single-assassin theory is still viable, because all of the elements of the parallel plot could be considered unrelated coincidences.

The second theory is that Castro, or his intelligence service, directed Oswald to kill Kennedy. This was the theory advanced by Thomas Mann, who was U.S. ambassador to Mexico in 1963. Mann told me in an interview that, on the basis of what was reported by the CIA station in Mexico about eye witnesses to Oswald's activities and intelligence intercepts of conversations, there was an "indictable case" against Castro. Like the Warren Commission, Mann did not know about the CIA's parallel plot. If he had, he might have better understood why he was abruptly recalled from Mexico in 1964 when he pressed the U.S. government for a further investigation. More recently, Castro's involvement in the Kennedy assassination has been advanced in two books. The first one, *Brothers in Arms: The Kennedys, the Castros, and the Politics of Murder*, by Gus Russo and Stephen Molton, published in 2008, is based on interviews with Cuban intelligence officers who revealed that Oswald's activities in Mexico, including previously unknown meetings outside the embassy, were reported to Havana prior to the assassination. The second book, *Castro's Secrets: The CIA and Cuba's Intelligence Machine*, published in 2012, is by Brian Latell, who worked for the CIA at the time of the JFK assassination. It reports that Florentino Aspillaga, who defected from Cuban intelligence in 1987, revealed in his CIA debriefings that on November 22, 1963, just before Kennedy was assassinated, he had been ordered to switch all the intelligence-gathering antennae under his command from monitoring Florida to monitoring Texas. He then was told to report any transmissions of interest to the top command in Havana. Latell suggested that these and other activities of Cuban intelligence, which the CIA only learned about a quarter century after the assassination, point to the possibility that Castro had advance knowledge about the assassination.

My own assessment, after a nearly fifty-year investigation of this enduring mystery, is that Cuban intelligence had influenced, if not directed, Oswald's actions. If this were an ordinary police investigation, detectives would have motive, means, and opportunity. As for the motive, we now know that Castro had the most powerful of all motives: self-preservation. In dangling his double agent Cubela before the CIA, Castro ascertained not only that the CIA was actively planning to assassinate him, but that, with the involvement of FitzGerald in the president's speech, the plot appeared to have the backing of JFK himself. As for means, his intelligence service had Lee Harvey Oswald in the palm of its hand. As Marina Oswald testified, Oswald's purpose in going to Mexico in September 1963 was to arrange a new life for himself in Castro's Cuba. He was desperate to serve Castro, so desperate that he had considered hijacking a plane to get there. He also said that he could kill Kennedy, as Castro himself disclosed in early 1964 to his associate Jack Childs, who was also an informant for the FBI. So here was a potential assassin, asking to obtain a visa.

The Cuban intelligence service also had opportunity, since President Kennedy often traveled through cities in an open car, and a sniper could be positioned in a high building along the route. Even if the sniper missed his target, the attempt would send Castro's message that American leaders who attempted to assassinate Cuban leaders were themselves vulnerable.

Finally, we are now aware of a number of overt acts by Cuban officials, including Castro's warning and threat, the conditional visa issued to Oswald, and the request by Castro's double-agent, Cubela, for a weapon similar to the weapon that Oswald used in Dallas. We do not know whether Oswald was informed of his conditional visa approval, but, if he was, the knowledge could have provided him both with an incentive to commit the act, and—in his mind at least—an escape route. John J. McCloy had been high commissioner for Germany before serving on the Warren Commission. When I interviewed him on June 7, 1965, he told me he had insisted that the report itself leave the door slightly ajar because the possibility that Oswald was an agent "could not be precluded." So Chief Justice Warren inserted a sentence into the Warren Report stating that it was not possible to prove a negative proposition, such as that Oswald had no sponsorship. It turned out to be a wise decision in retrospect because, as it now turns out, it cannot be precluded that Oswald was used by Castro's intelligence service in retaliation for the CIA's efforts to assassinate Castro. Indeed, in my view, that is the most likely explanation of what happened in Dallas on November 22.

FURTHER INVESTIGATION

To pursue any of these unsolved crimes, I recommend the following books as starting points.

Chapter 1: The Assassination of President Lincoln
Michael W. Kauffnan, *American Brutus: John Wilkes Booth and the Lincoln Conspiracies* (2004), Random House, New York

Chapter 2: The Reichstag Fire
Ian Kershaw, *Hitler 1889–1936* (1999), W. W. Norton & Company, New York

Chapter 3: The Lindbergh Kidnapping
Jim Fisher, *The Lindbergh Case* (1987), Rutgers University Press, Piscataway, New Jersey

Chapter 4: The Assassination of Olof Palme
Jan Bondeson, *Blood on the Snow: The Killing of Olof Palme* (2005), Cornell University Press, Ithaca, New York

Chapter 5: The Anthrax Attack on America
David Willman, *The Mirage Man: Bruce Ivins, the Anthrax Attacks, and America's Rush to War* (2011), Bantam Books, New York

Chapter 6: The Pope's Assassin
Paul B. Henze, *The Plot to Kill the Pope* (1983), Scribner, New York

Chapter 7: The Mayerling Incident
Frederic Morton, *A Nervous Splendor: Vienna 1888–1889* (1979), Little Brown Company, Boston

Chapter 8: Who Killed God's Banker?
Charles Raw, *The Money Changers: How the Vatican Bank Enabled Roberto Calvi to Steal 250 Million for the Heads of the P2 Masonic Lodge* (1992), Harvill, London

Chapter 9: The Death of Dag Hammarskjöld

A. Susan Williams, *Who Killed Hammarskjöld?: The UN, the Cold War, and White Supremacy in Africa* (2011), Columbia University Press, New York

Chapter 10: The Strange Death of Marilyn Monroe

Anthony Summers, *Goddess: The Secret Lives of Marilyn Monroe* (1985), Macmillan, New York

Chapter 11: The Crash of Enrico Mattei

Nico Perrone, *Enrico Mattei* (2001), Mulino, Bologna, Italy

Chapter 12: The Disappearance of Lin Biao

Ming-le Yao, *The Conspiracy and Death of Lin Biao* (1983), Alfred A. Knopf, New York

Chapter 13: The Elimination of General Zia

George Crile, *Charlie Wilson's War: The Extraordinary Story of the Largest Covert Operation in History* (2003), Atlantic Monthly Press, New York

Chapter 14: The Submerged Spy

Jim Hougan, *Secret Agenda* (1984), Ballantine Books, New York

Chapter 15: Jack the Ripper

Paul Begg and John Bennett, *Jack the Ripper: CSI, Whitechapel* (2012), Andre Deutsch, London

Chapter 16: The Harry Oakes Murder

John Marquis, *Blood and Fire: The Duke of Windsor and the Strange Murder of Sir Harry Oakes* (2005), LMH Publishing Company, Kingston, Jamaica

Chapter 17: The Black Dahlia

Steve Hodel, *Black Dahlia Avenger: The True Story* (2003), Arcade Publishing, New York

Chapter 18: The Pursuit of Dr. Sam Sheppard

James Neff, *The Wrong Man: The Final Verdict on the Dr. Sam Sheppard Murder Case* (2001), Random House, New York

Chapter 19: The Killing of JonBenet Ramsey
Lawrence Schiller, *Perfect Murder, Perfect Town: JonBenet and the City of Boulder* (1999), HarperCollins, New York

Chapter 20: The Zodiac
Robert Greysmith, *Zodiac Unmasked: The Identity of America's Most Elusive Serial Killer Revealed* (2002), Berkley, New York

Chapter 21: The Vanishing of Jimmy Hoffa
Arthur A. Sloane, *Hoffa* (1991), MIT Press, Cambridge, Massachusetts

Chapter 22: Death in Ukraine: The Case of the Headless Journalist
The International Federation of Journalists, *The Gongadze Inquiry: A Preliminary Investigation* (2005), International Federation of Journalists, Brussels, Belgium

Chapter 23: The Dubai Hit
Michael Bar-Zohar and Nissim Mishal, *Mossad: The Greatest Missions of the Israeli Secret Service* (2012), Ecco, New York

Chapter 24: The Beirut Assassination
Nicholas Blanford, *Killing Mr. Lebanon: The Assassination of Rafik Hariri and Its Impact on the Middle East* (2006), I.B. Tauris, London

Chapter 25: Who Assassinated Anna Politkovskaya?
Anna Politkovskaya, *Is Journalism Worth Dying For?: Final Dispatches* (2011), Melville House, Brooklyn, New York

Chapter 26: Blowing Up Bhutto
James P. Farwell, *The Pakistan Cauldron: Conspiracy, Assassination & Instability* (2011), Potomac Books, Washington, D.C.

Chapter 27: The Case of the Radioactive Corpse
Mark Hollingsworth and Stewart Lansley, *Londongrad: From Russia With Cash* (2009), Fourth Estate, London

Chapter 28: The Godfather Contract
Alexander Stille, *Excellent Cadavers: The Mafia and the Death of the First Italian Republic* (1995), Pantheon, New York

---

Chapter 29: The Vanishings

Yoshi Yamamoto, *Taken! North Korea's Criminal Abductions of Citizens of Other Countries* (2011), Committee for Human Rights in North Korea, Washington, D.C.

Chapter 30: The Oklahoma City Bombing

Andrew Gumbel and Roger G. Charles, *Oklahoma City: What the Investigation Missed—and Why It Still Matters* (2012), William Morrow, New York

Chapter 31: The O. J. Simpson Nullification

Vincent Bugliosi, *Outrage: The Five Reasons Why O. J. Simpson Got Away with Murder* (1996), W.W. Norton & Company, New York

Chapter 32: Bringing Down DSK

Didier Hassoux, Christophe Labbé, and Olivia Recasens, *L'Espion du President* (2012), Robert Laffont, Paris, France

Chapter 33: The MacDonald Massacre

Errol Morris, *A Wilderness of Error: The Trials of Jeffrey MacDonald* (2012), Penguin, New York

Chapter 34: The Knox Ordeal

John Follain, *A Death in Italy: The Definitive Account of the Amanda Knox Case* (2012), St. Martin's Press, New York

Epilogue: The Enduring Mystery of the JFK Assassination

Gus Russo and Stephen Molton, *Brothers in Arms: The Kennedys, the Castros, and the Politics of Murder* (2008), Bloomsbury USA, New York

ACKNOWLEDGEMENTS

I am deeply grateful to those who assisted my investigation of these unsolved crimes. I owe a particular debt of gratitude to Renata Adler, Natalie Altshuler, Robert Asahina, Richard Bernstein, Sidney Blumenthal, Svetlana Chervonnaya, Bob Coen, Carlo Calvi, Howard Dickman, Andrea DiRobilant, Chuck Downs, Susana Duncan, Harold Edgar, Ben Gerson, Andrew Hacker, Stuart Jacobson, Haroon Khan, Humayan Khan, Billy Kimball, Jules Kroll, Jim Hougan, Grant Manheim, Zhores Medvedev, Fred Miller, Eric Nadler, Jeff Paul, Magui Nougue-Sans, Mario Platero, Seth Roberts, Fabrice Rousselot, John Rubenstein, Gus Russo, Ko Shioya, and Robert Silvers.

Finally, I want to thank my editor Kelly Burdick at Melville House. The book benefitted enormously from his thoughtful suggestions and brilliant editing.

Parts of this book were adapted from reporting that I did for *Vanity Fair, The New York Sun, The Wall Street Journal,* and *The New York Review of Books.*

A portion of Chapter XIII, "The Elimination of General Zia," is taken from an article I wrote for *Vanity Fair* (September 1989); a portion of Chapter XXVII, "The Case of the Radioactive Corpse," is taken from an article that appeared in the *New York Sun* (March 19, 2008); portions of Chapter XXIII, "The Dubai Hit," and Chapter XXIV, "The Beirut Assassination," are taken from articles I wrote for the *Wall Street Journal* (March 27, 2010 and November 26, 2010). A portion of Chapter XXXII, "Bringing Down DSK," appeared in *The New York Review of Books* (December 22, 2011), which was later expanded as *Three Days in May: Sex, Surveillance, and DSK,* published as an ebook in April 2012.

INDEX OF NAMES

Canesi, Carlo, 84, 96
Carboni, Flavio, 72, 87, 94–95
Casaroli, Cardinal Agostino, 94
Castellito, Tony, 172
Castro, Fidel, 10, 307–308, 327, 329, 330–333
Castro Ruz, Fidel, 308–323, 325, 327
Castro, Raul, 308–309, 331
Chaika, Yuri, 202
Chapman, Annie, 140
Charles, Roger, 246–247
Chávez, Hugo, 13
Chimura, Yasushi, 238
Chowdhury, A.C., 281
Christie, Harold, 145–146, 148
Churchill, Winston, 215
Clark, Dr. Percy, 141
Clay, Clement, 22, 25
"Cleveland Torso Killer, the", 153
Connally, Gov. John, 324
Connally, John, 324
Cook, Andrew, 141
Coppola, Francis Ford, 92
Coriam, Rebecca, 170
Corrocher, Graziela, 78–79
Crater, Joseph Force, 14, 170
Cubela Secades, Rolando, 10, 313–326, 328–333
Curie, Marie, 210
Curie, Pierre, 210
D'Andria, Mario Lucio, 93
Dagaev, Maj. Gen. Yuri, 180, 186
Daschle, Tom, 47
Davis, Jefferson, 10, 22–23
Davis, Lanny, 284
de Duran, Silvia Tirado, 319–320, 322, 326–327
de Gaulle, Charles, 10
de Kock, Eugene, 45–46
de Marigny, Alfred, 147, 149
de Sá Carne, Francisco, 99
de Strobel, Pellegrino, 86

de Vosjoli, Philippe Thyraud , 111–112
Degnan, Suzzane, 153
di Jorio, Cardinal Alberto, 83
Di Maggio, Baldassare, 233
Diallo, Nafissatou, 259–266, 268–272, 274–284, 286–287
DiCarlo, Francesco, 93
Dimitrov, Georgi, 30
Diesel, 170
Donahoe, Capt. Jack, 153
Donovan, James, 312
Donovan, William "Wild Bill", 37
Dreyfus, Capt. Alfred, 17
Dubberstei, Waldo, 132
Dunlap, Jack, 132
Dunne, Dominick, 254
Durkin, Ethel May, 158
Durrani, Mahmud, 129
Dwight D. Eisenhower, 309–310
Earman, Insp. Gen. J.S., 330
Eberling, Richard George, 158–159
Eddowes, Catherine, 140
Egge, Gen. Bjorn, 100
Eisenstadt, Eric, 16
Elkin, Dr. Charles, 157
Emmanuel, King, 80
Engelberg, Dr. Hyman, 103
Esterhazy, Maj. Ferdinand, 17
Estigarribia, José Félix, 99
Faraday, David,
Fenjves, Pablo, 165
Ferdinand, Franz, 8
Feres, Eduard, 180, 186
Fernandez, Rosemary, 221
Ferrer, Mel, 65
Ferrin, Darlene Elizabeth, 165, 167
Firrao, Donato, 111
Fisch, Isidor, 38
FitzGerald, Desmond, 311–312, 315, 317, 321–323, 325–326, 329–330, 332
Fong, O.Y., 281

Forsyth, Frederick, 10
Fortier, Michael, 246–247
Foskett, Walter, 148
Fouks, Stéphane, 258
Franz Josef I, Emperor, 65
Frazier, Buell Wesley, 324
Friar, Jimmy, 295
Friel, Lisa, 272–273
Fung, Dennis, 252
Gandhi, Indira, 127
Gandhi, Rajiv, 126
Gelli, Licio, 89–92, 235
George VI, King, 145
Ghazali, Gen. Rustam, 196
Giacalone, Tony, 171
Giuliano Mignini, 302
Goldfarb, Alex, 185, 210, 216, 227
Goldman, Ronald, 251, 253, 254
Gongadze, Georgiy, 177–188
Göring, Hermann, 29–32
Gow, Betty, 35–36
Graff, Xavier, 265
Grapentin, Edeltraud, 11, 132
Greenson, Dr. Ralph, 103
Greer, Insp. K.E., 330
Grimm, Lt. Col. Johannes, 11, 132
Gu, Kailai, 116
Guede, Rudy, 301–305
Guerri, Cardinal Sergio, 83
Guevara, Che, 308–309
Gumbel, Andrew, 246–247
Gunn, Dr. Edward, 325
Habyarimana, Juvénal, 99
Hamamoto, Fukie, 238
Hammarskjöld, Dag, 97–101
Hand, Michael, 14, 99
Hansen, Mark, 152, 154
Haque, Syed, 259, 264, 266, 270, 281–282
Hara, Tadaaki, 238
Harden, Bettye, 166
Harden, Donald, 166
Hariri, Rafik, 195–197, 199

Harker, Daniel, 316, 318
Harris, Gen. Thomas, 24
Hartnell, Bryan, 166
Hassell, D. Christian, 55
Hassoux, Didier, 279
Hatfill, Steven J., 50, 51, 53, 56, 58
Hauptmann, Bruno Richard, 38–42
Hayes, Susan, 157
Hearst, William Randolph, 41, 151–152
Heer, Juerg, 90–92
Heirens, William, 153
Hekmatyar, Gulbuddin, 125
Helms, Richard, 311–313, 326, 328–330
Henze, Paul, 60–61
Hepburn, Audrey, 65
Herold, David, 21–25
Heywood, Neil, 116
Hindenburg, Paul von, 29
Hitler, Adolf, 29–33
Hoffa, James Riddle, 14, 169–173
Holler, Dr. Gerd, 67
Holt, Harold, 170
Honcharov, Ihor, 182
Hoover, Herbert, 37
Hoover, J. Edgar, 37–38, 107
Hosty, James, 107
Hougan, Jim, 16
Houts, Marshall, 148
Hussein, Saddam, 188
Ijaz ul-Haq, 129
Illuzzi-Orbon, Joan, 272, 278–279
Ipekci, Abdi, 59
Ishioka, Toru, 238
Ivins, Dr. Bruce, 51–58
"Jack the Ripper", 14, 139–142, 151, 153, 166
Jackson, Judge Melissa, 273–274
Jeffries, Norman, 105–107
Jensen, Betty Lou, 165
John Paul, Pope, 85
John Paul II, Pope, 59, 61, 75, 85

Mao Zedong, 113–116
Marchuk, Yevhen, 185
Marcinkus, Archbishop Paul Casimir, 75–77, 79, 83–87, 96
Markozani, Renata, 262–263, 266, 270
Mash'hood, Wing Cmdr., 122–123
Matlock, Jack, 126
Matsuki, Kaoru, 238
Matsumoto, Rumiko, 238
Matsumoto, Kyoko, 238
Mattei, Enrico, 109–112
May, Derek, 262
McCloy, John J., 9, 333
McConnell, John "Artie," 272–273, 278–279
McGinniss, Joe, 293
McHale, William, 110
McVeigh, Timothy, 245–249
Mehlis, Detlev, 195–197
Mehsud, Baitullah, 206–207
Melchen, Edward, 146
Melnychenko, Maj. Mykola, 179, 181, 183–185, 187–188
Mencken, H.L., 35
Mennini, Luigi, 86
Merkel, Angela, 257
Mezzetti, Laura, 300
Mica, Kenneth, 294
Mikesell, Perry, 50
Mir, Miguel, 316
Mitchell, Greg, 295, 297
Mitchell, John, 16
Molton, Stephen, 331
Mongiello, Det. John, 269
Monier, Stephen 40
Monroe, Marilyn, 103–108
Montini, Giovanni Battista, 82
Moore, Julianne, 237
Moro, Aldo 232, 235
Moroz, Oleksandr, 178, 182
Morris, Errol, 294–296, 298

Morrow, Ann, 35
Mueller, Robert, 56
Mumcu, Ugur, 59–61
Münzenberg, Willi, 31
Murad, Abdul Hakim, 248
Murray, Eunice, 103–106
Murtaza, Mir, 126
Musharraf, Pervez, 205–207
Mussolini, Benito, 80
Nasrallah, Hassan, 198
Nawaz, Shah, 126
Nevzlin, Leonid, 212, 216–217
Nichols, Mary Ann, 140
Nichols, Terry, 246–248
Nixon, Richard, 16, 114, 169
Nocera, Joe, 7
Nogara, Bernardino, 81
Noguchi, Dr. Thomas, 104
Norden, Albert, 31
Novitsky, Jacob, 39, 42
Ntaryamira, Cyprien, 99
Nugan, Frank, 14
O'Brien, Charles, 172
Oakes, Sir Harry, 145–149
Oakley, Robert Bigger, 129
Ocalan, Abdullah, 45
Odio, Sylvia, 319
Olson, Frank, 132, 134
Orlandi, Emanuela, 170
Oswald, Lee Harvey, 9, 107, 307, 314–315, 318–322, 324, 326–328, 331–333
Oswald, Marina, 314–315, 318, 321, 324, 332
Oswald, Robert E. Lee, 314
Pahlavi, Shah Reza, 109
Paine, Ruth, 321, 324
Paisley, John Arthur, 131–134
Palme, Lisbet, 43–45
Palme, Marten, 43
Palme, Olof, 43–46
Pan, Jungyin, 114

EDWARD JAY EPSTEIN